"This gem of a book could scarcely be appearing at a more opportune time. Internal auditing is in trouble, facing a perfect storm of threats to its future. It is under siege from increasingly fragmented flows of institutional accountability, from ruthless pressures to serve commercial interests rather than the public good, and from an intellectual exhaustion characterized by creativity-numbing, algorithmic thinking. Moreover, it faces an escalating risk of a takeover by artificial intelligence and other forms of machine learning. Bursting out of this bleak landscape, Lenz and Enslin, with the force of an unexpected thunderbolt, offer a powerful path to reform that pushes back against the prevailing pattern of decline.

The authors challenge the internal audit profession to consider the ramifications of their 5 P's model (People, Public, Performance, Purpose, and Planet), which collectively provide a route to a careful evolution of internal auditing. If implemented, the authors' suggestions might achieve more than simply rescuing the internal audit profession by shoring up its relevance – they hold out the prospect of reorienting internal auditing once more to fully serve the public good. The gardening metaphor has already captured the hearts of many internal auditors. I commend this visionary, courageous, and prophetic book to the global internal audit community."

-**David J. O'Regan**, *Auditor General at WHO/PAHO, Washington, DC*

The Gardener of Governance

This book builds on the popular **GARDENER OF GOVERNANCE** article, which enjoys amazing traction in the professional community globally and has been translated into 25+ languages. The Lenz and Jeppesen (2022) thought-piece introduced **the 5 "Ps"** as paths for the betterment of internal auditing: **People, Public, Performance** (Prosperity), **Purpose** (Profession) and **Planet**. These main fields of action and focus for the internal audit profession may determine the future role of internal auditing, its legitimacy, relevance and significance. The book aims to provide practical guidance for performing impactful internal audit assignments. Some readers will no doubt view the authors as unorthodox and the book may be a stretch for the purist, insisting on adherence to traditional rules.

It is pleasing to see that the new Global Internal Audit Standards advocate a pragmatic and holistic approach, which should further stimulate internal audit functions moving into uncharted territory that may require from them to become more resourceful in their approach as advocated for by the authors. This book is an inspiration and encouragement for all internal auditors who want to do better and aim higher, particularly the forthcoming generation of internal auditors who are open-minded and who may sometimes doubt themselves because of opposition or insecurity. We believe that internal auditors who absorb the knowledge and make it their own will benefit from this book on their career trajectory.

This easy read is relatable, engaging and convincing to support internal auditors globally who are seeking to widen their repertoire on their journey to become modern and effective internal auditors. This book is relevant and will be insightful to internal auditors, students and lecturers, as well as other stakeholders including senior and executive managers and board members. Drawing on Rainer's vast practical expertise gained from over 300 audits in more than 50 countries, along with his series of publications and adding Barrie's hands-on advice benefitting from 30 years of entrepreneurial experience, the authors create an interesting blend of creative authoring that challenges the status quo and advises emerging internal auditors on becoming more impactful and effective.

We're dropping the pebble in the pond. Let's see how far the ripples spread and to what effect.

Security, Audit and Leadership Series

Series Editor: Dan Swanson, Dan Swanson and Associates, Ltd., Winnipeg, Manitoba, Canada.

The ***Security, Audit and Leadership Series*** publishes leading-edge books on critical subjects facing security and audit executives as well as business leaders. Key topics addressed include Leadership, Cybersecurity, Security Leadership, Privacy, Strategic Risk Management, Auditing IT, Audit Management and Leadership

The Shortest Hour: An Applied Approach to Boardroom Governance of Cybersecurity
Lee Parrish

Global Audit Leadership: A Practical Approach to Leading a Global Internal Audit (GIA) Function in a Constantly Changing Internal and External Landscape
Audley L. Bell

Construction Audit: Building a Solid Foundation
Denise Cicchella

Continuous Auditing with AI in the Public Sector
Lourens Erasmus and Sezer Bozkus Kahyaoglu

Ironwill 360° Leadership: Moving Forward: Unlock Twelve Emerging Trends for Forward Thinking Leaders
Douglas P. Pflug

The CISO Playbook
Andres Andreu

Leveraging Blockchain Technology: Governance, Risk, Compliance, Security, and Benevolent Use Cases
Shaun Aghili

The Closing of the Auditor's Mind?: How to Reverse the Erosion of Trust, Virtue, and Wisdom in Internal Auditing
David J. O'Regan

Radical Reporting: Writing Better Audit, Risk, Compliance, and Information Security Reports (Second Edition)
Sara I. James

Team Intelligence: A New Method Using Swarm Intelligence for Building Successful Teams
Mohammad Nozari

The Gardener of Governance: A Call to Action for Effective Internal Auditing
Rainer Lenz and Barrie Enslin

Navigating the Cyber Maze: Insights and Humor on the Digital Frontier
Matthias Muhlert

The Gardener of Governance

A Call to Action for Effective Internal Auditing

Rainer Lenz and Barrie Enslin

Forewords by Mervyn King, SC and Kato Plant

CRC Press
Taylor & Francis Group
Boca Raton London New York

CRC Press is an imprint of the
Taylor & Francis Group, an **informa** business

Designed cover image: © Pixabay

First edition published 2025
by CRC Press
2385 NW Executive Center Drive, Suite 320, Boca Raton FL 33431

and by CRC Press
4 Park Square, Milton Park, Abingdon, Oxon, OX14 4RN

CRC Press is an imprint of Taylor & Francis Group, LLC

ISBN: 9781032858166 (hbk)
ISBN: 9781032886701 (pbk)
ISBN: 9781003539001 (ebk)

DOI: 10.1201/9781003539001

Typeset in Sabon
by KnowledgeWorks Global Ltd.

Contents

Foreword

Prof. Mervyn King, SC
Internationally known as the "Godfather of Corporate Governance"

The directors of a limited liability company are the heart, mind, soul, and conscience of that legal fiction. Being a legal fiction, the company is an incapacitated person that has no heart, mind, soul, or conscience. Through the governance architecture, the directors become the heart, mind, soul, and conscience of the company.

When something goes wrong the wrath of society should turn against the directors and not the incapacitated, and by definition, innocent company.

At the beginning of the 21st century, the issue of the primacy of the shareholder became debunked and value creation replaced the primacy of the shareholder.

The purview of the internal auditor changed as the board focused on inputs, outputs, and the outcomes of its activities in producing its product or rendering its service. With externalities such as climate change the IA teams became differently resourced.

The internal auditor was a profession of hindsight to work out a system that did not result in some wrongful doing recurring. It then became a professional service of insight knowing what was going to happen and making suggestions as how to improve the systems within the company in making its product.

Today it is a profession of foresight where it applies its mind to the future outcomes of the company's product and the long-term health of the company. The question of shareholders owning the company and the primacy of the shareholder has been debunked. The important issue is the collective mind of the board ensuring that its judgment calls are made in the long-term best interests of the health of the company.

The internal auditor has a contractual obligation to the company, whereas the external auditor has a statutory obligation. The chief audit executive must act independently and is usually appointed by the audit committee on behalf of the employee company and reports to the audit committee.

The internal auditor has a risk-based approach today, no longer a reactive and controls-based approach.

There are 21st-century merging technologies with which internal auditors have to familiarize themselves in order to keep up to date in the work they do, such as the Internet of Things, Augmented reality, Virtual reality, Blockchain, Artificial intelligence, 3D printing, Drones and Robotics. A lack of technology adoption will result in diminishing value for organizations.

One cannot successfully run an organization without strong internal auditing. It is the oil which ensures that the engine runs smoothly.

The internal auditor of today is not the internal auditor of yesterday. The internal auditor with foresight advises directors as to whether their strategy can be controlled successfully. It will also advise the executives if another skill is required in the internal audit team, which today is not made of only accountants with the ESG factors becoming so prominent.

The book "The Gardener of Governance – A Call to Action for Effective Internal Auditing" challenges legacy wisdom in the profession and explores what is beyond "objectivity" and "independence" and sets out the behavioral dimensions of the internal audit profession in the corporate governance ecosystem. The authors show how the profession can be more interesting and exciting by moving away from yesterday's ineffective traditional ways of internal audit.

One should read the new global internal audit standards as these standards prompt the internal auditor to become more resourceful.

The book "The Gardener of Governance – A Call to Action for Effective Internal Auditing" will aid internal auditors to become more resourceful. It is a must read for internal auditors and combines well with my thesis that the collective mind of the board must make business judgment calls which, with original intellectual thought, they honestly believe will be in the best long-term interests of the health of the company.

The authors consulted ChatGPT about their and my thoughts about the long-term value of a company and the internal auditor being the "Gardener" and ChatGPT advised as follows: "The concept of directors and senior executives as guardians of governance combined with internal auditors as gardeners of governance offers a robust and comprehensive approach to corporate governance. This combination emphasizes both strategic oversight and continuous improvement fostering a governance culture that is both proactive and resilient. By working together, these roles can ensure that governance frameworks are not only well designed but also effectively implemented and adapted to meet the evolving needs of the organization. This has the potential to significantly enhance the effectiveness and sustainability of corporate governance practices".

The directors are the guardians of the company and as stewards, they look after the assets and business affairs of the company. In order to give effect to their strategies and the purpose for which the company exists, systems are needed. This is where the "gardener" comes into existence. With the ability of hindsight, insight and foresight the internal auditor today plays a huge role in ensuring that the business of the company operates smoothly.

Prof. Kato Plant
University of Pretoria

The internal audit profession is at a crossroads. While private- and public-sector organizations and their stakeholders expect internal auditors to be trusted advisors rendering "tangible value-adding services", internal auditors are still in a box-ticking mode, adding limited value. At this inflection point that has been reached, the internal audit profession needs to undergo a paradigm shift. Internal auditors should move beyond mere "procedural thinking" to "creative, innovative and out-of-the box thinking" to provide impactful internal audit services. Internal auditors need to transcend their traditional role of primarily providing assurance by being a "gardener (and guardian) of governance" to prevent corporate governance failures within organizations. The time has come to unlearn and relearn the theory and practice of internal auditing to enable internal auditors to be more efficient and effective.

The journey to becoming an effective internal auditor starts with a process of education and training. Traditionally, aspirant internal auditors learn the "basics" of internal auditing, including amongst others, the definition thereof, its assurance role, its governance responsibility, the types of services rendered, and the internal audit process, including internal audit reporting. These aspects can be classified as the "what" of internal auditing. Most of the internal audit textbooks provide information on the "what" of internal auditing, but *The Gardener of Governance: A Call to Action for Effective Internal Auditing,* provides answers to the "how" and "why" of internal auditing.

This book is the new "Sawyers" of internal auditing as it provides practical, hands-on, real-life guidance and examples that should enable internal auditors to *really* be effective. The esteemed authors, Rainer Lenz and Barrie Enslin collectively have more than 50 years of experience in internal auditing and are therefore in the ideal position to provide relevant guidance to aspiring and current internal auditors who want to do "more and better".

Also, the book highlights internal audit's role in five key focus areas, namely people, public, performance, purpose, and planet. It puts "practice into theory" and theory into practice by addressing key aspects of being an internal auditor, such as how to deal with a toxic organizational culture, difficult clients, addressing undue client interference, and dealing with your own oversights and mistakes. Enslin specifically highlights an elevated way of thinking when drafting the internal audit report to clients, also justifying the internal audit's legitimacy by practically demonstrating its contributions to the bottom line, "including quantifiable savings, increased revenue and improved efficiencies". Lenz challenges the role of internal audit in the combined assurance model by stating that "Internal auditing can be more than the 3rd line". He also highlights the key competencies needed by internal auditors, such as authenticity, empathy, and logic. Both authors challenge the concepts of "objectivity" and "assurance" which provide thought-provoking ideas that should be considered by internal auditors who want to be fit for purpose.

This book is therefore a call to unlearn and relearn the theory and practice of internal auditing, moving away from the traditional role of the internal auditor to the role of a "gardener of governance and change agent", operating in "complex and chaotic contexts". Internal auditors are "actors in the pioneering zone", who ask "what if" type of questions and who "champion the governance, risk and compliance (GRC) and Combined Assurance arena". These internal auditors continuously "reconsider their audit approaches and techniques".

I trust that *The Gardener of Governance: A Call to Action for Effective Internal Auditing* will become an important and trusted companion for internal audit educators, students, practitioners, and other stakeholders who want to relearn the theory and practice of internal auditing, who want to be effective and who aspire to make a positive contribution to the global internal audit landscape.

Preface

This is NOT just another book about internal audit. This is OUR book about the profession and this is our only book about it. We are internal audit practitioners and this book is for you, an internal audit practitioner wondering what does modern, effective internal auditing look like. This has been our leading question since entering the profession. Between us, we, Barrie and Rainer, have been working in the internal audit profession for 50+ years. Barrie founded his internal audit service company, Pro Optima Audit Services in 1997. Rainer, after a career in Chief Financial Officer and Managing Director type roles, joined the profession in 2007. This book summarizes our perspectives thereby benefiting from our travelogue: Rainer has performed 300+ projects in 50+ countries all around the world as Chief Internal Auditor of three different global organizations, with revenues in the ballpark of EUR 2 billion, always in industry, heading small internal audit functions. Barrie's journey complements Rainer's. Barrie has performed most of his projects on the African continent, in Ghana, Guinea, Mali, his native South Africa and Tanzania, beyond this he additionally had assignments in Australia, Papua New Guinea and Fiji.

We, Barrie and Rainer, first met at the ECIIA 2019 conference in Luxemburg. Rainer was speaking about "WRAPS – How to make better decisions" and we've stayed connected since then. In the winter of 2023–2024 Barrie invited Rainer to join him on a project authoring a book for internal audit practitioners. An invitation Rainer happily accepted. We delivered our draft manuscript on 21 July 2024.

We decided to use the popular 2022 GARDENER article as reference. That Lenz and Jeppesen article has been enjoying amazing traction in the profession globally. This article, originally written in English, is by far the most read article of all time at EDPACS (part of Taylor & Francis Group) and there are 25+ translations. This 2022 GARDENER article is based on Rainer's presentation as keynote speaker at the IIA Nordics' 70th anniversary. Back then, Rainer spoke about "The Future of Internal Auditing", about megatrends, the 5Ps, five paths to strengthen the value proposition of internal audit and suggested the GARDENER metaphor as mantra for the effective internal auditor. We build on that in this book.

We invite you to read and ponder. We have chosen to cite Hervé Gloaguen (the former Chief Audit Executive and Chief Compliance Officer at Allianz Group) who, in his introduction to our book wrote:

> "The Gardener of Governance" by Dr. Rainer Lenz and Barrie Enslin proves to be a foundational work in the field of internal auditing, a profession at a crossroads of transformation. This book proposal promises a comprehensive and innovative approach to redefining the practice of internal auditing beyond its traditional boundaries. With their combined experience of more than five decades, the authors bring a wealth of knowledge and a fresh perspective on the functions of internal audit.
>
> What makes this book special is that it is based on the metaphor of the "gardener of corporate governance" introduced by Lenz. This metaphor, which symbolizes the nurturing role of internal audit in the corporate governance ecosystem underscores the need for internal audit to evolve beyond mere enforcement of regulations to become a value-adding partner to corporate governance.
>
> The structure of the book, outlined by five thematic pillars – People, Public, Performance, Purpose, and Planet – promises to be a holistic guide for practitioners. It aims to equip internal auditors with the tools, strategies and mindsets necessary to effectively navigate the complexity of modern business environments. With a blend of theoretical insights and practical guidance, the authors aim to challenge conventional wisdom and encourage auditors to adopt innovative, effective audit practices that can contribute significantly to a company's success.
>
> The timing of this publication, which coincides with the introduction of new global internal audit standards, makes it an indispensable resource for professionals looking to adapt their practices to these forthcoming standards.
>
> "The Gardener of Governance" aims at redefining the role of internal audit as a strategic partner in corporate governance. It is a call for auditors to cultivate a more proactive, creative and value-driven approach to their work. As such, it is a must-read for anyone committed to the future of internal audit and corporate governance.

We are confident that you will find something new in this book about internal audit, something you did not already know, though you might find some of our ideas provocative, they are always carefully considered. As this short preface is no excerpt from the book, we invite you to read the book from A to Z. Having done so, we would love to hear from you. All feedback, whether appreciative or critical is welcome.

Many will find this book unorthodox, maybe extreme, something which conservative readers may find challenging. But hey, we all have a role to play; the conservative and protector of values must keep the liberal in check, while the liberal should challenge the status quo. With the internal auditor being one of the most opinionated species on Earth, this is about to become interesting ...

July 2024

Dr. Rainer Lenz, Frankfurt am Main Barrie Enslin, Johannesburg

About the Authors

Dr. Rainer Lenz, *Corporate Audit and Financial Expert, University Lecturer, Independent Board Member and Mentor,* is a pioneering practitioner and an impactful researcher. He is a positive, high energy and hands-on leader and finance and corporate audit professional with 30+ years of international experience as CFO and Chief Internal Auditor in global organizations. Since 2007, he has been Chief Audit Executive with 300+ assignments in 50+ countries. He holds PhD in economics and management science from the Louvain School of Management in Belgium, is an Independent Board Member, is teaching Governance and Internal Auditing at the Johannes Gutenberg University in Mainz (Germany) and has earned several awards for exceptional contributions to the Internal Audit Profession, including the 2023 Bradford Cadmus Memorial Award from the Global Institute of Internal Auditors. Nominated Awardee (5×) as Global Internal Audit Thought Leader (by Richard Chambers). He is the author of a series of articles in peer-reviewed journals with over 1,200 citations to date (LinkedIn: https://www.linkedin.com/in/rainerlenz/; Google Scholar: https://lnkd.in/euwxX5yZ).

Barrie describes Rainer as:

> Passionate and energetic, freely sharing his knowledge of and insights into the internal audit profession – a wild thinker, provocative, and he continuously challenges the status quo, which is the hallmark of a true thought leader. He was the first internal auditor I encountered who has these qualities.

Barrie Enslin, *Founder, Managing Director – Pro Optima Audit Services (Pty) Ltd (Pro Optima),* is a Bachelor of Accounting Science (North-West University, Potchefstroom, South Africa, 1984) and certified internal auditor (TheIIA, 1993) (https://www.linkedin.com/in/barrie-enslin-6934621b/; benslin@prooptima.co.za).

Barrie has five years of accounting and 35 years of internal audit experience, both in South Africa and internationally. He identified the need for operational audits in the mining industry and decided in 1997 to start Pro Optima. Five of the eight biggest mining companies in South Africa now count under Pro Optima's clients. Services provided include internal audit outsourcing and co-sourcing, second line assurance services, business process analysis, and other consulting work. Pro Optima has contributed over 2.5 billion South African Rands (ZAR), i.e., ±USD 170 million (considering exchange rate fluctuations) in quantified value added to its clients, with approximately 40% of its projects showing significant quantified value adding, mostly recoupment and prevention of overpayments to vendors and institutions, reduced pricing, curbing of wasteful spending, and improved efficiencies.

Rainer describes Barrie as follows:

> The Pro Optima success story is attributable to the team leveraging on the often-unexploited power of internal auditing. Barrie is pragmatic, does not stick to the script, and aspires to seek a fine and healthy balance between a systematic approach and the freedom to be creative. I believe Pro Optima's unorthodox approach is key in providing the much-needed value adding services to its clients.

Rainer and Barrie met first at the ECIIA 2019 conference in Luxemburg. The duo soon realized their views on internal auditing were very similar and identified the need for practical guidelines for effective internal auditing, which they started work on in January 2024. While writing this book it became even clearer how similar their thinking is. Although they did not agree beforehand about any of the specific content, their contributions dovetail superbly.

Acknowledgments

Rainer:

September 2019: We are grateful to the European Confederation of Institutes of Internal Auditors (ECIIA) for connecting people from all over the world, as they did in September 2019, the origin of our journey to co-creating this book. Both authors attended the annual event of the ECIIA in Luxemburg about "Embrace Change and Innovation in Internal Audit" and met at the Welcome Reception at Bourglinster Castle on the evening before the event. Rainer mentioned that he had a speaking slot the next day – speaking about "WRAPS – How to make better decisions".[1] Barrie expressed amazement after that session saying that he had momentarily realized that we were speaking the same language, which wasn't German or Afrikaans, our respective native tongues – it was the same internal audit "dialect".

January 2024, fast forward, Rainer contacted Dan Swanson, the Managing Editor of EDPACS (part of Taylor & Francis Group), informing him that Barrie invited him to co-author an original and practical book building on the Lenz and Jeppesen (2022) article, the 5Ps and the suggested metaphor for internal auditors. Dan confirmed his interest on the same day and that train promptly started to leave the station. We thank Dan Swanson for the opportunity.

In March 2024, we had to provide references for our book proposal. We thank our first three reviewers on behalf of all others forthcoming, Hervé Gloaguen, Prof. Dr. Florian Hoos and Dr. David J. O'Regan. We thank all our professional peers in advance who will comment on the book.

In June 2024, while crafting the book in night shifts and on weekends we also discussed the title of our book and we considered diverse options. We are grateful to Nabanita Sadhu from IIA India for her advice.

In July 2024, we submitted the first draft version of our manuscript. We thank Gabriella Williams (Editor at Taylor & Francis Group) and her dedicated team for reviewing, editing, formatting and so much more to complete the publication process.

In Autumn 2024, I thank my friend, David C. Jackson FCMA, CGMA, for proofreading parts of the manuscript.

In January 2025, one year from idea to ink, we are grateful for all the minds and hands supporting us on the journey, some we know, some we don't. Thank you all! We are grateful for everybody supporting us on this journey publishing our only book about internal auditing.

Without the amazing traction of the GARDENER article, this book would not exist. We thank the 30,000+ readers of the original Lenz and Jeppesen article, published in 2022. There are 25+ translations. We thank all translators and supporters. That strong interest and the encouraging feedback from our professional peers have been a continuous source of motivation and inspiration.

I thank Prof. Kato Plant and the Department of Auditing at the University of Pretoria (UP) for creating the Dr. Rainer Lenz – The Gardener of Governance annual award for the best performing postgraduate student in both internal audit research and internal audit practice. In her announcement she adds: "We would like to mirror and honor the life and work of Dr. Rainer Lenz, who is both a pioneering practitioner and an impactful researcher."[2] Thank you, dear Kato and faculty at UP, for your vote of confidence. Furthermore, I thank Timo Neumann (Chief Internal Auditor) and the WÜRTH Group for sponsoring this award in the first three years, from 2025 to 2027.

Finally, I thank my friend Barrie for our inspiring conversations all along the way, for his kind invitation to co-author this book and for his energy and originality. To me, Barrie is part of the "9% Proactive" group of internal auditors referenced as role models in the Vision 2035 project report from The Internal Audit Foundation (2024). Barrie and his team at Pro Optima Audit Services leverage the often-unexploited power of internal auditing, thus benefitting from a fine and healthy balance between a systematic approach and the freedom to be creative. Pro Optima's unorthodox approach is key in providing much-needed value adding services to its clients.

Barrie:

While concurring with Rainer's acknowledgment of the contributors above, I thank him for agreeing, without hesitation, to allow me co-authoring this book based on the acclaimed GARDENER article. Thanks for your valuable contribution to the contents of this book, your advice, prompt responses, and amiability. Working on our book with a thought leader of your caliber was a privilege.

To Barbara, my wife and our children Lana and Cilliers with their spouses Tiago and Nadia, thank you for the support throughout the process, including being sound boards and advisors as the book progressed. Special thanks to Lana who spent many hours with me on linguistics and contributed to the contents. What an amazing time of dad and daughter bonding it was!

I thank the Pro Optimates. Whoa, what a team you are! Each team member contributed. Special thanks to my righthand man, business partner and CEO of Pro Optima, Donovan Reeve, and the following employees who contributed to the contents and/or reviewed sections of the book: Elvis Sefithlolo, Brenda Newman, Katlego Monyae, Annelise Steenekamp, and Brandan Pillay.

My sincere gratitude to Beaulah van der Merwe for reviewing the final draft manuscript as well as the other persons who assisted with reviewing sections of the book – Darryl Reid, Wayne Swanepoel, and my dear friend Duard le Roux who is a great encourager.

Several other people contributed to this book due to their involvement in Pro Optima over the years. Noel and Marian Fitzgibbon played a key role in its establishment, although they did not realize that at the time. Businessmen Willem Steyn, Willie Vermaak, and Johan Kruger† provided valuable advice at the onset. Past employees who contributed to Pro Optima's success. Frik Coetzee, who was the first mine manager to see the value in the services that I offered to provide. Our clients, without whom Pro Optima would not flourish as we are. Too many individuals to name.

Most importantly, my Lord and Savior who called me into business in early 1997 when I had no prior business experience. He provided me with a clear vision and immediate equipping for the task ahead while opening the necessary doors. It all felt surreal at the time. He has been sustaining the business in an awesome way.

Introduction

THERE IS MORE

There is more to internal auditing than merely auditing. The response to the Gardener[3] metaphor has shown that internal auditors want more and want to break free from dogmatic auditing mindsets – from self-inflicted constraints and limitations of the conceptual past – to understand why effective internal auditors should become pioneers and learn how to get there. Internal auditors worldwide show an interest and even a hunger, to learn more, to develop and improve their skills on their journeys towards success. We have a passion for wanting auditors to realize there is much more to internal auditing than merely performing audits and producing findings. Moving away from traditional ways may open a new world for those caught up in a boring job. If that is you, know that **There Is More**.

We've identified the need for practical guidelines to building and maintaining effective internal audit functions and are positive that this book will foster a notion in internal auditors' and its stakeholders' minds that the internal audit function should and can be an indispensable value-adding partner; a strategic partner, a strategic advisor.[4] This book challenges legacy wisdom and explores what is beyond "objectivity" and "independence" and sees the value and potential in better understanding the behavioral dimension of our profession in the corporate governance ecosystem.

We must make the profession more interesting and exciting by moving away from ineffective traditional ways. The successful auditor knows that tangible value-adding, such as savings, recoveries and efficiency improvement, are mere outflows from effective auditing. One does not have to focus on these per se. Barrie shares some of the methods and techniques his internal audit practice uses and how these methods contribute to the successes referenced in this book.

KNOWLEDGE IS POWER

Knowledge, combined with talent, original thinking, excellence and interpersonal skills are prerequisites for continuously improving development into an effective auditor and to be valued as such by its main stakeholders. Without sufficient business insight, including knowing the operational side of the business, internal auditors may not be able to effectively support their clients in achieving their corporate objectives. Gaining the necessary knowledge and awareness of adverse human behavioral patterns may open a new world when we're equipped to deal with them because the saying "**knowledge is power**" is particularly true in this instance.

We encourage you to study and apply the new Global Internal Audit Standards (GIAS),[5] as these standards prompt us to become more resourceful and in some respects explicitly require this from us. This book can aid its readers in becoming more resourceful for those inside and outside our profession.

As authors, we do not wish to present this book as a complete guide to effective internal auditing, nor do we pretend to have all the answers. We do not expect everybody to agree with its content. We would, however, be delighted if professional peers would read the book and take time to ponder.

THE ART OF INTERNAL AUDITING

Talent is not limited to the arts, but stretches over into all spheres, including internal auditing, with some auditors being more talented than others. For the less-talented person, excelling may not come as naturally as for the talented which requires them to attentively develop and master the necessary skills, including original thinking. The good news is that most people can develop such skills as we explain in this book. Excellence is an added ingredient to mastering the art of internal auditing, without which, one may fall short of being an effective team member. We also introduce a different approach to communicating results, i.e., "building" as opposed to writing the audit report, further demonstrating the art of internal auditing and countering some of the enemies of our profession, like playing it too safe and shoddy auditing. We point to unexploited potential in practice when rendering internal audit services.

INTERNAL AUDITING CAN BE MORE THAN A THIRD LINE

Let's re-think. Let's not take anything for granted. Let's challenge legacy wisdom. Internal Audit can do more. We can do better. We need better: a new paradigm. The Three Lines Model, while useful, falls short in addressing the complexities of our hyperconnected, fast-changing world, where VUCA (Volatility, Uncertainty, Complexity, Ambiguity) and BANI (Brittle, Anxious, Nonlinear, Incomprehensible) realities dominate.

Many people tend to stereotype auditors as socially awkward and boring. Many still perceive internal auditors as the "fun police". Judging by the abstract 42-word definition of internal auditing,[6] we don't blame them. We have not come far as a profession to change this narrative. We ask why it remains essentially unchanged in the new Global Internal Audit Standards (GIAS). To better the perception of internal auditors, we need a better narrative. We need a positive perception that sticks. Simple, unexpected, concrete, credible, emotional and inviting storytelling are supporting features of sticky ideas. We suggest the GARDENER metaphor as a promising purpose when seeking to become a strategic advisor.

We suggest a bold move. We suggest viewing internal auditing no longer as the third line, but rather as a hinge, a connector, a central player in the communication network of an organization. The time for moving beyond the Three Lines Model[7] is ripe. We can do more. We can do better. Internal audit can champion the GRC agenda, the Governance, Risk and Compliance activity. It can be THE driver of nurturing, strengthening, building an Aligned Assurance Program. We suggest that internal auditors get out of the third line box and become a driving force in the governance arena, nurturing the corporate governance ecosystem. Internal audit can be a strong(er) pillar in the overarching governance system, connecting the dots and more effectively helping to prevent governance failures.

We suggest viewing the effective internal auditor as THE GARDENER OF GOVERNANCE. This positioning beautifully complements Professor Mervyn King's concept of directors and senior executives as GUARDIANS OF GOVERNANCE, *"the heart, mind, soul and conscience"* of an organization with the overriding priority *"to ensure the long-term health of the company"*.[8] In Professor Kato Plant's perspective, *"The guardians and gardeners work together to enhance ethical and effective governance"*.[9]

THERE IS NO NEED FOR HUMANS WHO BEHAVE LIKE ROBOTS

We wonder how robots and internal auditors will work together in this unprecedented digital age. Nobody can answer this question reliably at this stage. The profession is at significant risk of providing false assurance if we behave like robots, e.g., applying a tick box approach. Demonstrating efficacy and the profession's true value requires a transition to original thinking for individuals and functions still trapped in a procedural mindset. An internal audit activity may unknowingly or even knowingly, provide some level of false assurance, which is one of the major risks to internal auditing. We're concerned that false assurance may be more prevalent in our profession than what one would wish to believe.

Business is about people working together. Internal auditing is a people business, which requires us to have good insight into human behavior and to be equipped to deal with demanding situations such as toxic work cultures, including bullying, client pushback and other undue interference in the work of internal audit. Healthy collaboration and camaraderie are key to the internal audit function achieving its goals. However, this is easier said than done. As authors, we have been through the mill, now sharing our experience and shedding light on the human side of our profession as we see it. After all, we are humans with Authentic Intelligence (AI), not robots with Artificial Intelligence (AI).

CHAPTER LAYOUT

Each of the five chapters starts with a synopsis of the Gardener article on which this book is based, followed by an introductory thought and a list of the chapter's learning objectives. The main body of each chapter has two parts. In the first part Rainer shares his perspective and reflections gathered over the course of his career, working as Chief Internal Auditor in the profession since 2007. In part, two Barrie shares personal insights reflecting on his audit trail during his over 35 year internal audit career.

We're dropping the pebble in the pond... let's see how far the ripples spread.
We invite you to read:

THE GARDENER OF GOVERNANCE

A Call to Action for Effective Internal Auditing

We look forward to hearing your feedback, appreciative or critical, all welcome.
Please comment. Please get in touch.

NOTES

1 https://drrainerlenz.files.wordpress.com/2019/09/eciia-2019_wraps_dr.-rainer-lenz_final.pdf
2 Prof. Kato Plant on LinkedIn, 14 October 2024, https://drrainerlenz.wordpress.com/2024/10/14/the-gardener-of-governance-award-university-of-pretoria-thank-you-dear-prof-kato-plant/
3 Lenz, R. and Jeppesen K.K. (2022), The Future of Internal Auditing: Gardener of Governance, EDPACS, 66:5, 1–21 https://www.tandfonline.com/doi/full/10.1080/07366981.2022.2036314
4 The Internal Audit Foundation (2024), Internal Audit: Vision 2035, US, Lake Mary, July
5 GIAS://www.theiia.org/globalassets/site/standards/editable-versions/globalinternalauditstandards_2024january9_editable.pdf; accessed online 06 June 2024
6 The Institute of Internal Auditors (The IIA) (2024), Global Internal Audit Standards, Lake Mary, Florida, US, January; glossary (page 12): "internal auditing: An independent, objective assurance and advisory service designed to add value and improve an organization's operations. It helps an organization accomplish its objectives by bringing a systematic, disciplined approach to evaluate and improve the effectiveness of risk management, control, and governance processes".
7 The IIA'S Three Lines Model - An Update of The Three Lines of Defense, 2020, https://www.theiia.org/globalassets/documents/resources/the-iias-three-lines-model-an-update-of-the-three-lines-of-defense-july-2020/three-lines-model-updated-english.pdf
8 Williams, David (2024): The Corporate Revolutionary - Mervyn King's Life in Law, Business and Governance, Tafelberg, July
9 Professor Kato Plant (University of Pretoria), 04 September 2024 on LinkedIn, https://www.up.ac.za/auditing/article/38069/staff

Chapter 1

The 1st P is about People ... because business is about people working together

GARDENER OF GOVERNANCE ARTICLE SYNOPSIS

All strategies ultimately deal with people and change begins with people. Internal auditing must remain flexible, adapting to the unknown future and learning continuously. People skills are the key to success, including communication skills, especially listening skills, i.e., the origin of the profession. Interpersonal skills, communication, and listening are and will remain mission critical, in fact, key to the internal auditor's success. Increased cooperation between the Institute of Internal Auditors (TheIIA) and universities is important to enhance awareness of internal auditing as a career path. Being pragmatic, not dogmatic, helps.

LEAVING A LEGACY

We occasionally recall the people who helped shape us in our life's journey, both personally and career-wise. From some, we have learned how TO, and from others how NOT TO. Much of what shaped us were the people skills rather than the tasks we learned. Leaving a legacy of guiding people to perform their duties well is important, although cultivating life skills may be more impactful in the long run.

In the American Psychological Organization's 2023 Work in America workforce survey, 19% of respondents described their workplace as very or somewhat toxic, with more than 20% claiming their work environment has harmed their mental health at work. Surely, this is an alarming statistic and one to which many internal auditors can relate to in their workplaces.

Internal audit management should create a healthy work environment for staff to experience job satisfaction where people can work in a positive environment free from toxic behavior, which too many employees are subjected to. For a workplace to be free from toxic behavior is nearly impossible because we are all human. However, removing or preventing some of the elements of a toxic work environment will certainly help. Several elements are required to facilitate

DOI: 10.1201/9781003539001-1

job satisfaction. This book deals mainly with two of these elements, namely healthy relationships and performing successful value-adding projects.

Managers and staff alike must be properly educated in developing an awareness of the importance of people's skills, and how they can enhance effective collaboration among colleagues and with the clients they serve. Whereas leaders play a major role in creating and maintaining a profitable, enjoyable workplace, dissident staff can affect the atmosphere, making the workplace a less than desirable environment. Creating and maintaining a positive workplace culture requires nurturing and time. Bad culture can subtlety creep in and, like sourdough, permeates the organization, gradually pushing the cart down the slope.

LEARNING OBJECTIVES OF THIS CHAPTER

- It is important to create and maintain a healthy work environment.
- Collaboration and camaraderie are key elements in accomplishing an effective internal audit function.
- Good people skills are key to effective collaboration.
- Awareness is key in preventing and mitigating toxic cultures and behaviors.

This section has two parts. In Part One Rainer references his co-authored Lenz and Jeppesen (2022) article and further published work underlying that internal audit is a people business in essence. Part Two is about Barrie's personal insights reflecting on his audit trail since 1989.

Part ONE (Rainer)

HOW HUMANS AND ROBOTS WILL WORK TOGETHER

In the digital age, we must address the fundamental question, being how will humans and robots work together in the future. There will be new opportunities, new dangers, new peaks and new troughs. A robot (generative artificial intelligence like ChatGPT or other such) can respond to any question at the speed of light. Algorithms per se, however, will not consistently provide reliable responses. Neither will humans. We must examine and better understand the roles and contributions of both, humans and robots.

The time is ripe to revolutionize internal auditing: Eulerich et al. (2023) state that "*accountants, auditors and tax preparers having a 100 percent exposure to significant automation*". Emett et al. (2023) report "*that Uniper, an international energy company, is using ChatGPT in the internal audit function, testing its use in audit preparation, fieldwork and audit reporting. Initial reports suggest efficiency gains ranging from 50 to 80 percent*".

We must ask ourselves:

What are machines/robots good/better/best at doing?
What are the particular/superior strengths of human beings?

THERE IS NO NEED FOR HUMANS WHO BEHAVE LIKE ROBOTS: THINK!

Human beings should focus on what they can do better than robots. We have the ability to think, to connect the dots, to connect the pieces of a puzzle to form a picture. Most of all, that competence deserves strengthening: Think!

I expect right listening and questioning will remain a specialty of human beings.

When I asked the audiences during recent presentations whether they could cite the 28-word-long purpose statement of the new Global Internal Audit Standards, none of the 300+ professional peers were able to do so.[1] That fact leads to two observations:

First, not knowing the purpose of the internal audit profession points to a fundamental flaw of the internal audit value proposition. If we don't know our WHY, i.e., the reason for our profession, our legitimacy is not solid. We will discuss PURPOSE in a separate chapter of our book.

Second, in the digital age, ChatGPT provides answers to almost everything in no time. Human beings cannot compete with that. At that point, I deliberately paused my presentation to enjoy the sound of silence for a moment: "**Think!**" Human beings have the ability and potential to think, to reflect, in other words, "not knowing" is part of their repertoire and "not knowing" is not per se a bad thing, on the contrary, "not knowing" can become an excellent beginning. Hence, as my topmost contribution to the human role in internal auditing in the digital age, I suggest "not knowing" as a promising starting point of the "Think! model".

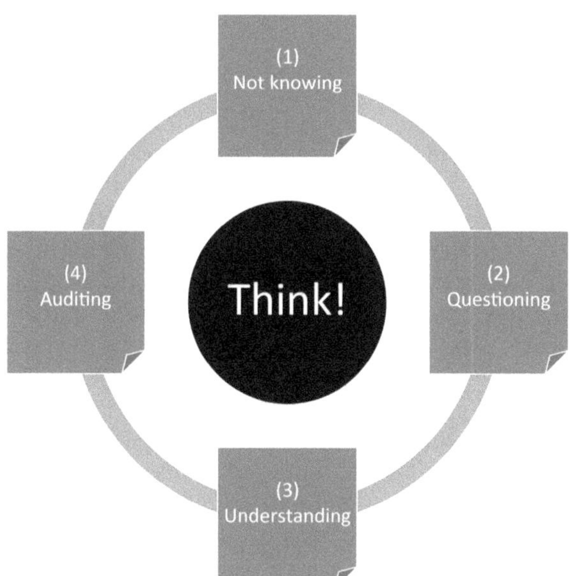

Figure 1.1 Think! A model of internal auditing in the digital age.

My basic premise is to think a fresh any time you audit, since I view internal auditing as contextually bound, the specific context deserves due appreciation. Thinking goes beyond applying an algorithm.

Right questioning is crucial: Think!

Choosing the right prompt is needed to obtain helpful results from ChatGPT. Right questioning is crucial. Inspired by Walger[2] and discussions with Braun,[3] I suggest Think! as a model to acknowledge the paramount importance of auditing with a fresh pair of eyes, not getting misguided by preconceptions or other distracting paths. Effective internal auditing requires good listening skills and right questioning. Right questioning demands an open mind. Only when we understand the essence of the audit subject, can we perform an effective audit. Hence, my model as presented here has four components (1) Not knowing, (2) Questioning, (3) Understanding and (4) Auditing.

Right questioning is super important in the digital age with ChatGPT giving you answers to everything in no time.

1. **Not knowing**
   Not knowing is a good starting point. The Greek philosopher Socrates[4] (c.470–399 BC) wisely said "I know that I know nothing". Not taking anything for granted, not assuming is helpful as an attitude. Embracing the Socratic method, I recommend commencing each audit with the mindset that "I know that I know nothing". This humility opens doors to meaningful inquiries and fosters deeper understanding.
2. **Questioning**
   As stated in my PhD thesis (Lenz 2013): The Latin word "audire" means "to hear" in English. As Ridley (2008) states, "*the right questions will always be the key to effective internal auditing. So will be right listening!*" There is a deeper meaning in the fact that humans have two ears and one mouth (so that we can listen twice as much as we speak). That may be particularly good advice for internal auditors.

   Starting with a blank slate allows for genuine engagement and discovery, making internal auditing a continuous journey of learning and growth. This approach is also a plea for being critical when using checklists. Questions, after all, are far more productive than answers.

   When on assignment, on site, we literally start with a blank sheet of paper. "I know that I know nothing" (Socrates). Of course, we have done due preparatory work, but we put that aside when arriving on site, meeting with our clients face-to-face. That makes good sense, for I know nothing really about the company to be advised/audited. Not knowing makes it possible to ask the necessary questions.

3. **Understanding**
   When carrying out the internal audit engagement, we seek to gain insights about core questions, including: What does the organization want to achieve? Do we know where we want to go? Do we know where we are? Do we know how we get there, get from A to B? What are helpful parameters in tracking our course? What are potential stumbling blocks?
4. **Auditing**
   Knowing the goal, we can reflect, think and rethink, to what extent the organization (or a specific process we audit) is on a good path, on a goal-oriented path and delivering on its ambitions. We typically take a snapshot that way. Once our audit is completed, life goes on. To be effective, there is more to audit than a point in time assessment. We suggest Internal Audit becomes a companion, helping to check progress, ideally constantly.

Right questioning is crucial.

We see value in the metaphor Gardener of Governance to illustrate our understanding of internal auditing. We are not simply taking a snapshot of the organizational context in focus at a given point in time, we prefer continuously supporting, nurturing and strengthening.

The Vision 2035 of The Internal Audit Foundation (2024) suggests positioning internal auditors as strategic advisors. We are doubtful whether that truly can be the role of internal auditors. We see a risk of overpromising and underdelivering. Many corporate actors claim to be strategic advisors, develop strategic plans, facilitate strategic planning sessions, design and implement performance measurement systems, or to advise on potential mergers and acquisitions. This is NOT what internal auditors do. This is NOT what internal auditors are good at.

Creating is harder than judging. We know that. We offer an alternative leitmotif. We suggest the GARDENER metaphor as purposeful for the effective internal auditor.

THE GARDENER OF GOVERNANCE

We concur with Pav Gill, the whistleblower at Wirecard, that the quality of governance determines the success of organizations:

> Not investing in corporate governance will eventually lead to your downfall.
>
> *Pav Gill*[5]

Governance is one of the central themes and challenges in the 21st century. We suggest personifying the effective internal auditor as THE GARDENER OF GOVERNANCE. This positioning beautifully complements Prof. Mervyn King's concept of directors and senior executives as GUARDIANS OF GOVERNANCE (Williams 2024). The guardians and the gardeners work together to enhance ethical and effective governance. Both strengthen corporate governance, top-down and bottom-up, so to say. Guardians have the authority and the mandate to take decisions. Internal auditors as gardeners have no formal authority. Internal auditors do not change processes or people by themselves but can rather inspire other people to change. Understood that way, the internal audit position in the corporate governance mosaic becomes clear and "play your position" gives context and content to the effective internal auditor.

Internal auditors are not the Chief Executive Officer (CEO). The Chief Internal Auditor is the Chief Audit Executive (CAE), a very different role. The term Executive is misleading. Internal auditors work indirectly, requiring a plethora of skills; human, leadership, communication, listening and the ability to influence. Focusing on the essence of what it means to be human when performing internal auditing work, I introduce the Trust Triangle and authenticity (Lenz & O'Regan 2024) as anchor term to the discourse and suggest the refined leitmotif of *"The Gardener of Governance: Our Nature is Nurture"* as a purpose for internal auditing (building on Lenz & Jeppesen 2022). With the suggested Gardener metaphor, we build on Chambers (2017) who coined the term "Trusted Advisor".

Jacka (2019) defines the leading paradigm of internal auditors as:

> A trusted advisor is one of the first people you turn to when you have a decision to make, need feedback, or just need an honest appraisal of a situation. It is someone with whom you can freely share information; someone who can help you analyze the current situation; someone who will be honest; and someone who will provide valuable, critical and constructive advice in times of need.

Internal auditors who matter are a cherished resource, in demand when decisions must be taken. When everything is crystal clear, when there is no leeway and when there is exactly ONE right answer (or best practice) then there is nothing (little) to decide. Decisions are only required when there is a degree of uncertainty. Maneuvering under uncertainty is the constant challenge of leadership today, in the age of permacrisis. Here, the effective internal auditor can be a resource and can become a more treasured one. To become such, the internal auditor should have antennas for the behavioral dimension of his organizational context, which includes the impact of applied heuristics and the biases of human nature. While I am challenging the Global Internal Audit Standards (The IIA, 2024) by stressing the existence and value of objectivity, I look forward to the research results of Nuijten (2024) who studies how heuristics and cognitive biases influence risk behavior and decision-making preferences.

The Gardener of Governance helps decision making.

"MUST-HAVE" HUMAN SKILLS

Effective internal auditors have strong human skills, including authenticity. Authentic internal auditors benefit from awareness, honesty, consistency and sincerity. I introduce the TRUST TRIANGLE as pinnacle of my suggested pyramid of competencies with the additional elements of empathy and logic.

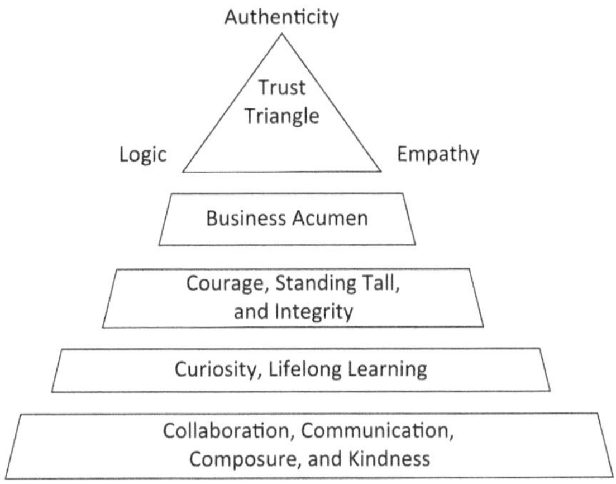

Figure 1.2 Lenz' pyramid of competences (2025).

With the introduction of AUTHENTICITY as a new anchor term to the discourse of the effective internal auditor, I stress the need that clients experience "the real you". That REAL YOU is not about objectivity, as I view it, it is about YOU, it is about who you are as a person, it is, hence, more so about subjectivity, how you make sense of the world around you. Moreover, empathy, the ability to put oneself into someone else's shoes and to not only understand their position but also to appreciate their feelings, is the key to people's hearts. Logic represents analytical and critical thinking where reasoning and judgment are sound.

Internal auditors should be curious and lifelong learners and should be enablers of learning and change (Lenz et al. 2024). There is a long way to go. The survey results of the Internal Audit Foundation (2024, 19) show that only 14% (15%) view internal auditors as curious learners (holistic thinkers) while every other internal auditor is seen as compliance-focused (54%) and as "police" (48%).[6] Since internal auditors operate in the political space, our ethical compass must be sound. There are toxic workplaces where internal auditors must demonstrate courage, stand tall when it matters. The effective internal auditor understands the business they work in. Kindness and caring are fundamental. We have no idea what the other person we are speaking with is going through in life. "Treat People with Kindness" (Harry Styles) is mandatory. Don't confuse kindness with softness though. Strong messages can be conveyed in style, with respect and in a kind manner. As for caring, Isabel Verstraete (2021) wrote a beautiful book about CARE. Her CARE principles are people-centered, and she recommends starting with **your own people**, secondly **your clients**, then your communities, and eventually the world:"Start at the heart of the matter: your own people"! (Verstraate 2021, 34). Collaboration and communication are indispensable skills too. We must be able to work with and through others. In this updated version of my pyramid of competences (Lenz & O'Regan 2024), I add composure, thereby underlining that the further you progress in your career in internal auditing, the more important it becomes to master human (soft) skills. Effective internal auditors stay calm, thoughtful and in control of themselves especially in complex and chaotic contexts. That helps making better decisions.[7]

Kindness and caring are fundamental.

In Part Two, Barrie shares his original viewpoints benefitting from over three decades of offering internal audit and associated services as an entrepreneur.

Part TWO (Barrie)

CREATE AND MAINTAIN A HEALTHY INTERNAL AUDIT FUNCTION

Someone recently told me how she experienced workplace satisfaction in a happy office for many years, only for a new manager with a toxic management style to be appointed, causing undue stress and unhappiness among the staff. Peace returned to the workplace two years later when that manager left. It is not fair that one person's toxic behavior dictates the culture, causing unhappiness, stress, anxiety, or even depression.

As with most things in life, striking the right balance between give and take is the challenge, i.e., business leaders and staff should care for each other. Positive behavior and consistent mutual respect maintain equilibrium and keep the work environment stable, peaceful, and pleasant. For the human body to continue working effectively, the vital organs must remain healthy. We generally do not feel our vital organs when they are healthy but become acutely aware of them when experiencing pain or discomfort in one or more of them. However, some illnesses can only be diagnosed through medical tests, which, if left undetected, can cause serious health issues, including terminal illness, that could have been prevented with early diagnosis. Thus, we can be seriously ill without feeling it. Similarly, an organization can be seriously or even terminally ill without the key players feeling or realizing it. Just as regular medical check-ups are necessary to identify any health issues that we may be unaware of, the organization should undergo health checkups periodically through, among other self-assessments, as well as external and internal audits. If it is important for you to work in a healthy work environment, whether you are the leader or not, being mindful of it is key to fostering healthy collaboration to assist in achieving the desired results.

Be intentional to creating and maintaining a healthy internal audit function.

Healthy collaboration and camaraderie

Effective collaboration between colleagues and with clients is key to the internal audit function achieving its goals. It is difficult, if not impossible, to operate effectively without a high level of collaboration and camaraderie. To be effective, the internal audit function needs a combination of displaying the characteristics of likable people and excellent service delivery. Favor from the clients is attracted through collaboration, likeability, fairness, good judgment, and when the clients perceive the internal audit function as a value-adding partner. Maintain the right balance between a stoic professional image and humanity by being approachable. But be careful how much personal information you share with others, as this can render you vulnerable, allowing for someone to leverage such information.

We attract respect from others through our conduct and attitude. Respect is also an earned dynamic; it cannot be forced. Mutual respect and valuing relationships are fundamental to our endeavors to create and maintain healthy relationships.

Yes, but ... there are two sides to every coin. Everyone has their own beliefs, preferences, strengths, and shortcomings. What is suitable for one may not be appropriate for another, and what is good for one internal audit function may not be feasible, desirable, or may simply not work for another due to, among other things, appetite, size, structure, culture, vision, and strategy. **But, yes ...** as with many things in life, there should be a balance between caring and knowing when to invoke authority.

Figure 1.3 Relationships is one of the six principles of the Pro Optima Culture Model.

Before discussing some guidelines for building and maintaining healthy relationships, let us do a high-level health check by considering the following two statements:	
It is important for me to create, maintain, and/or contribute to a healthy work environment.	True/False
My work environment is generally a happy and healthy place.	True/False

Be likable. Some people are inherently more likable than others, either by personality or having learned important people skills over time. Mastering the following will help:

- **Be genuine.** *Keeping up Appearances*, the British comedy series (circa 1990) is an example of the opposite of this principle. The main character is a snobbish middle-class woman named Hyacinth Bucket, who insists that her surname is pronounced "Bouquet". Everyone (except her) knows she is not the upper-class person she presents herself to be, and for this reason nobody likes her. Whereas *Keeping up Appearances* is an extreme example, most people can relate to it because we all know someone somewhere whose character and behavior resemble Mrs. "Bouquet" in some way. The takeaway is that being pretentious serves no good purpose because disingenuous behavior can be identified right away and is repellent.

  Some people are naturally likable, while others must work harder to come across that way.

- **Being trustworthy** is key to effective collaboration and requires, among others, the following important attributes to be part of our ethos so that everyone enjoys working with us.
  - **Be reliable in keeping your word,** even to your own detriment, or communicate honestly if you cannot fulfill the undertaking.
  - **Be honest.** It is quite common, in my experience, for people to shamelessly lie about everyday things, such as providing a false reason for being late, or not addressing a matter listed in the notes of a meeting that was assigned to them. When someone tells a white lie in my presence, it immediately reduces my trust in that person. As auditors, we should not tell lies, not even half-truths.
  - **Treat personal information shared as private and confidential.** An easy way to lose trust is to tell someone else what a colleague or auditee has told you during a private conversation. How often does it happen that someone tells you what another person has said about you, for example "John told me you sold your house"? While it may not be strictly confidential, it is a personal matter; a matter which one may not want everyone else to know about. Let's guard our mouths; think twice before saying "I heard from *John* that you ...". Let our default setting be to assume personal information shared with us is private and confidential. We can easily feel betrayed when hearing secondhand information about ourselves. It is even worse when the two of us have agreed to keep shared information confidential. There are exceptions though. We're talking about the principle in general here.
- **Stick to your guns when necessary** and do what you know is right, and you will earn respect from others.

Speak well of others. There is something I call distant affirmation. It is the opposite of gossip, where one speaks well of the person, complimenting them in their absence.

A gossip betrays a confidence, but a trustworthy person keeps a secret: Proverbs 11:13

Show empathy. When we are mindful of people's feelings, we are less likely to hurt them. Putting ourselves in the other person's shoes may help us be more sensitive to how they perceive things. It is particularly relevant for internal auditors to be appropriately empathic in their interactions with clients, such as when requesting information and reporting adverse findings. We must be reasonable in our expectations when requesting information because our clients are generally busy and under time pressure, just as we are. Be wise when reporting adverse findings by using the softest tone to still get the right message through.

Primarily listen to hear and understand, not to respond. Developing good listening skills is key to being a successful auditor because the auditee will be more likely to confide in you and less likely to deprive you of important information. Attempts to impress the auditee with your knowledge of the audit area may cause irritation and negativity toward the audit. It's better not to:

- Interrupt others while they are speaking.
- Jump in and finish someone else's sentence.
- Talk about ourselves without asking other people about their health, family, work, etc.

Be modest, not smug. Gloating is a sickness among internal auditors. It is even worse when an auditor feels smug gratification when catching people out. This is a narcissistic trait, contrary to the objectivity principle. But rejoicing when discovering wrongdoing to improve the control environment is another matter. There is nothing wrong with seeing justice served, obviously without being haughty.

I find that too many of us find our self-worth in finding findings.

Deal with clients respectfully. People often experience visits from the auditors negatively, and for different reasons, which may include:

- Previous bad experiences with auditors.
- A fear that the auditors may identify anomalies.
- Expecting work pressure will increase due to the time taken up by the audit.

Don't be judgmental. Having an open mind is crucial for an internal auditor because it is directly linked to the principle of objectivity. Being judgmental can be blatant or subtle, and we can easily judge others without realizing it. Besides the clash with objectivity, a judgmental attitude tends to alienate us from others. Obviously, some things are blatantly wrong and harm others, e.g., corruption, violence, and cruel words. But when it comes to personal beliefs, not respecting someone's personal truth when they share it with us can jeopardize trust. Being judgmental comes with a type of arrogance that makes a person think their personal truth is "The truth" and should therefore apply to others. Especially sensitive subjects such as religion and morals can become landmines very quickly. Even our belief in what is right or wrong in each other's audit approaches and methods may have an element of judgment. If we do not accept each other's truths, there may be constant animosity between us. Mistaking one's personal truth for the ultimate or objective truth is arrogance. Being judged is not a good feeling.

A judgmental attitude contrasts with objectivity.

Ponder this.

Of the guidelines mentioned above:

- Which one manifests the strongest in me?
- Which one concerns me the most?

Cultivate kindness as a way of life

Our first thoughts toward others may be negative, often distrust and/or offense. Whether consciously or not, these thoughts are often deeply embedded, pervasive, and negatively biased. Whereas it can be detrimental to be too accepting of others we do not know well, we should find a fair default position.

Kindness is a choice. Just to put the records straight; I'm a work in progress. Kindness does not always come naturally. I must continuously choose to be kind to others ... and I haven't arrived yet. There are many ways to express kindness. For centuries, people showed hospitality, kindness, and unity by sharing food. Consider packing something extra in your lunchbox to share with a colleague. Kindness is contagious. If you initiate kindness at the workplace, it will likely permeate throughout. When starting my graduate studies at Potchefstroom University in 1981, it was mandatory to greet everyone every time, irrespective of how many times you would walk past the same person. This habit is still part of me. Upon starting my career, one could tell who studied at this university. They were the ones who greeted everybody every time in the corridor. Other acts of kindness include being friendly, offering to make coffee, holding the door open for a colleague, and helping a colleague with a difficult job or big workload. The key is to be mindful of being kind.

Make kindness a habit.

When traveling by train from Cologne to Frankfurt in November 2022, the railway company did not hook the car with my allocated seat, causing the passengers from the three first-class cars to cramp into two cars. The isles were choked with the standing passengers traveling on this approximately one-and-a-half-hour trip. A young man seated near me offered his seat to an elderly lady about 20 minutes into the trip, who I guessed, was in her eighties.

He prompted another young man to offer his seat to an elderly man, but the young man refused. While pondering the incident, I decided to give him one of the high-quality branded umbrellas I had with me and told him: "Young man, this is to honor and thank you for doing the right thing today. Please take this (umbrella) as a token of my appreciation". The following thoughts ran through my mind afterward:

- First, it was appalling that the lady stood for about 20 minutes before someone would offer her a seat, while no one would give up a seat for the elderly man. I would think it is a given in most cultures to give up your seat for an elderly person. "Should it even be regarded as an act of kindness?", I thought.
- On the plus side, the lady must have been grateful being offered a seat, while the young man's action moved me to acknowledge him for the kind act. My action probably encouraged him, and I wondered what happened after he exited the train. Did kindness extend any further? Maybe this event encouraged him to do acts of kindness more often, and he probably shared this feel-good story with others.
- The takeaway is that a young man's (very) small act of kindness potentially had far-reaching effects. It is in our power to do the same, and it does not require much from us. Unfortunately, the opposite is also true, i.e., one act of insolence can have long-term and far-reaching adverse effects. This story may encourage our readers to be kind more often.

Deal with offense promptly and effectively. Offense can be like poison and will affect our ability to be kind to others, which can lead to a toxic work environment. A healthy self-awareness of our offense-related behavior can be life-changing, with positive effects on our well-being and potential positive ripple effects in the workplace. Being defensive when reprimanded can cause us to repeat the mistakes because we concentrate on our emotions instead of the matter at hand. Not being able to handle constructive criticism is a career hindrance and can stop growth in its tracks. If it isn't personal, don't make it personal.

What causes us to be offended so easily?

- Our insecurities can make us feel threatened and are often caused by past bad experiences.
- Being self-conscious and over-sensitive, for example, perceiving oneself as less intelligent or not good enough.
- Getting into a mental habit of taking offense because offense breeds offense.
- Being generally pessimistic causes a person to first see or believe the negative, for example, assuming the other person has bad intentions.
- Having difficulty seeing things from the other person's perspective.

Set your default position to acceptance and kindness. Our underlying attitude toward colleagues and loved ones should generally be acceptance and kindness. We should cognitively set our default as such, as opposed to being argumentative, distrustful, and rude. Being on the road, for example, is an excellent way to practice kindness by deciding I will not get unnecessarily upset by other drivers' behavior and will even give way where it is not mandatory, obviously considering safety. Try this at least once before shrugging off this idea. It works well for me.

Do not hastily take offense because it often proves to be unnecessary as the situation causing the offense may merely be a misunderstanding. Giving the other person the benefit of the doubt may prevent or diffuse a potentially explosive situation. If you are easily offended, consider changing your mindset instead of expecting others to change. Once offended, we tend to see ghosts and soon our thoughts spiral into a pattern of unfounded negative thoughts toward the other person.

Have a good chat with yourself. I recently behaved contrary to what I have resolved as a good road user, by reacting in an unsafe and rude manner in a situation that did not warrant such behavior. I had a serious talk with myself, which was so intimidating that I would think twice before repeating such behavior.

Postpone taking offense (indefinitely). Our uniqueness and life experiences cause us to be offended by different things and to different degrees. When someone pushes your buttons continuously, it may gradually become difficult not to get offended. The question is then:

- Is the "offender" wrong?
- Is it fair of me to expect the "offender" to change?
- Is it merely a matter of own preference, such as the way the toilet roll is hung, or the toothpaste is squeezed?
- Can it be resolved through a sensible discussion?

Examples of behavior that can cause offense include the following:

- Another person's mannerisms or habits can put you off but should not necessarily cause offense.
- A person being inherently abrupt or obnoxious. A frank, open discussion may resolve the situation and assist that person in improving their self-awareness.

These matters obviously mostly relate to trivial situations, with a different approach required otherwise. I started applying the technique of postponing offense indefinitely some 20 years ago, and it works well. By forming a habit of postponing your offense (indefinitely) will greatly enhance your ability to maintain good relationships because you mentally detach yourself to a degree from that person the moment you decide to take offense. So, merely decide: "I won't be offended now, maybe next time. Next time I do the same, and the next time and..." On the other hand, we should not unduly suppress our valid feelings. So, find a healthy balance between postponing offense and attending to your feelings.

Shortly after starting my internal audit career in 1989, I observed the animosity between two colleagues. Something that caused the two to offend each other was him starting the office pool vehicle before she was in the car, as he wanted to be at the destination well before the scheduled time. The combination of her credence and him being quite chauvinistic and generally stubborn, while obsessed with being punctual fueled the unresolved irritation. I wonder what would have happened had one or both applied the above principles.

Lana's purge journal. My daughter keeps a purge journal, which she explained as follows: "When a person upsets or offends me, I have to get the anger out of my system. Instead of discussing or venting, potentially causing conflict, I use a 'Purge Journal'. I have formed a habit of writing my raw feelings in the journal as soon as I'm seriously offended by splashing the poison on the page. When angry, I record my feelings no matter how horrible they sound. We often say things we don't mean when feeling hurt or angry. Our cruel words in that moment of retaliation can have far reaching consequences. Rather take all your anger out on paper. All the horrible things I say stay in the book. After my cathartic session, I close the book, carry on with life and no one gets hurt".

Purge the urge to say something you can't take back.

Ponder this.

- Am I easily offended?
- Which one or more of the above techniques do I consider helpful?

Appreciate and celebrate others

Developing the habit of expressing appreciation to others is a great way to encourage our colleagues. Many find it extremely difficult to accept a colleague's promotion, and those who are highly competitive find it generally hard to celebrate others' success. Rather set your default to celebrating your colleagues' successes and deal actively with jealousy if you find it difficult to do so.

Small talk is important

Our families, pets, and hobbies are important to us. I recently had a discussion with two gentlemen I had just met and asked them about their families. Both were married with a single child, and their expressions brightened when talking about their kids. The one talked about how smart his seven-year-old daughter was, including being able to read before going to school. I guess this prompted the other man to share something about his three-week-old baby son's milestone. When he had the opportunity, he said: "my son started making babbling noises recently". For many, this would sound like a mundane event but for him it was a priceless accomplishment and a delight to talk about him. Seeing these men talk about their children with such love and enthusiasm was a precious experience. I still cherish the memory because there was something so wholesome and beautiful about it.

Let's realize that our lives may not interest others as much as we may think. Rather be the one who shows interest in the other person, yet without stimulating another's self-absorbency. It can be draining listening to people who mainly talk about themselves while showing little to no interest in the other person's life. Be mindful to talk less if you tend to be self-absorbent.

Talking with colleagues also requires balance, for example:

- Unnecessary chit-chat during work time may reduce productivity, which isn't ethical.
- Do not make colleagues dependent on you for personal advice – don't be their shrink.
- It is not wise to share too much of your life with colleagues because it may increase your vulnerability.

Ponder this.

Do I talk too much?

A gossip betrays a confidence: so, avoid anyone who talks too much: Proverbs 20:19

Display basic good manners

- Greet friendly.
- Be polite and professional. Always say "Please" and "Thank you".
- Do not interrupt.
- Do not use vulgar language. It is a bad habit and both disrespectful and generally offensive.
- Do not eat when you talk to other people over the phone. It sounds bad and disrespectful when you chew in someone's ear.

However, consider that good manners in one culture may be offensive in another.

DEALING WITH A TOXIC CULTURE

There is a growing sense of awareness that a toxic corporate culture is a key risk due to the far-reaching effects it can have on businesses. Dealing with difficult customers and troubled colleagues is one of the auditor's challenges in life, which requires them to be equipped with the right tools. This may be on a corporate or divisional level, or even closer to home, the internal audit function. A company can be "born" toxic or can become toxic over time. A key to stomping out a toxic culture is awareness, including self-awareness. People at all levels can cause a toxic culture to manifest. It is therefore necessary for leaders to be aware of the red flags because the failure to recognize abuse and the undermining of authority are two reasons for toxic behavior to prevail in the workplace. A friend often tells me how he and around 300 colleagues in the division of a large international company have been suffering under a toxic senior manager despite the company's website showing the high premium the company places on a healthy culture, including staff's mental health. One wonders how such toxicity can prevail in a large company priding itself in being caring.

Identify bad patterns of behavior before they become destructive.

Signs of a toxic culture/work environment, include:

- Uncertainty about our vision, values, and roles.
- Authoritarian and unfriendly.
- Stress, fear, and anxiety.
- Distrust, gossip, criticism, politics, unfairness.
- Staff's mental and emotional health is not a priority.
- Task-focused, excessive workloads, staff show physical signs of work stress.
- Unfriendly competition, rivalry, jealousy, favoritism, blaming.
- Overcontrolled, rigid rules, and boundaries.
- Moving along, merely existing.
- Frustration, displeasure, fear of losing your job.
- Small dogs take the fall for the big dogs' mistakes.

Attachment 1 may assist the reader in evaluating self and others for healthy and potentially toxic behavior and personality traits.

My attitude and behavior affect others

Be the one who creates and stimulates a healthy work environment by not involving yourself with toxic talk, such as:

- Initiating gossip and whining discussions.
- Airing frivolous, petty, malicious, and troublesome complaints.
- Starting and/or spreading rumors.
- Using triangulation to turn colleagues against each other with devious intent.
- Forming clicks where discontent, cynicism, and bitterness brew and stew.
- Stimulating toxicity by joining and fostering the above.

One person's sense of entitlement affects the entire team.

People tend to believe the first account of gossip or a rumor and often do not probe these further, which may leave us with a potentially false "truth", sometimes for life. It may help curb the gossip and undue complaining if you visualize being vomited over when drawn into a gossip session. Rather tell or show the initiator politely you're not part of this.

Any story sounds true until someone tells the other side and sets the record straight. Proverbs 18:17.

Such conduct tends to send one's thoughts into a negative toxic spiral that can give rise to bad and irrational behavior. Peoples' legitimate concerns should, however, not be suppressed. Rather create a safe setting to effectively deal with discontent and grievances through proper grievance procedures. For everyone's protection, staff should be strongly discouraged from engaging in toxic talk and conduct. They should be encouraged to follow the grievance procedures instead. You'll probably find that little, if any, of the toxic talk will present itself as legitimate grievance. This advice obviously relates to companies with healthy corporate structures providing mechanisms for lodging grievances without fear of retribution.

Toxic talk must be stopped in its tracks. Act now if this dynamic rears its ugly head in your workplace.

Dealing with troubled colleagues and dissident staff

To the toxic leaders, my advice is to either turn or burn because we must rid our profession of toxicity. Being well-equipped to deal with the different people inside and outside the workplace is necessary to prevent the auditor from falling prey to the adverse effects that troubled people can have on us. People are often unaware of tactics used by persons who exhibit narcissistic traits. Basic awareness should assist the auditor in identifying dangerous behavior more easily and promptly. This book will not deal with the topic in detail but we advise the readers to research narcissistic personality disorder (NPD) because the saying "knowledge is power", is particularly true in this regard. This can hold the key to preventing you from falling into a narcissist's trap, and help breaking free from their tyranny, whether it involves a boss, peer, subordinate, friend, family member, romantic partner, or stranger. However, guard against labeling a person a narcissist, or worse, diagnosing a person with NPD as this is NOT an auditor's, but a psychologist's role. I recommend Dr. Ramani Durvasula's YouTube videos on this subject.

Most people tend to first blame a toxic workplace culture on leadership, which is mostly valid when it occurs on a macro scale, like at a corporate level. On a micro level, dissident staff tend to bully colleagues and undermine leadership. They are the ones who often play "the victim" and everything to do with constructive criticism may be viewed as unfair treatment and they often have an unfounded feeling of being wronged. Failing to effectively deal with dissident staff can cause them to become a festering wound in the workplace, which may affect everyone around them. Ignoring the situation is usually not the best option, although I've learned people may show their true colors when you wait it out a bit, especially if it is not immediately clear who the primary instigator is. This is where the importance of community in the workplace will show. The troublemaker cannot stand up to a united group when we all back each other. A team converging under the umbrella of unity and espousing the correct values and morals will win the day. But you must set clear rules, such as an anti-bullying and unreasonable behavior policy. It must be clear to everyone that such behavior is unacceptable. By creating awareness, a safe channel for reporting unreasonable behavior, and outlining the consequences, should reign in the troublemakers.

Keep a watchful eye on the habitual complainer.

> **Ponder this.**
> Do we have a toxic workplace problem in our organization?

DEALING WITH DIFFICULT CLIENTS

Be alert to trends manifesting in a person or department/company. The sooner the auditor identifies potential toxic trends, such as the following, the better:

- Bullying and argumentative tactics.
- Constant pushback on legitimate findings, including attempts to gaslight the auditors by creating the notion that they are petty and/or stupid. When pushback and argumentative tactics appear to permeate throughout a department or division, it may point to an orchestrated attempt to undermine the internal audit function. You may even find that management implemented internal audit's recommendations during or after the audit, which indicates they may have agreed with the finding all along but merely pretended to disagree to have the finding removed from the report.
- Overreaction to matters affecting the audit, including audit processes, protocols, audit reports, and perceived auditors' mistakes.
- Being overly sensitive to looking bad in audit reports.
- Showing undue discontent with the internal audit function at management meetings, including the audit committee meeting, either blatant or subtle.

However, be careful not to play "victim" if such criticism may be valid. We must keep our side of the street clean, including performing our work prudently, treating clients with respect, and leaving our egos at home. The following replies to my question of "What annoys you most of internal auditors' behavior?" show some common perceptions out there.

- Obnoxious and unprofessional behavior and attitudes, such as throwing their weight around, i.e., I'M THE AUDITOR, you're the auditee.
- Different auditors requesting the same information, which may include members of the same audit team or different sets of auditors.

- Auditors not following the appropriate reporting protocols, for example, discussing findings with others before discussing or clearing them with the relevant auditee.
- "Auditors live in a perfect world"; they think there's enough time and resources to implement their "unfeasible" recommendations.
- Having a "one size fits all" mindset.
- Being picky.

ADDRESSING UNDUE CLIENT INTERFERENCE IN THE WORK OF INTERNAL AUDIT

Own experiences and discussions with peers indicate that undue management interference to sabotage internal audit's work may be a widespread occurrence. This includes using their influence to sanitize audit reports and to refute audit findings because they may not want internal audit to report on shortcomings in their areas of responsibility. Unfortunately, they are more concerned about the perceptions of others than addressing the audit findings. It may be a form of damage control to soften the blow of adverse audit outcomes and/or an inherent fear of looking bad in the eyes of other people, mostly their seniors and/or the board. Richard Chambers articulates this adversary well in his 2021 article, Courageous Internal Auditors Are Storm Chasers. "*We have all likely encountered one or more C-level executives in our organizations who bristle at real or perceived criticism in our reports. When taken to the extreme, these executives can become open adversaries of internal auditing. When this happens, we must not shy away from risk-based audit coverage in their areas of responsibility. That takes courage, and courageous internal auditors are willing to push against closed doors and sail toward turbulent storms*".

Standard 7.1 [Organizational Independence] of the GIAS states that the internal audit function must be free from interference when determining its scope, performing internal audit engagements, and communicating results.

Signs of undue interference

Blurred reporting lines. Unhealthy protocols being established or creeping in over time, such as:

- Insisting the audit team must share findings with them as soon as they are discovered, even if they are not yet confirmed.
- Involving themselves in the different phases of audits that do not directly relate to their area or level of responsibility, particularly attending the kick-off meetings and draft report discussions.
- An executive "assigning" the responsibility to a senior official to act as a buffer between internal audit and the board to refute findings and dilute the significance of findings and/or the overall outcome of audits.
- Executives who insist that the audit report may not be issued as final without their consent.

Motivating the postponement or cancellation of an audit because of believing they may not "pass" an audit due to substandard controls, or they may be aware of or even involved in misconduct.

Stalling the audit or intentionally causing frustration and delays by not providing the correct information they know is important to the audit. This tactic sometimes surfaces when performing audits at remote locations where you have limited time on-site and can't easily revisit the site.

Hovering over the audit team to see what the auditors are testing and what they have found so far.

Creating an atmosphere where the auditors feel they must walk on eggshells so as not to offend the auditee. Fostering an objectivity mindset of people being all equally important may help navigating through these challenging situations.

Tiring you out with protracted processes, including delayed responses and multiple argumentative report clearance meetings, arguing, for example, against general good practice and/or established company rules, and the tone of the audit report. The auditor should take care not to succumb to unwarranted pressure but also not to be stubborn.

Stalling the audit and hovering over the audit team may be fraud red flags and may concern auditees at different levels out of fear that an internal audit will identify irregularities. A staff member told me he felt uneasy when the auditee constantly followed him around during the audit. The reason for the auditee's peculiar behavior soon became clear when he confessed to lodging false refund claims after realizing the auditor was about to pick up the fraud.

Ponder this

Is undue interference in the work of internal audit a concern in our organization?

Deal strategically with perceived pushback

Undue pushback may be subtle, and the audit team may only realize this after this has formed a trend. Keep your radar switched on to identify it sooner rather than later to address it strategically, including raising the matter at the appropriate level. However, always keep your side of the road clean before blaming difficult situations on client pushback. The appropriate response to perceived undue pushback is key in addressing the situation. Instead of withdrawing and evading contact with perceived difficult clients, try building relationships with them because our response to opposition can improve or worsen the situation.

Ponder this.

Is client pushback on audit findings a concern in our organization?

Dealing with bullies and argumentative people

Auditors should educate themselves on the tactics of bullies and argumentative people as they can be ruthless. Their tactics may be subtle and may take time to recognize if we're not mindful. Awareness is the key to preventing us from falling prey to such tactics. Many auditors are afraid of being bullied, and because of this, bullies may succeed by inducing fear, and unfortunately, often get away with it.

Be mindful of their tactics. We can easily excuse the bully for merely being a "difficult person". No; a bully is a bully and should be viewed as such. The informed and mindful auditor has acquired the tools to recognize and counter bullies' tactics. But be wise in dealing with bullies because they are not all the same. My daughter, Lana, has prepared an opinion piece which is attached as Annexure 2, providing advice on how to approach the different types of bullies.

Bullying by internal auditors. The GIAS deals with bullying in the Considerations for Implementation section of Standard 1.3 [Legal and Ethical Behavior]. It advises that internal auditors should behave in alignment with ethical and professional values and mentions **bullying**, harassment, and discrimination as examples of discreditable behavior.

The tactics used by bullies and argumentative persons are listed below. We use this to prepare for meetings when expecting an argumentative person will attend, and assess the behavior after the meeting, among others to train staff on human behavior.

Tactic		*Applied?*
1	Arguing in bad faith. Not caring about or trying to understand your point.	
2	Seeing interaction as a win-lose situation and would rather turn a meeting into conflict.	
3	Using word salads, i.e., confusing reasoning which leaves you with a sense of "what is the person trying to say?".	
4	Putting you on the spot by throwing in analogies that do not really prove their point but is merely an attempt to unsettle you; although they claim it does prove their point.	
5	Bullying and intimidation to dominate and be perceived as right at all costs.	
6	Redefining to change the narrative.	
7	Diverting from the subject.	
8	Deflecting, attacking, projecting to shift the attention from what they are doing wrong or have done wrong.	
9	Gathering loyalists by involving others to side with the argumentative person.	
10	Pushing buttons to lure you into aggressive/negative reaction, which is then used against you.	
11	Invoking authority, for example, (mis)quoting stats from a "reliable" source to bolster a weak argument, but which you are not able to verify during the argument.	

12	Insisting the other person gives a yes or no answer only; no "buts".
13	Nit-picking.
14	Attacking your credibility and trying to create the belief, for example, IA is not competent.
15	Being revengeful if you don't play their game.
16	Talking over the opponent and not giving them the chance to speak.

Awareness is key in identifying people playing the argumentative tactics game for the auditor to be able to counter it strategically. Staying calm, respectful, and refraining from being lured into fruitless arguments, I find, are helpful. When the person, for example, attacks your integrity, try to avoid the "I'm not, you are, I'm not, you are" fight. Rather respond friendly, saying "This is not a nice thing to say about me". Pro Optima have recently started to consider anticipated adverse situations such as dealing with difficult auditees in our audit programs per the following example.

Counter argumentative tactics strategically.

Anticipated adversities affecting the audit:

Potential adversity	*Reason for concern*	*Strategic action plan*
Client pushback: Dismissing and downplaying findings.	Recent experiences	Obtain convincing examples of risk materialization. Prepare well for meetings. • Anticipate behavior and questions. • Team unified, one spokesman. • Be mindful to remain calm. Have high-quality working papers at hand. Maintain a robust auditing mindset. Positive reporting tone.
Delays in obtaining supporting documents.	Limited time at remote site.	Request info at early stages, escalate soonest in case of default/ delays.

This enables the team to strategically deal with the potentially toxic situation, for example:

- **Choose the right person/team for the job,** which will typically exclude persons who tend to be timid or aggressive, from dealing directly with the difficult auditee, or ensuring effective oversight if that auditor must deal with such person.
- **Prepare the audit team well** for a meeting where an argumentative situation is anticipated. Break the fear dynamic through mutual understanding, collective confidence, and solidarity.

Counter the bully's bad behavior

Donovan Reeve, my business partner, and CEO of Pro Optima offers the following advice.

> "A bully in the workplace, by my definition, is a bombastic person 'full of sound and fury, signifying nothing,' as Shakespeare would say. Remaining peaceful and present, I find, is the best way to handle them. Their attempt to railroad you into their atmosphere of aggression cannot be competed like with like; so, don't be lured into their playground where they can pick a fight with you. Understanding that there is nothing behind a bully's harsh words and/or personal attacks, let them huff and puff, but they will not blow the house down. Your house will stand as you let them run out of air and, once again knowing you stand on the foundation of facts and truths. However, I have a caveat: in standing up to bullies, make sure your foundation is sound and solid, and do not waver on the facts. A single sign of weakness is blood in the water for a bully, and they will attack. Peace and truth are your shield and sword".

- **Don't give in to power plays.** Stand your ground, no matter how uncomfortable. About four years into my internal audit career the CFO requested that I perform a special audit of a production section at a gold mine I was employed at. He warned that the head of the department was a difficult person, which proved to be true during my first encounter with him. Fortunately, I was forewarned and went prepared. He was a big guy with a loud voice, and he immediately started to argue in an extremely aggressive way while gradually moving closer toward me, and well into my personal space. I instinctively knew that if I retreated, I would lose all credibility. He tried his luck, with his face eventually about 30 cm (12 inches) from mine, I thought: "You can try to kiss me, but I will keep eye contact and won't move". He retreated when realizing this auditor had no intention of retreating. His attitude immediately changed, and he fully cooperated from then on.
- **Grow a thick skin.** As internal auditors, we should start building immunity early in our careers because many auditors experience abuse at the hands of auditees, including rudeness, hostility, accusations, intimidation, and physical threats. We must also learn to deal with the emotional stress of reporting situations that can significantly affect an auditee's future, such as when having to report gross negligence and fraud, which I find more challenging than dealing with perceived abuse. As with many things in life, being well-equipped is the key to overcoming obstacles. Like a tree growing annual rings, we must grow layers of "durable skin".

Ponder this.

- Do we have a bully problem in our organization?
- Do I regard myself as a bully?
- Do others regard me as a bully?

Enabling and truth-telling

The abuse may intensify if enabled. We can enable a toxic environment without realizing it. There are two kinds of enablers, i.e., passive and active enablers.

Passive enablers do not have awareness and do not see the situation for what it is. Their take on the matter includes, for example, he/she:

- Is merely a difficult person.
- Does not mean any harm.
- Is just a blunt and straightforward person/tells it like it is.
- Had a difficult upbringing.

Active enablers are aware of what is happening but fail to act. They can combat toxic behavior but hesitate to speak up for different reasons, such as self-preservation, thinking it is not their duty, not wanting to offend or upset the offender, or assuming someone else would be the truth-teller. However, by not being the truth-teller, they effectively choose to support the toxic behavior. Whereas passive enablers must learn to develop an innate awareness, active enablers must learn how to speak up wisely.

The truth-teller calls out toxic behavior, but beware, being the truth-teller may come at a cost. Consider wisely and cautiously how to deal with each situation because bullies can be dangerous and vindictive. Calling out bad behavior for being wrong and damaging is important but stay clear of pathologizing people by labelling them narcissists.

Ponder this.

What role can I play in a potentially toxic work environment?

EFFECTS OF A TOXIC CULTURE ON THE WORK OF INTERNAL AUDIT

It's time to take a stand

I would imagine many readers either have or are experiencing a toxic work environment. The time has come for internal auditors to fight this, whether in its ranks or the wider client organization because it can adversely affect our work as follows:

Impaired auditor's judgment. Constant pushback on legitimate findings and recommendations may unduly sway the auditor's assessment of the significance of a finding or the overall audit opinion. Once the auditee sees the tactic is successful, the pushback may intensify, which may further impair the auditor's judgment.

Reduced self-confidence. This can cause the auditor to be scared to deal with that person, or to downplay the significance of a finding, or worse, not reporting a legitimate finding. While subcontracting on an internal audit assignment many years ago, it was concerning that the seemingly intimidated auditor-in-charge frequently reminded the team to be extra vigilant when reporting findings, out of fear for the client's argumentative line manager. Yes, the person was surely intimidating but an auditor must learn to effectively deal with such situations; and allowing oneself to be intimidated is not an option.

Fear of dealing with difficult clients, which can be challenging for the auditor who is unassertive and who battles with social anxiety. Unfortunately, a toxic person can be inhumane by using an auditor's timidity as an opportunity to walk over them, which requires the leaders to identify and empathically assist staff dealing with their dilemma. As leaders, we should protect our staff against bullies while developing their confidence through mentoring and formal assertiveness training.

Don't feed your staff to the lions.

Poor client relationships and undue stress on the auditor are obvious effects of a toxic work environment.

Additional time spent on projects, which may adversely affect the internal audit function's efficiencies and costs.

Guard against getting unsettled

When you are easily unsettled and tend to panic when confronted with a perceived adverse situation, your life would generally be more stressful than people who take things in their stride. Setting your default to staying calm in all situations helps, particularly perceived adverse situations, should aid our mental and emotional health, instinctive reactions, and decision-making ability. Rather stay calm and assess the situation before reacting because it may prove to be trivial or harmless. If the situation seems more serious, with potential adverse consequences, you should still be able to better deal with the situation by staying calm. Be alert to others' tactics to deliberately unsettle you for own gain, such as an auditee airing discontent about a trivial situation or even a non-event, for example, by accusing you of not following protocol, or complaining about the risk rating of a finding. The natural reaction of a panicky person may be to unduly apologize and hastily commit to "rectify my mistake" to the detriment of our work. Getting unsettled can cause us to behave irrationally, like "jumping on" the audit team or auditor when the client questions a finding or accuses the team of something. Rather stay calm and resolve the situation outside of that meeting as appropriate.

Perfectionism

Many auditors suffer from this seemingly harmless condition, including me. Such behavior can take its toll on relationships and increase anxiety due to higher stress levels people work under. Perfectionists can exhibit one or more of the following narcissistic traits because of an obsession to make sure everything is flawless:

- Over-controlling.
- Overly critical and picky.
- Setting unrealistic standards.
- Being too task orientated.

If this behavior describes you in part or fully, a self-assessment and action plan would be wise. It is easy to confuse perfectionism with excellence though. They are not the same as further discussed in Part Two of Chapter 2.

> **Ponder this.**
> Do I have a perfectionism problem to deal with?

DEALING WITH OWN OVERSIGHTS AND MISTAKES

Believe it or not, internal auditors aren't perfect; we do make mistakes. Mitigating the potential adverse effects in the face of an upset client or colleague is about how to best handle the situation.

A leader should not cast blame.

Own up to your and the team's mistakes. Blaming others and making excuses are bad ways to deal with our mistakes. Throwing others under the bus will likely bite the blamer sooner or later. Blaming others will over time reveal the blamer's inability or unwillingness to address their shortcomings because subconsciously, they have resolved that blaming is a way out. GIAS Standard 1.3 [Legal and Ethical Behavior] mentions "failing to accept responsibility for mistakes" as discreditable behavior.

Do not allow someone to weaponize your mistakes to outmaneuver you. Being overly embarrassed and apologetic can put you on the back foot. Obviously, there are mistakes, and then there are MISTAKES, requiring different responses depending on the severity. Be wise whatever the situation is. Stay calm and consider the appropriate response to limit the opportunity for others to take advantage of your mistakes and oversights, particularly in the face of a bully.

Be honest without oversharing.

Effective corrective action is essential to demonstrate the situation has been or is being addressed, and to prevent a recurrence of the same or similar adverse situations. This may include communicating corrected information to all parties who received the original communication if it contains significant errors or omissions per Standard 11.4. [Errors and Omissions].

THE LEADER'S ROLE

Leadership is one of the most written and discussed topics. The intent here is not to deal with the topic extensively but to share my "two cents" worth.

Build relationships of trust and loyalty, rather than fear and cynicism.

Show the team that you care

- Relate to them; do not act like you are above them.
- Show interest in aspects that are important to the employee, like family and hobbies.
- Back them up when they experience opposition from clients or others.
- Make time for them.
- Be kind and do not hold mistakes against them for long.
- Our people's well-being is important. Demonstrate this to all team members. It is a principle of Pro Optima to not try to make a profit at all costs.
- Go above and beyond to personally help them by keeping your eyes open to ways to assist, both in the work situation and with personal issues.

Work within team limits

- Don't over expect. Understand where you were at as a junior.
- When identifying gaps, address this in their development plans.
- Do not be overly critical to the point of breaking their spirits.

Don't be the hero

Develop the habit to make other people heroes, including your team members, the client, and seniors. It is a strategic move that may eventually make you the hero, i.e., as opposed to presenting yourself as the hero now, only to later lose your hero status. The following may assist:

- Cognitively consider ways to make other people heroes until it becomes a habit.
- Make others part of projects that are likely to be a great success instead of doing it by yourself so as not to have to share the credit.
- Habitually referring to we, our and us, instead of me, my, and I when talking to team members, the client, and seniors. Even when the client or team member made a mistake, rather refer to it as "our mistake".

Enable and empower staff

- Recognize and reward good work.
- Let our default setting be to believe in our people.
- Do not write people off before you have tried to uplift/develop them.
- Help to develop your team members' careers.
- Identify opportunities for employees to master new soft skills, for example, invite a team member to high-level management meetings.
- Identify any auditing skills that your team lacks and implement a plan to upskill them.
- Give direct feedback and be careful to hide truths behind a shield of politeness. However, never do it in a rude way.
- Focus on employee strengths. Generally, deploy employees in areas of strength, while assisting them in their development areas.

Be open to new ideas

Encourage staff to keep an agile and open mind to see when operations can be improved. Evaluate each employee's ideas supportively and guard against stifling your employees' creativity when they raise new ideas.

Learn to handle pressure well

One of the key qualities of a manager is to be able to handle pressure well. As a manager, you are held accountable for the performance of others, which brings about more pressure. Some pointers to assist in this regard are listed below. Take good care of your emotional stability to help you think clearly during periods of stress. The key is to always remain calm. This will demonstrate that you can take things in your stride and complete your tasks even in the face of difficult circumstances. Force yourself to think positively and instill the same attitude in your team members.

Guard against burnout

I have experienced burnout some ten years ago, which affected my life considerably. Recognizing the signs of burnout in your life and that of your team members can aid greatly in preventing a full-blown burnout.

- **Feeling drained, tired, lacking the energy to get work done.** I have even experienced it exhausting to take a one-hour trip home after spending a day at a client's premises.
- **Experiencing the job as increasingly stressful and frustrating**, and at times, feeling unable to cope with the workload, which previously would have been a normal workload.
- **Having trouble coping with everyday life matters** such as lodging an insurance claim, resolving an account query, and dealing with a trivial disagreement you have with someone.

- **Having trouble concentrating,** such as forgetting where or how to find an electronic file stored on your laptop, that would normally be second nature.
- **Experiencing a much lower brain functionality,** which affects your creativity and ability to perform the more complicated tasks. For me, it felt like a pole vaulter constantly gliding underneath the bar at a height that was previously easy to sail over.
- **Physical symptoms,** such as anxiety, becoming emotional, headaches, and intestinal issues.

Guard against a toxic corporate culture. Leaders set the tone for creating and changing the culture of the business. It is important to create a culture conducive to contentment in the workplace.

Overseeing the audit project/assignment

Being a good auditor does not automatically make you a good senior or manager as different dynamics come into play when moving up in the hierarchy. Remember how little you knew when you started your career. So, do not expect junior team members to be at a level where you have not been at that stage of your career.

Lead the team throughout the project

A leader is part of the team and should not reign and rule from on high.

- **Carry the workload with your team members.** This will show them that you are part of the team and not merely a delegator (or abdicator) of work.
- **Review the project rules and the processes with your team** to make sure everyone knows what is expected and what to do. Discuss any concerns and make it clear you are available for any team member that has an issue.
- **Provide input from your experience** and training when the team needs it.
- **Do not wait until the fieldwork is close to completion,** or halfway, or even a quarter of the way before getting involved in the detail of the project. When there is a mess-up late in the audit, the senior and manager are at fault. This obviously depends on your departmental structure and your role in it.

Stay in touch with the auditor in you as well as with the auditor on the coalface

As people move up in the hierarchy, they can become detached from the auditor on the coalface. They, (understandably) have an increased focus on the macro level. However, this can cause them to neglect those who must still tap into their knowledge and skills to learn from the best. The "best" usually moves up early in their careers; often leaving the coalface just as they have reached an advanced level of knowledge and skill, which they should still use to build into the staff. This leaves a gap where the auditor must further develop without the best being around to mentor them. What the best may regard as second nature may not be second nature for the developing auditor. The best do not always realize they have developed a second nature ability, and therefore may easily expect the developing auditor "to know what I know". The right balance between macro- and micro-management is necessary for the best to effectively impart their advanced knowledge and skills to others.

Do not withdraw from the battlefield, leaving the soldiers who have theoretical knowledge but are not yet sufficiently skilled to attain the victory.

Leave a legacy by raising successors.

> **Ponder this.**
> What aspect mentioned in this section can aid in my development as leader?

TAKE AWAYS

For the internal audit function's leadership

A health check could assist in gauging where you are. Would you say staff generally experience the workplace as a happy place?

Good	*Not so good*
1. A clear vision, values, and roles.	Uncertainty about our vision, values, and roles.
2. A friendly work environment, with relaxed interaction at all levels.	Authoritarian, unfriendly, and stress filled.
3. Mutual trust and respect.	Distrust, gossip, criticism, politics, unfairness.
4. Staff are mentally and emotionally cared for.	Staff's mental and emotional health is not a priority.
5. People-focused and manageable workloads.	Task-focused, excessive workloads, staff show physical signs of work stress.
6. Teamwork, collaboration, support, equity, and accountability.	Unfriendly competition, rivalry, jealousy, favoritism, blaming.
7. Freedom, flexibility, promote initiative and original thinking.	Overcontrolled, rigid rules, and boundaries.
8. Empower and develop staff.	Stagnation, hire from outside.
9. General pride in own and team's achievements.	Moving along, merely existing.
10. Job satisfaction and security.	Frustration, displeasure, fear of losing job.

Work culture may be considered as an audit area, although it may be wise to use a subject expert like a psychologist to enhance credibility of the audit results.

Don't let "too much" overwhelm you.
Start somewhere, implementing something.

For the internal audit staff and professionals in general

Healthy collaboration and camaraderie, as well as knowledge and awareness of toxic behavior, are key to internal auditing's ability to best serve our clients.

For senior and executive management, and the board

Have you resolved that people and their mental health are important in your organization? I am confident that most employers, at least the large corporations, have. However, with the statistics showing that many people are still subjected to toxic work environments, management and the board members should establish what the reality is in their organizations.

NOTES

1 The Institute of Internal Auditors (2024, 15), Purpose Statement (Domain I): "Internal auditing strengthens the organization's ability to create, protect, and sustain value by providing the board and management with independent, risk-based, and objective assurance, advice, insight, and foresight".
2 Gerd Walger was one of my Professors at the University Witten/Hedecke, 1987 to 1991, https://www.brandeins.de/corporate-services/mck-wissen/mck-wissen-it/fragen-pruefen-verstehen-vergessen, accessed online on 11 June 2024
3 Thomas Braun is the founder and CEO of Sokrates Group, https://www.linkedin.com/company/sokratesgroup/; his profile on LinkedIn: https://www.linkedin.com/in/thomas-braun-68b98a7/, accessed online on 11 June 2024
4 Accessed online 11 June 2024, https://en.wikipedia.org/wiki/Socrates
5 When sharing some Wirecard reflections in an unplanned standup interview with The Banking 50 and Fintech Netherlands, June 2024.
6 Vision 2035 Survey, Q22, In general, how do you think internal audit is viewed? (Choose all that apply.) (n=6506)
7 My presentation from 19 September 2019: "WRAPS – How to make better decisions", https://drrainerlenz.wordpress.com/wp-content/uploads/2019/09/eciia-2019_wraps_dr.-rainer-lenz_final.pdf

REFERENCES

Chambers, R. (2017), Trusted advisors: Key attributes of outstanding internal auditors. Internal Audit Foundation.

Chambers, R. (2021), Courageous Internal Auditors are Storm Chasers.

Emett, S. A., Eulerich, M., Lipinski, E., Prien, N., & Wood, D. A. (2023, July 18). Leveraging ChatGPT for enhancing the internal audit process – A real-world example from a large multinational company. SSRN Electronic Journal. Available at SSRN: https://ssrn.com/abstract=4514238

Eulerich, M., Sanatizadeh, A., Vakilzadeh, H., & Wood, D. A. (2023, November 17). Is it all hype? ChatGPT's performance and disruptive potential in the accounting and auditing industries. Available at SSRN: https://ssrn.com/abstract=4452175 or http://dx.doi.org/10.2139/ssrn.4452175

Jacka, M. (2019), Trying to define trusted advisor, blog, April 16, a publication of TheIIA.Org. https://internalauditor.theiia.org/en/voices/20192/trying-to-define-trusted-advisor/

Lenz, R., Karmann, O., & Druckenmueller, J. (2024), Internal Auditors as Change Agents: What a Difference a Year Makes! EDPACS, 69:5, 26–38. https://doi.org/10.1080/07366981.2024.2348283
Lenz, R., & O'Regan, D. J. (2024), The Global Internal Audit Standards – Old Wine in New Bottles? EDPACS, 69:3, 1–28 https://doi.org/10.1080/07366981.2024.2322835
Lenz, R., &Jeppesen K.K. (2022), The Future of Internal Auditing: Gardener of Governance, EDPACS, 66:5, 1–21. https://www.tandfonline.com/doi/full/10.1080/07366981.2022.2036314
Lenz, R. (2013), Insights into the effectiveness of internal audit: a multi-method and multi-perspective study, Université catholique de Louvain – Louvain School of Management Research Institute, Doctoral Thesis 01|2013 https://drrainerlenz.wordpress.com/wp-content/uploads/2013/03/lenz-r.-2013-diss..pdf
Nuijten, A. (2024), Gardening Behavioral Governance: creating fertile grounds for better decisions, Presentation at the ECIIA 2024 conference in Budapest, September, https://eciiaconference2024.iia.hu/program/
Ridley, J. (2008), Cutting Edge internal auditing. John Wiley & Sons, Ltd, Chichester, England.
The Holy Bible, New International Version, 2011.
The Holy Bible, The Living Bible translation, 1971.
The Institute of Internal Auditors (The IIA, 2024), Global Internal Audit Standards, US, Lake Mary, January.
The Internal Audit Foundation (2024), Internal Audit: Vision 2035, US, Lake Mary, July.
Verstraete, I. (2021), Does your brand care? Lannoo Campus Publishers.
Williams, D. (2024), The Corporate Revolutionary: Mervyn King's Life in Law, Business and Governance, Tafelberg; 1. Edition (5. Juli 2024). https://www.apa.org/monitor/2023/09/toxic-workplaces-psyctherapy

ATTACHMENT 1

PERSONALITY/ BEHAVIORAL TRAITS QUESTIONNAIRE

pro optima Audit Services

Instructions:

1. Mark one box only with an 'X' against each trait/ statement
2. Do not skip any line item
3. Complete the questionnaire honestly

Name:

Date completed:

SECTION A – POSITIVE TRAITS

A	Trait/ statement	High/ true	Leaning to high/ true	Leaning to low/ false	Low/ false
1	Integrity				
2	Ability to talk				
3	Ability to listen				
4	Good written communication				
5	Self-awareness				
6	Gratitude				
7	Learning agility				
8	Influence				
9	Empathy				
10	Respect				
11	Courage				
12	Strategic thinker				
13	Working in excellence				
14	Ability to delegate				
15	Flexible				
16	Conform to (positive) company culture				
17	Good judgement				
18	Empower others				
19	Actions match your words				
20	Self-development				
21	Self-motivated				
22	Able to deal with conflict effectively				
23	Responsible				
24	Accountable/ take responsibility				
25	Loyal				
26	Visionary				
27	Assertive				
27	Personal happiness				
28	Confident				
29	Networker				
30	Likeable				
31	Task focused				
32	Results-orientated				
33	Attention to detail				

A	Trait/ statement	High/ true	Leaning to high/ true	Leaning to low/ false	Low/ false
34	Curious and having the ability to ask good questions				
35	Open to new ideas				

SECTION B – POTENTIAL TOXIC BEHAVIOR

B	Trait/ statement	High/ true	Leaning to high/ true	Leaning to low/ false	Low/ false
1	Arrogant				
2	Self-centered				
3	Demanding				
4	Controlling				
5	Manipulative				
6	Vindictive				
7	Confrontational				
8	Irresponsible				
9	Inability to apologize				
10	I do it better than others				
11	My-way-or-the-highway mindset				
12	Write people off easily				
13	Focus on weaknesses rather than strengths of team members				
14	Badmouthing and exposing team members' weaknesses/ mistakes				
15	Often having excuses for not achieving				
16	Not taking responsibility				
17	Blaming others				
18	Talk too much and don't listen to others				
19	Rationalizing poor or unethical conduct				
20	Unpredictable				
21	Know-it-all				
22	Preoccupied with power, success, and appearance				
23	Become unhappy, angry, and confused when things don't go your way				
24	Have a sense of entitlement and require constant, excessive admiration				
25	Expect to be recognized as superior				
26	Exaggerate achievements and talents				
27	Nit-picking				
28	Believe you are superior and can only associate with equally special people				
29	Monopolize conversations and belittle or look down on people perceived as inferior				
30	Expect special favors and unquestioning compliance with their expectations				
31	Take advantage of others to get what you want				
32	Have an inability or unwillingness to recognize the needs and feelings of others				
33	Unhealthy competitiveness - Be envious of others and believe others envy them				
34	Coming across as conceited, boastful, and pretentious				
35	Insist on having the best of everything — for instance, the best car or office				
36	Become impatient or angry when they don't receive special treatment				
37	Have trouble handling anything perceived as criticism				
38	Have significant interpersonal problems and easily feel hurt/ insulted				
39	React with rage or contempt and try to belittle others to make myself appear superior				
40	Have difficulty regulating emotions and behavior				
41	Experience major problems dealing with stress and adapting to change				

B	Trait/ statement	High/ true	Leaning to high/ true	Leaning to low/ false	Low/ false
42	Feel depressed and moody because you feel you fall short of perfection				
43	Indecisive				
44	Take credit for others' hard work				
45	Tendency to divide instead of uniting people				
46	Highlighting my strengths as the most important requirements for the job/ position I am in, or I aspire to				
47	'Bank' on selective good deeds/ achievements instead of consistency in performance that will be self-evident over time				
48	Gather loyalists				
49	I thrive when I am the center of attention				

ATTACHMENT 2

BULLYING IN THE WORKPLACE

OPINION PIECE BY LANA ENSLIN

People have a natural tendency to spend time around those who share their interests, opinions and hobbies. This usually leads to natural hierarchical structures being forced into place by those who are considered stronger, (e.g. performance, physical strength, size, and ability to lead), and usually starts in school. Just like high school, the workplace is riddled with bullying.[1] Many people who "climb the ladder" to better their own careers, step on others to get to the top. Some people may use their charm or likability to deceive and scheme in attempts to force their perceived competition out. Others may use more overt bullying tactics that antagonize and harm others. Different types of harmful behavior can stem from various aspects of that person's background. Understanding why the bully is doing what they're doing greatly helps one navigate these difficult situations. "It is crucial to identify where each power imbalance lies[2]."

These are all simply my own opinions, drawing from my own personal experience in the workplace throughout the years.

I am of the opinion that bullying is simply leadership gone wrong. It occurs when someone with the ability to lead takes advantage of that trait and uses their gift to manipulate others for personal gain. "When leaders demonize 'the other' it creates an 'Us vs. Them' ideology where people who don't need to be enemies are turned against each other."[3] The learnt fear of "the other" is so powerful, that it can foster enough hate to mentally justify terrible offenses if believed long enough. This divide-and-conquer approach is extremely effective in controlling people.

If a leader is persuasive and subtle enough, time enables them to obtain power and loyalty from those around them. Eventually enough people will be on this person's side, defending them without knowing

[1] Dr. Ramani Duvarsula, An Insidious Type of Narcassistic Bullying, 2023 (Online lecture)
[2] Dr. Ramani Duvarsula, Don't You Know Who I Am, 2019
[3] Steven Hassan, Combatting Cult Mind Control, 1988 [p53]

1 | Page

why and following them down a dark path where they are often discarded when they no longer serve a purpose. My Dad refers to this as "gathering loyalists."

Malicious leaders use their followers to achieve their own objectives. For some it's purely about having power over others, for others it's financial gain. There's a potential leader with these traits in every field, and the workplace is by no means excluded. Sometimes I wonder how many cult leaders and dictators began their reign through business ventures. We must be vigilant and able to spot that person who gathers people around them to cause unrest. You'll feel it in your gut.

Tiny cult-like bubbles can form anywhere; invisible microcosms disguised as a normal group of peers. It could be anyone. It could be the nice secretary with dirt on the boss, planning a coup. It could be the mid-level manager interfering with relationships, using triangulation to turn trust into suspicion. It could be Betty from accounting getting you to conspire against an innocent person she has personal issues with.

These insidious traits are more destructive than we realize. People who get away with antagonistic behavior constantly without a sign of remorse must be watched out for. Disruptors, as I call them, are people who thrive on creating chaos. The thrill of gossiping about salacious things and having the spotlight is worth the destruction to these types of individuals. Their actions can do irreparable damage to a team once the trust has been destroyed. People who don't value relationships are dangerous. People who intentionally destroy them even more so. When the fabric of trust is torn, years of solidarity can turn into instant discord.

Talking about others: The difference between Slander, Moral Obligation and Talking in Confidence

Knowing when to discern between an actual victim of a bully's abuse and someone attempting to cause a tear in the fabric of trust is crucial. Know the difference between a moral obligation of warning someone before they get hurt, and gossip with malicious intent. Often, due to the shame of having been fooled by the perpetrator, the victim's pride will prevent them from broadcasting the abuse to everyone. In many cases, fear of the perpetrator causing significant drama in their life at best, and making life dangerous at worst, would discourage a victim of emotional/financial/physical abuse from revealing something so personal to everyone. Healthy people want unnecessary drama out of their lives. In the case of a victim who prefers to broadcast such a personal truth, one should be wary. Someone is

2 | Page

not to be trusted if they thrive off conflict. A healthy person would confide in someone they trust. A healthy person will only talk openly about the person in question if they have a moral obligation to prevent someone else from getting hurt (e.g., "before you go into business with Bob here's why you need to be careful"; Bob is a scam artist, *ergo* a moral obligation to warn someone before they are financially abused). Breaking the fabric of trust can cause people to lose their jobs. This fabric of trust tears when suspicion enters via gossip and rumors. If enough people believe the untrue rumor, the unfortunate subject's personal reputation can be severely damaged, possibly irreparably.

Tools to identify bullying and how to handle each situation

Ask yourself, "why are they behaving in such a way?"

Possible reasons

- **Asserting power.** If an individual is insecure, and has felt weakness or powerlessness in the past, the fear of being vulnerable will always be there. The bully often wants to assert their position as the "alpha", even in the form of a physical standoff so they never have to feel weak again.

What to do: stay calm, stand your ground, don't get angry or show that it affects you.

- **Distracting from wrongdoing.** If someone has committed fraud or stolen money, the aim is sometimes to cause others to feel uncomfortable enough to end the meeting due to personal insults. The bully may feel that if the auditor is scared off, the meeting will end too early for anyone to become suspicion of the bully's crime.

What to do: don't react, give them the opportunity to lose their temper and give themselves away. Stay quiet pretend you don't know that they're suspicious

- **Prejudice.** Unfortunately, prejudice can be something that becomes an integral part of their worldview and cannot easily be changed.

What to do: understand there's not much you can do to change the person's mind when met with hostility due to prejudice, other than realizing it's not your problem. Keep a professional, stoic

3 | Page

demeanor and be acutely aware of their fragile ego. Calling the bully out on their prejudice may embarrass them, possibly risking an unsafe situation due to loss of temper. In this case, nobody is safe

- **Unregulated emotions.** Unresolved childhood trauma, PTSD from war or even someone who was spoiled by their mother and never learned how to process healthy anger or grief can become unhinged. With these individuals, rage and anger can be a form of emotional release; a catharsis, so to speak. Someone who becomes verbally abusive must be put in their place.

<u>What to do:</u> everyone as a team must stand in solidarity with the victim. Immediately refuse (collectively) to accept any of this type of behavior. When it's many against one, the bully may feel embarrassed and leave.

Excuses and Enablers

Many people who excuse the bully's behavior are the problem too. This is how they keep getting away with it. Common excuses are: "they've just always been this way", "they had a rough childhood", "They've had a traumatic past". Well, guess what, we're all traumatized to some degree. We've all had difficulties in the past, but it's no excuse to treat other people badly. Messed up kids have an excuse. But messed up adults get therapy and carry on with life without hurting others. Call out the enablers who sit by, listen, and do nothing when they see bullying, especially if it's being collectively excused or enabled. Of course they are scared too, but solidarity should apply here as well.

There will always be power dynamics in every workplace, but being aware of which tactic is being used in which situation will help maintain the equilibrium. When someone gossips and uses buzzwords without being able to recount any examples, claiming that they have been abused financially or emotionally by a "narcissist/sociopath/psychopath" it may be an attempt on that person's character. Labeling anyone as such with buzzwords is irresponsible unless one is a mental health professional. While pathologizing the behavior of others is not our place, I believe it is our moral duty to call out bad behavior and condemn it collectively.

Lana Enslin, 8 July 2024

4 | Page

Chapter 2

The 2nd P is about the Public's perceptions ... because no appreciation, no internal auditing

GARDENER OF GOVERNANCE ARTICLE SYNOPSIS

To gain acceptance, relevance, and heightened impact, internal audit's services must be seen and appreciated. To promote internal auditing, it is crucial to influence regulators and boards alike, heightening awareness and appreciation of internal audit's value proposition. Stakeholders should understand how internal auditing differs from external auditing. The benefits of mandatory internal auditing come with the price of internal coercion.

IT'S NOT SO EASY

Most internal auditors think internal auditing is relatively easy provided the individual is academically qualified with a few years of experience. WELL, IT IS NOT. At least not if we want to do it well. Think of the internal auditor as a formally trained musician with a few years of experience. Assume a group of 50 students started their undergraduate studies in music, with 20 dropping out over the three-year course. Of the 30 who obtained their degrees, maybe five are exceptionally talented while ten are very talented. This leaves 15 (50%) individuals who are moderately talented and below. The odds are high that the five exceptionally and ten very talented musicians will do well in the music industry, provided they work diligently at their craft. What are the prospects for the remaining 15? Good question. We should be able to get an answer later in this chapter.

Talent is not limited to the arts but stretches over into all spheres, including internal auditing, with some auditors more talented than others. But just as the talented musician or athlete must exercise and train well to improve and maintain their form, so too must the internal auditor. For the less-talented person, excelling may not come as naturally as for the talented, which requires them to attentively develop and master the necessary skills.

It's a whole package.

DOI: 10.1201/9781003539001-2

LEARNING OBJECTIVES OF THIS CHAPTER

- To gain acceptance, relevance, and heighten impact, internal auditing must be seen and appreciated.
- Excellence and original thinking are prerequisites for delivering impactful audit results.
- You can develop and enhance your original thinking skills.
- The audit report can be used as a tool to enhance audit quality and to demonstrate excellence.

Part ONE (Rainer)

INTERNAL AUDIT IS STILL SEARCHING FOR AN IDENTITY AND A UNIQUE SELLING PROPOSITION

STANDING TALL when it matters is a challenge. Most know what is the right thing to do so, in fact, doing the right thing makes all the difference. Pav Gill,[1] the whistleblower who unearthed the multi-billion fraud at Wirecard, is a shining example of that.

Lenz and O'Regan (2024) challenge the role of Internal Auditors in the Corporate Governance Ecosystem. Lenz (2013) stated that *"IA has not generally been seen to have a significant role in the financial crisis, neither as part of the problem nor as part of the solution" and "IA is still searching for an identity and a unique selling proposition (USP) in order to play a more important role in the governance debate"*. More than ten years on, that observation, that judgment is still valid – unfortunately.

THE LINES OF THE THREE LINES MODEL ARE BLURRING

The Three Lines of Defense Model used to be the leading paradigm of Internal Auditing until 2020. According to the widely known model, operational management represents the first line. Compliance, risk management and quality and other management control departments are the second line. The third line is Internal Audit. I value the simplicity of the model.

However, in the past I was already critical of it, talking as it did, exclusively about defense. The model was an undue over simplification. Business is about both, offense and defense. I see value in the old sports aphorism that "offense wins games, defense wins championships." To win a football game, the team must score one more goal than the opponent. What makes good sense in sports may work in business too. Modern play seeks to incorporate offense (value creation) and defense (value protection). An overhaul the Three Lines of Defense Model was due. Weighing up the pros and cons, I was in favor of an evolutionary adjustment at the time, to include both aspects of the game, defense and offense. Since 2020, the Three Lines of Defense Model has become the Three Lines Model, a helpful evolution it.

I still value its simplicity. A model is always a reduction of complexity, however, five years on, in 2025, I have increasing doubts whether this is truly the best way of positioning Internal Audit going forward.

The moment has come to move on from the IIA's Three Lines Model.[2] The third line no longer portrays an adequate and attractive value proposition. We need something else. We need something better. The Internal Audit Foundation (2024, 30) says more diplomatically: *"As the needs of the profession and organizations continue to evolve, this may prompt future research to reevaluate The IIA's Three Lines Model".*

The new Global Internal Audit Standards (GIAS)[3] have come into effect since January 2025. The GIAS demand "Coordination and Reliance" in Standard 9.5, referencing "Combined Assurance" twice in the document:

> *In a* ***combined assurance*** *approach, the chief audit executive coordinates the internal audit function's assurance engagements with other assurance providers to reduce the frequency and redundancy of engagements, maximizing the efficiency of assurance coverage.*
>
> (Own emphasis)

As an example of evidence of conformance, the GIAS suggest *"Assurance maps and/or combined assurance plans that identify which provider is responsible for assurance services in each area"* among other aspects.

We fully concur with this ambition demanding the chief internal auditor to initiate and drive coordination among the mosaic of assurance providers. Along with The IIA, we believe that the Internal Audit Function (IAF) is well, possibly best, placed to drive that agenda. Internal auditors are ideally well-educated professionals with a holistic perspective. Today, that is, in parts, aspirational. Internal auditors have the privilege to travel to places and getting to know the business and the people on site locally. That way internal auditors can gain invaluable insights across the entire organization.

We doubt that the legacy Three Lines Model, even after migrating from the former Three Lines of Defense Model, is the best paradigm to meet that purpose of creating "Combined Assurance". The alleged beauty of being the third line no longer meets the needs and demands of the permacrisis we have been experiencing in the 21st century. To achieve more peer and public recognition, the more promising path may be to be for our role to be so much more on several levels; proactive and visible, contributory and dynamic, and one that delivers more tangible outcomes.

INTERNAL AUDITING CAN BE MORE THAN THE THIRD LINE

There are professional voices who argue in favor of adding more parallel lines to the model. I doubt more parallel lines would make the model more convincing. I do not think PARALLEL LINES are the right response in the hyperconnected world we live in. We need to more fully cater for considerations of aligned (combined, integrated) assurance and thinking. We need to allow for diverse practices while preserving the model's simplicity.

As described in Lenz and O'Regan (2024), shared goals, shared knowledge, mutual respect and effective communication (frequent, timely, accurate and problem-solving minded) are key ingredients of a successful value-adding internal audit function. These are the elements of Jody Hoffer Gittell's Relational Coordination Theory (also referenced and applied to the context of IA by Lenz 2013).

Internal Auditors are uniquely and best positioned to help prevent corporate governance failure. We are on deck all the time and should know how the organization ticks, how leadership is exercised and whether in "moments of truth" portrayed core values truly matter. Internal audit can become the key coordinator in the corporate governance ecosystem (Lenz and O'Regan 2024): a key coordinator, center-stage, not a third, all too often marginalized, line. In other words, I challenge the Three-Lines-Model,[4] the present paradigm about internal auditing, as it is commonly known. Alternatively, I suggest viewing internal auditing as connector, a central player in the communication network of an organization, providing the power of context (Gladwell 2000) and aiding decision-making.

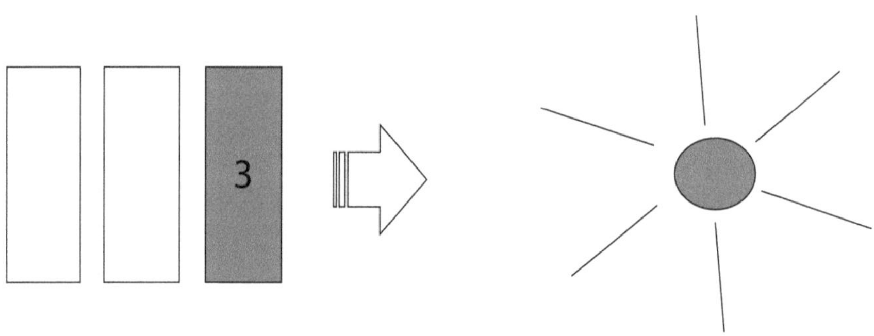

Figure 2.1 Internal Auditing can be more than the Third Line.

In 2013, in my PhD thesis (Lenz 2013), I judged that:

> Internal Audit has not generally been seen to have a significant role in the financial crisis, neither as part of the problem nor as part of the solution and Internal Auditing is still searching for an identity and a unique selling proposition (USP) in order to play a more important role in the governance debate.

In 2024, over ten years on, Drasček (2024) still, rightfully questions our WHY and HOW of internal audit:

> *What is Internal Audit uniquely good at?*
> *How does Internal Audit create value?*

The time is on us to move beyond the Three Lines Model. It has been a step forward to remove the focus on defense in the last update. We must challenge the adequacy of the revised Three Lines Model, especially in the industrial sector, the world I have been working in and where I have been socialized over decades. This might be different in the more compliance minded context of financial services and banks.

Internal Audit can be THE driver of nurturing, strengthening and building an Aligned Assurance Program, or some might prefer calling that Combined or Integrated Assurance.[5] It is not about the name. It is about the content. I suggest internal audit gets out of the third line box and to become a driving force in the governance arena, nurturing the corporate governance ecosystem.

Practically speaking, internal audit can champion the GRC agenda, the Governance, Risk and Compliance activity. Internal Audit can take an organization toward Aligned/Combined/Integrated Assurance. Chairing, co-creating, or leading assurance mapping, for example, holistically demonstrating how gross risks are mitigated and who is rendering what type of assurance can be an outcome of such work. Thus assurance rendered can be raised to a higher plateau. Such an undertaking could visualize on one page what are the top risks, what is being done by whom to mitigate the exposure and what further steps must be taken. The internal audit work program may derive from that exercise, too. To succeed, this requires internal auditing to perform center stage, liaising with all relevant faculties. Being sometimes isolated in the third line will no longer suffice.

In June 2024, I contributed with a presentation to the success of the 20th European Academic Conference on Internal Audit and Corporate Governance.[6] This was my fifth participation in this amazing event.[7] In the 2010s, 10+ years ago, as a doctoral student, in the 2020s as a guest speaker. This conference aims at "*Uniting academics and professionals with a shared interest in the domains of corporate governance and internal audit*". I find it important that the global community of internal auditors truly benefits from its international membership. I would recommend the profession to continue learning from all constructive and professional minds around the planet, thereby heightening the share of other voices to supplement the still pre-dominantly North American (US) driven discourse.

The European Academic Conference on Internal Audit and Corporate Governance has chosen a beautiful logo.

Figure 2.2 Logo of the European Academic Conference on Internal Audit and Corporate Governance (www.eiacg.com).

That logo – as I view it – resembles a blossoming flower. A change in thinking at this time is justified. We can do more. We need better: a new paradigm. The Three Lines Model, while useful, falls short in addressing the complexities of our hyperconnected, fast-changing world, where VUCA (Volatility, Uncertainty, Complexity, Ambiguity) and BANI (Brittle, Anxious, Nonlinear, Incomprehensible) realities dominate. Internal auditing is about connecting the dots.

Adding more parallel lines – external auditors, regulators and others – will not provide the adaptability we need. In a nod to the new EIACG logo above, I advocate a new paradigm: the blossom. Internal auditors, like petals, contributing across the entire organization, with each petal representing areas where they can add value, provided the board (the management board and the supervisory board in two-tier board structures) agrees. This metaphor reflects the true nature of internal audit – holistic, flexible and serving both the internal purposes of the organization and the broader public good. Let us rethink, innovate and embrace a more integrated, forward-thinking approach.

The Vision 2035 report (The Internal Audit Foundation 2024, 28) references changing personas on the road to strategic advisors. In order to flourish, the profession needs fewer than the current 37% "purist" type of internal auditors, i.e. those who hold traditional views about internal audit. The lion's share of internal auditors, currently 54%, is classified as "practicalist", those who advocate or adhere to what is practical. The report is a plea for a more "proactive" type of internal auditor, currently a mere 9%, who embraces new ideas and new ways of working and drives change that creates value. These three personas resemble the rough typology of internal auditors as presented in Lenz and Jeppesen (2022): type 1 (by-stander), type 2 (swimmer) and type 3 (surfer).

Internal Auditing can be more than the Third Line. Internal audit can be a strong(er) pillar in the overarching governance system, connecting the dots. My own practice and insights into internal auditing in the industrial sector clearly indicate to me that the Three Lines Model is outdated, the lines are blurring. That may be different in the financial services sector, possibly still, largely compliance driven. I see value in the logo of the European Academic Conference on Internal Audit and Corporate Governance. I suggest we challenge the Three Lines Model and consider alternative modes of illustrating the role and contribution of internal audit.

In Part Two, Barrie speaks about excellence, original thinking and building the audit report.

Part TWO (Barrie)

IT'S ABOUT PERCEPTIONS

To be seen and appreciated, internal auditors must be perceived as professionals who apply their minds, embrace a culture of excellence and are ingenious collaborators. The profession should adopt the appropriate mindset and audit methodologies, among other thinking innovatively and moving away from external audit approaches. This should enhance internal auditing's ability to demonstrate its true value to stakeholders and to overcome the potential adverse effects of mandatory internal auditing by changing the oft-unwanted notion of "we tolerate the internal auditors because we have to" in favor of "we want internal auditing because it makes business sense". Governance frameworks, laws, and regulations regarding controls over financial reporting (ICOFR), such as SOX, have contributed to internal auditors adopting external audit methodologies and perspectives to our profession's detriment. ICOFR and SOX are important, yes very important but so are general internal controls and operational internal auditing. The internal audit function must be perceived as indispensable by being earnest in our striving to add value. It comes back to wanting to work, wanting to improve, wanting to do well, and wanting to be wanted.

THE "ULTIMATE" VISION OF INTERNAL AUDITING

When asked about their vision, internal auditors often refer to it as providing an effective, efficient, and/or value-added service to the client, with action plans stating that we will do more of this and less of that to achieve the objective. What if our vision is to steer the internal control environment of the client to maturity and the mission is, come hell or high water, we will achieve this within the next five years? There will be no excuses, not taking no for an answer, not blaming management and the board. We will get there whatever it takes, if the board doesn't seem to support us, we will make sure they do. This is extreme and a tall order but if we don't try, we won't know, right? In any event, even if we're only 80% successful, we probably did better than "we did more of this and less of that, resulting in controls to improve, although we're still far from the desired maturity level, and we're not sure when or if we'll get there". Consider incorporating into your internal audit function's vision helping the client achieving the desired internal control maturity. Maybe this notion should feature in the GIAS' purpose statement of internal auditing as well.

EMBRACE A CULTURE OF EXCELLENCE

Excellence, in short, is the quality of being extremely good. This is exactly what must be on people's minds when they think and talk about their internal audit function. Excellence is a complete package comprising accuracy, punctuality, quality, integrity, accountability, self-discipline, neatness, going the extra mile, innovation, adding value, good personal relationships, and acting in a way that let the client feel important because their internal audit function responds to their requests promptly and effectively. If internal auditors do not strive to achieve and maintain excellence, the activity will not grow and may not even survive. The in-house internal audit function may still get away with mediocracy, but the outsourced practice will put itself at great risk. Let's, however, not confuse excellence with perfectionism as the line between the two is easily blurred. Whereas excellence produces the desired results, perfectionism can be poisonous if not promptly diagnosed and effectively treated. Find the fine balance between excellence on the one hand and the available time and resources on the other. Excellence and original thinking are closely related and are two of the six principles in the Pro Optima culture model.

Figure 2.3 Excellence and original thinking are principles in the Pro Optima Culture Model.

Be intentional about it

As with many things in life, unless we are intentional, we seem to often fail in our endeavors to follow through on good resolutions. Our project teams are encouraged to decide at the beginning of each project: "We're gonna hit this one out of the park" and we record in the audit program HOW we'll hit it out of the park. This mental attitude motivates the team to deliver an excellent product with each project.

Start somewhere – with something today enhancing your level of excellence.

Diligence and discipline

"Don't care to do the job well" is not the mark of a person operating in excellence. Auditors must be disciplined and comply with the Internal Audit Standards and their organization's standards and ethics. Leaders should deal effectively with negligence and laziness, which are enemies of our profession.

It is possible to be too lazy to apply your mind.

"It looks right" should not exist in an auditor's vocabulary. We should not base audit results on "it looks right". The question is: "Is it right?", not "Does it look right"? This can only be achieved by doing thorough audit testing in conformance with Standard 14.1 [Gathering Information for Analysis and Evaluation] requiring, among others that internal auditors must use professional skepticism to evaluate whether information is reliable. Standard 14.1 further states that "Reliability is strengthened when the information is:

- Obtained directly by an internal auditor or from an independent source.
- Corroborated.
- Gathered from a system with effective governance, risk management, and control processes".

Attention to detail is a hallmark of excellence. Failing to pay attention to the (important) details, you will make mistakes, waste time, harm your and the department's reputation as well as cause undue stress for yourself and others. Attention to detail contributes to the capacity to foresee challenges and to address them proactively, and this is key to delivering excellent results. Anticipation is key to the ability to pay attention to detail, i.e., to anticipate constructively; not fear-based anticipation of expecting disaster to strike. Anticipate things in your everyday life, for example, anticipate the driver of the other vehicle may not see you when approaching the intersection. Aspects that each staff member must actively and cognitively pay attention to, particularly if it is not yet part of your "make-up", include spelling (emails, reports), neatness (dress, working papers, office), completeness (project planning, testing, reporting), and accuracy (spreadsheets, working papers, timesheets, findings) to mention a few.

Promptness. Start and finish projects within schedule. A late start may, while a late finish will rob you from receiving the laurel wreath.

Professionalism in all correspondence, reporting, and workpapers. Edit your work, including grammar, spacing, font, and the correct names and designations in correspondence before issuing it.

Neatness (even in the small things), like the design of spreadsheets, must be of a high standard without wasting time seeking perfection, for example:

- Descriptive headings and headers.
- Be consistent with letter size and fonts as well as use the appropriate horizontal and vertical alignment.
- Use decimals appropriately.
- Use check totals to identify potential formula errors.

Meetings with auditees require planning and cognitive attention to detail, including:

- Always be on time.
- Acquire and practice effective communication skills.
- Mostly listen to understand rather than to respond, e.g., nod to show you're listening.
- Be well prepared to start strong and to be in control as circumstances dictate.
- Present logically, which requires prioritizing and sequencing of your thoughts.
- Have all audit evidence handy and logically arranged to locate and present it immediately when needed.

Our managers and seniors are encouraged to demonstrate and instill a culture of excellence by ensuring it permeates throughout the business.

> **Ponder this.**
> Which area of my job can I increase the level of excellence?

Never audit on autopilot.

THE INTERNAL AUDITOR AS AN ORIGINAL THINKER

Internal audit leaders who do not intentionally develop their staff's creative thinking abilities may struggle to show real value to their clients. **Initiative** is the ability to assess and initiate things independently, for example, identifying and leading the process of redesigning a working paper template when the current version requires revision or implementing improvements in the workplace by introducing others' innovations and ideas such as audit management software. Initiative is important but not enough; creativity is a powerful added ingredient to the mix. **Creativity** is the art of creating something original by using imagination. Since creativity is often associated with the arts, the terms creativity, original thinking, and outside-the-box thinking are used interchangeably in this book. Original thinkers are more inclined to identify significant and value-added findings that are not part of the testing program. These findings surface because the auditor is pragmatic and does not stick religiously to the audit program, like a talented actor enhancing the scene by not sticking to the script. Rather, they think outside the box and keep their eyes and ears open. Auditors with blinkers on will continuously identify mainly superficial findings, like documents not signed, and reconciliations not promptly performed. Pro Optima instills a culture of creativity and innovation throughout the team to best serve clients. Some team members are intuitively creative and proactive, while others need the tools and encouragement to step out and stay out of their comfort zones. When researching the topic of creativity and innovation in the internal audit profession in 2018 while preparing the Pro Optima DNA Manual, titled *Beyond the Obvious*, I was surprised to find no website that provided satisfactory practical guidance on the topic. Information about this topic was presented academically and theory-based, with a few hints on how auditors can be creative or innovative. The topic of original thinking has since been written about more often, although I did not come across any website providing detailed practical guidelines at the time of writing this book.

Initiative and innovation are brothers –
innovation is the big brother.

Creativity does not have a recipe. It's not doing exactly as others do, neither is it doing things the same way as the previous time. Employees sometimes say: "But last time you showed me to do it this way". My usual reply is "Creativity does not have a recipe", or I would say, with friendly sarcasm, "That must have been a Monday. Today is Thursday", to get the point across.

> **Ponder this.**
> Do I regard myself as creative?

You can develop the ability to become an original thinker

Some auditors are naturally divergent thinkers, while others must be taught. Some practical advice for developing yourself follows.

Be intentional about it. You will only be able to develop and improve your original thinking skills if you are mindful to do so. Believe in your capability.

If you are an "I cannot", cognitively get out of this mindset. Remove the psychological barriers by developing your creativity.

Start somewhere – with something today enhancing your creativity.

Identify your own ideas first. Try coming up with your ideas or solutions before asking someone else will assist in naturally developing your imagination. I decided not to do research before completing the first draft of this book because I wanted it to be authentic. Although time-consuming and challenging I pressed through with this resolve and did limited research shortly before submitting the manuscript to the publishers.

Become more proactive. Develop an innate ability to be proactive and to anticipate change, rather than being reactive to situations and changes after they happen. Driving a vehicle provides ample opportunity to develop this innate ability by anticipating what the other driver may or may not do that poses a risk to you.

The internal audit profession provides ample opportunity for developing our original thinking abilities.

Force yourself out of your comfort zone. Identify your comfort zones and cognitively force yourself out of them, which usually requires taking risks. For example, if you are not a natural public speaker, find an opportunity and (just) do it.

Start doing things differently.

- Learn to be okay with disrupted routine; in fact, embrace it.
- Broaden your horizon, travel outside your district, travel outside your country. If you can, travel to the moon.
- Take different routes when traveling to the shop, work, relatives, etc.
- Develop an interest in a different sport. Start exercising if you become passive.
- Take up a class in something outside your frame of reference, e.g., pottery, piano, ballroom dancing, or a different language.
- Discuss among the family and record an action plan to make life more joyful and interesting.
- Observe how outside-the-box thinkers operate as motivation to become more creative.
- Attending a critical thinking training course can be a valuable investment.

Become part of the subject/audit area. Auditors lacking business insight tend to be shackled in an abstract work environment, which will limit their value-adding ability.

- **Increase your exposure to the operational aspects of the business.** This will broaden your horizons and stimulate your creative thinking ability. Spend time in the factory, go underground at a mine, take a tour of the processing plant, visit various sites/branches of the business, or join a truck driver on a day trip.

Business insight is key to effective internal auditing.

- **Be on site.** I have difficulty believing remote auditing is generally better than being mostly on-site. Performing sit-throughs as opposed to proper walkthroughs has become the norm for many internal audit functions. We refer to this phase of the project as a "hawk-through" which implies the auditor/team is observant to get true insight, instead of information only, while being attentive to identify value-adding opportunities with hawk eyes. See, interact, feel, touch, taste, and get your hands dirty because auditing only from behind a desk is unlikely to give the same good results as being present.
- **Perform proper research** on the topic at hand; even for audit areas that are regarded as run-of-the-mill audits, such as revenue recognition, payroll, and procurement because this opens our minds to best practices and opportunities to add value. The internet is a powerful tool – use it. While searching ideas for a payroll audit to demonstrate how easy it is, ways to improve the workplace experience came up, including proper lighting and effective workstation layout. Spending time in the payroll office during an audit provides the opportunity to see, feel, and hear. Now that I have determined that inadequate lighting and workspace can affect the payroll staff's performance and well-being I can observe and evaluate these conditions. If this test resulted in an improved work environment, I would have added value, and even if it didn't bring improvement to the payroll office, I took a step in developing my original thinking capability.

Go where your fear is.

Ponder this.

Which one or more of the above tips can I apply to develop or enhance my creativity?

Be one step ahead. A smart auditor is one step ahead and will not just fall for an auditee trying to lead you (by the nose). Blindly accepting what the auditee tells you will easily lead you astray. People sometimes tell you what they think, what you may think is the right answer. An auditor should not arrive at the test result by merely asking someone how the risk is mitigated and taking that answer as the truth and basing the finding on hearsay, just as you cannot believe everything shared on social media. Avoid, for example: "it seems" in reporting because this creates the impression you did not bother to find the real issue or cause.

Do not be led by the nose.

Apply logic. Use your brain. Guard against including illogical findings and recommendations in the audit report. Auditors who do not operate at a high level of excellence can easily fall into this trap because of imprudence. It is good practice to pulse the auditee before presenting the first draft to test your logic regarding a finding and/or recommendation, which may save you getting egg on the face later.

Gullibility and auditing are enemies.

Look beyond the paper. Interpret audit "evidence" with insight. It is easy to fall into the habit of accepting the audit information obtained at face value, which may sometimes turn out not to be evidence. For example, records that match exactly may indicate anomalies, such as an order that is generated after the invoice date is likely a confirmation order, which may be a circumvention of the purchasing procedures. Auditors who do not apply their minds may merely tick off on the checklist that an order supports the payment, which may be true, but also wrong. The GIAS deal with this aspect under Professional Skepticism, defined as questioning and critically assessing the reliability of information.

Follow your intuition when sensing that something may be wrong with a document or activity. Skilled auditors have developed this innate ability over time. Several of our most significant findings reported over the years were identified by listening to (and following) our intuition, many of which fell outside the immediate scope of the projects.

The good news is that you can develop the ability to become an original thinker.

Keep your radar switched on for opportunities to add value. Be observant, make the connections in your brain, and actively consider how you can add value with each project. Gather strategic information that can guide you. Listen, look, and understand to be able to read the situation. Observant persons will often see opportunities to add tangible value to the business.

Should-be vs. As-is audit approach. Adopting Pro Optima's Start with Intuition Methodology (SWIM) is an excellent way to develop your original thinking ability because it requires the audit team to apply their minds to design and test required controls (Should be), instead of mainly relying on the client's designed controls (As is). Chapter 4 of this book explains SWIM. The smart auditor will likely identify the control gaps, but the below-average auditor may not. We are the internal control experts, so let's use this knowledge and skills to identify the required controls. Exceptions may include some compliance and financial reporting audits.

Brainstorming. Our project planning process starts with a brainstorming session. Everything the team members can think of regarding the subject/audit area is recorded without criticizing or telling someone their contribution is incorrect or irrelevant. The brainstorming results largely form the basis for developing the audit program. The habit of some internal audit functions to download checklists and/or mainly use audit programs passed on from generation to generation without first applying their minds inhibits the team's original thinking development.

Will you still look good if return on investment is one of your scorecard metrics?

Use technology effectively but do not succumb to the "curse" of technology by hiding behind the computer to which many auditors have fallen prey to.

Start writing (building) the report early in the project, e.g., after the initial "hawk-through" as this will enhance the opportunity to identify control gaps. Refer to *Building the Audit Report* section below.

Do not let excitement get the better of you. Be patient and do not rush to conclusions and judgments.

Seek advice from others. Sitting in your corner, minding (only) your business when busy with a project will keep you shackled in a small world. Get out of the small world by interacting and asking for advice from others. Similarly, discuss your ideas with different people as they can become exponentially more valuable as you discuss them, including with those who think differently from you. But guard against falling into a habit of seeking advice before you have tried to come up with your ideas.

Think, speak, and sound strategically. Auditors who think with a strategic purpose are more likely to excel in their work. Prepare and deliberate before approaching the auditee to request information or providing feedback on the audit results. Prioritize and sequence your thoughts. Structure your verbal (and written) communication in a way that helps the audience focus on the core message.

Healthy interaction. Obtaining information only by email prevents the auditor from having regular eye contact and observing what happens in the audit area. An online meeting is a better alternative to sending emails only and a site visit may be even better.

Great ideas and thoughts require time to develop into a great audit.

Think of creative ways to perform audit tests, for example:

- **Include creative testing in the project plan and think creatively throughout the audit.** Our standard audit project program template has a section for creative testing. The auditor/team must think of one or more creative ways to perform tests that are outside the normal audit testing framework. Whereas we have many examples of how creative testing opened our eyes to significant findings and value-adding opportunities, I will mention an example relating to a financial controls audit.

  In addition to the sample of 25 payments selected from the ledger, we obtained all supplier invoices, with their supporting documents for three months and scanned through them. We identified at least three significant anomalies that would have been missed had we only relied on the limited (normal) sample testing, including:
  - The capital approval process was bypassed by absorbing significant capital-related expenditure in working costs.
  - Prepayments were capitalized and depreciated long before the asset was delivered.

- Incorrect expense cut-off.
  Some can argue that this technique is biased. Here's my take: This was not an external or ICOFR audit in which materiality is a crucial concept. The purpose of the internal audit was to assess the adequacy and effectiveness of internal controls. Good luck if you believe that a sample of, say, 25, as time permits, can provide assurance of control adequacy and effectiveness. The audit team may at most be able to confirm whether or not the system is operating as intended for the sample tested, whereas fraud and mistakes would have been found just by chance.
  The question is: Was it wrong to identify and report that significant capital-related expenditure was absorbed in working cost, that prepayments were capitalized and depreciated long before the asset was delivered, and expenditure was not reported in the appropriate reporting period? I don't think so, provided the findings are presented fairly and in the right perspective.

Ponder this.
What creative audit test can I apply in a current or next audit?

Find something you weren't looking for.

- **Change direction when necessary – also referred to as adaptive auditing.** Be wisely flexible and revise your audit program as needed, instead of religiously sticking to it. Be practical and consider the best option for each project. It may not always be the best option to continue with the audit per the audit planning if circumstances dictate otherwise, for example:
  - **Halt the audit in favor of a work-study or business process analysis (BPA).** During the audit of a service provider who bused mine employees between their residences (hostels) and workplaces (shafts), the auditor observed many of the buses carried only a few passengers at a time. We agreed with the client to perform a BPA, instead of continuing with the audit. The value-added effect was significant, with the client still commending Pro Optima years later for identifying the inefficiencies and proposing changes to the configuration of the bus fleet and bus routes, which reduced costs by approximately ZAR25 million per annum (equating to ±USD1.7m in 2018).
  - **Stop and move on to the next audit** if the initial testing shows an adequate standard of control to better use the available resources. This may be a challenging thought for the auditor erring on the conservative side. We have largely followed this approach when establishing an internal audit function for our first client. The audit universe consisted of about 100 audit areas for the five operations and a corporate office, i.e., about 500 audits to be performed by

three to five auditors. We spent the first three years trying to cover as many audit areas as possible at the different locations. When an audit outcome showed relatively good controls midway, we would consolidate, issue the report, and reallocate resources to the other scheduled audits. The audits were by no means superfluously done. In fact, about 40% of the audits during the first three years resulted in quantifiable savings and recoveries.

The impact of original thinking on the internal audit activity

The creative internal audit activity is more likely to show a positive return on investment. We keep track of the tangible savings and recoveries and have shown positive returns on investment for all our major clients every year since 1997, with only minor exceptions. Our culture of creativity has led to incredible cost-saving and production-efficiency interventions for our clients, now totaling well over ZAR2.5 billion. We only track savings for maximum 12 months despite most of the savings continuing way beyond and indefinitely. Attachment 3 presents examples of our audit staff's value-adding contributions. All our staff members have something to show; even the ones who have been with us for a mere few weeks or months. Some staff members had difficulty deciding which of the tens or hundreds of their projects/contributions to list here. Most staff are deployed at clients where we perform audits, investigations, business process analysis, and other consulting work as a Second Line service on a continued basis, with a permanent presence at three of these clients ranging from 15 to 22 years.

The internal audit activity earns greater respect because management is more likely to regard internal audit as a trusted partner if its positive contribution is evident.

It is easier to convince management to implement recommendations. Management will find it hard to argue once the risk has materialized as opposed to suggesting the risk may materialize.

The less creative auditor's *condition* is the creative auditor's *cause*. The original thinker often identifies the anomaly/error that has occurred due to the deviation from a specific control while the less creative auditor mostly identifies the deviation from the control only as per the following <u>basic</u> example.

Element of finding	*Generic finding*	*The original thinker's finding*
Condition	Bonus calculation sheets were not signed in evidence of review.	Production results for teams A and B were swapped around.
Cause	Oversight by the senior bonus coordinator.	Bonus calculation sheets were not subjected to diligent review.
Effect	Potential incorrect bonus payments.	Team A members were overpaid by $2 000 while Team B members were underpaid by $1 500.

Internal auditors become influencers for change. A recommendation should not merely be the response to the cause. Internal auditors can influence the destiny of the client when they regularly identify significant shortcomings and opportunities while providing out-the-box solutions.

Cultivate an environment for original thinking

Internal audit leaders should create an environment in which staff can develop and apply their original thinking abilities. Unfortunately, over-controlling is the fate for many in the profession. Several auditors have told us their strictly controlling internal audit environment inhibits their creative abilities. A common response is: "We are given an audit program and must work accordingly". Those who joined us from other employers often express appreciation for the training and encouragement to develop their original thinking abilities because they see the undeniable value added to project outcomes. Have open discussions with staff to assess the level of frustration that may exist due to over-controlling, and how this affects job satisfaction and career path planning.

> **Ponder this.**
>
> Is our work environment conducive to developing our original thinking abilities?
>
> What can I as a leader do to develop our staff's original thinking abilities?

Leaders should not inhibit or suppress their staff's creativity.

BUILDING THE INTERNAL AUDIT REPORT

Internal auditors often find it difficult to present audit results successfully and creatively. Most find it rather easy to relay the findings when discussing it among the team but get stuck when having to present the results in the report. I am an advocate for the audit report to be an artwork as opposed to a run-of-the-mill style. Audit reports can be presented artistically, yet simply. However, achieving this demands more from us than merely presenting the relevant facts accurately. A report prepared with an intended sense of creativity enhances the likelihood that the recipients will read it without unnecessary delay and understand everything in it without undue effort.

The primary purpose of the audit report is not to report findings, just as the purpose of an audit is not to find findings. Rather the purpose is to communicate engagement results in an accurate, objective, clear, concise, constructive, complete, and timely manner per Standard 11.2 [Effective Communication]. This mindset is key to internal auditing's endeavors to communicate audit results accurately and in the right perspective.

A logical layout and flow throughout the report are key elements in achieving the objective of building a good report that can be viewed as a work of art. Applying the following principles will assist in this process:

- Think report throughout the project, even, for example, while driving home from work.
- Plan the layout and start building the report early in the project.
- Group similar concepts together. Even though you may have 20+ findings, these can often be grouped into five or fewer sections and subsections to create a logical flow.

The (primary) purpose of the audit report is not to report findings.

Start with the big picture

Start building the report early in the process, which will assist greatly in developing a logical layout and populating the report as you progress with the project. You may find it easier for the report to evolve into a masterpiece over the length of the project.

Build the report throughout the project – instead of starting to write it only after the fieldwork.

Frequently climb out of the detail, move to higher ground, and look down to see the bigger picture. Assess where you are and where you need to go. Like an artist having to frequently step back and view the painting from a distance. Leave the report in progress, or portions thereof between revisions for an hour or longer, even overnight or over a weekend to gain a fresh perspective as the report grows.

Writing the findings requires effort

Reading is made considerably more difficult when findings are not presented in a well-structured manner. Rather than placing an additional onus on the readers to interpret the ambiguity, the auditor should take responsibility for clear writing to enable the readers to understand findings without having to read it again. The art lies in writing technical matters in a way that nontechnical readers will easily understand the findings.

It is the auditor's duty to write clearly, not to put more burden on the reader.

Let's not present a bag of findings and call it an audit report.

State the critical issue first. This will help to present the findings without feeling you get stuck in a mud pool. Readers want a brief description of the issue, the level of risk, cause, and how to address them. Practice by first writing (or saying) what the main point is, instead of building up to the main point. Ask yourself: "What is the problem or the real issue", or "What happened?" It may take time and regular practicing to easily find the real issue. Often the first thought of what the problem is may be the cause or the effect, rather than the real problem/condition. Consider the following basic example:

The situation – Overtime audit

i. An employee was overpaid by $141.12 in October 2024.
ii. His timesheet reflects sixteen hours weekday overtime, but his pay slip reflects eight hours weekday and eight hours Sunday overtime.
iii. Our investigation into the cause of the error revealed that the payroll clerk erroneously captured eight of the sixteen weekday overtime hours as Sunday overtime in the payroll system.
iv. The payroll supervisor did not identify the error during the review processes due to an oversight.

Which of the above sentences contains the real issue?

Whereas the responses may differ between auditors, I have structured the findings as follows:

Finding

Eight weekday overtime hours were incorrectly captured as Sunday overtime from a timesheet to the payroll. Oversight during the payroll review processes resulted in the error going undetected causing the employee's overtime pay being overstated by $141.12 in the October 2024 payroll.

Discussion

	Observation	*Element of finding*
i.	An employee was overpaid by $141.12 in October 2024.	This is the effect.
ii.	His timesheet reflects sixteen hours weekday overtime, but his pay slip reflects eight hours weekday, and eight hours Sunday overtime.	These two sentences encompass the real issue (condition).
iii.	The payroll clerk erroneously captured eight of the sixteen weekday overtime hours as Sunday overtime in the payroll system.	
iv.	The payroll supervisor did not identify the error during the review processes due to an oversight.	This is the cause.

Tip: Do not start the finding with something that isn't the issue, such as an amount or a date, for example, "The October 2024 payroll", because there's nothing wrong with this month, right? Every year has one. The issue is clearly something else.

Start the finding with a condensed introductory phrase of what will follow if it has more than one observation per the example below. This will help to avoid overstuffing of sentences and paragraphs, because you would present the different related observations in bullet points, thereby eliminating unnecessary transition words and phrases like also, in addition to, and moreover.

Instead of saying:
Review of the payments to on-site service providers revealed that some purchase orders were prepared after the invoice dates. Formal agreements were also not in place with two high-value service providers to confirm the accuracy of their charges. Moreover, adequate supporting documents did not accompany service providers' invoices to enable effective validation of payments, as well as the responsible company representatives did not sign any of the invoices tested as evidence that the invoices were reviewed and duly approved.

Rather say:
Controls were not adequate to ensure payments to on-site service providers were correctly made for services required and rendered to the applicable standards due to the following shortcomings:

a. Orders were created after the invoice dates instead of before work commenced as required by ...
b. Adequate supporting documents did not accompany service providers' invoices to enable effective validation of payments.
c. Formal agreements were not in place with two high-value service providers to confirm the accuracy of their charges.
d. The responsible company representatives did not sign any of the invoices tested as evidence that the invoices were reviewed and duly approved.

Formulate the findings in your mind when you have distance, e.g., while driving home. This will help you think of additional information or testing needed to improve the quality of the audit and to better present the findings. When it is not clear where the finding is heading within the first ten words, I normally refer it back to the author to redo.

Think report throughout the project.

Weave the criteria, condition, cause, and effect into the finding, but no need to state the obvious. I find it boring, and the report is usually much longer if the elements of a finding are reflected in separate columns as illustrated below.

Presenting elements separately			
Criteria	*Condition*	*Cause*	*Effect*
Section 2 of the Procurement Policy requires from the buyer to obtain at least one quotation for purchases with values ranging from $501 to $1,000.	Quotations were not obtained for ten of the 20 purchase orders selected for testing where the order values ranged from $501 to $1,000.	The Procurement Policy was not communicated to the buyer.	The Company potentially paid excessive prices for the goods acquired.

Elements weaved into finding
Quotations were not obtained for ten of the 20 purchase orders with values of $501 to $1,000 as required by Section 2 of the Procurement Policy. This was due to the buyer being unaware of the existence of the policy, which increases the risk of paying excessive prices for the goods ordered.

Quantify/bring perspective. Findings can be vague and incomplete if they are not presented from the right perspective. Quantification is important so that the reader can interpret the severity of the exposure and the associated risks. It even helps the auditor put things into perspective, for example, if quantified, you may find it is not as bad as you originally thought, or it may be worse.

For non-compliance-type findings, mention the section in the criteria which has not been complied with. This prompts the auditor (and senior) to confirm it is a real deviation and should eliminate the risk of including a finding that you mistakenly thought was a deviation. We can easily get confused with, for example, policies of the different clients or divisions, or different versions of a policy or regulation.

Avoid petty reporting. When a control weakness or anomaly has a low-risk rating and is easy to correct, you may consider including the finding in the draft report for discussion only. If justified, remove the finding from the report after obtaining proof that your recommendation has been satisfactorily addressed.

Clarity and consistency

Standard 11.2 [Effective Communication] advises that reporting should be clear, i.e., logically and easily understood by stakeholders. Applying the following advice should aid in achieving clarity and consistency when writing.

Think simply. It seems much easier to complicate things when writing because most people find it much more difficult to write in a plain, straightforward manner. This is a paradox, because how can simplicity be more complex than complexity itself? Auditors should practice the art of plain writing as further discussed below.

Develop the art of not writing complicated matters in a complicated manner.

Use the simplest words and expressions possible. Simplicity, but not oversimplifying to the point of missing out information which the reader needs to fully understand what you are trying to say. Replace longer/difficult words and phrases with shorter/simpler alternatives while writing and when editing, for example: why say "utilize" if you can say "use" ... or "documentation" if you can say "documents"? Use the simplest word without letting it sound common.

Conciseness. Standard 11.2 further advises that *"communication should be concise, i.e., succinct and free from unnecessary detail and wordiness"*. To avoid anything that can be safely omitted, consider whether it is (really) necessary to include the information, rather than whether I can include it. When suggesting to an auditor to remove unnecessary information during the report review process, the response is often "I want them to know", which readers probably don't want or need to know. If you're honest with yourself, you might find that the extra information is just to let the finding sound juicier, or worse, you want readers to know how well you did, which can sometimes be at someone else's expense.

Keep the report concise without omitting vital information.

Simplify ideas with lists or tables. Lists and tables are often necessary to enhance readability, to support the finding (by showing the severity) and/or to bring perspective. Tables are often more useful than graphs – in my experience.

Try not to think academically when you write but think in plain language – almost as you would speak to your colleague, spouse, or grandmother. See the following real-life example:

Auditor wrote:	*Changed to:*
"Upon inspection of numerous sheets, it was noticed that many failed to include the signature of the responsible engineer..."	"The mechanical engineer did not sign 11 of the 15 maintenance sheets selected for testing..."

Do not overstuff sentences. Cramming too many ideas into one sentence can compromise readability. Rather break information into shorter sentences and/or sub-sections (e.g., bullet points). Using words like also, furthermore, in addition to, and moreover is an indication of overstuffing.

Be direct and concrete instead of abstract and fluffy. We generally find it easier to write abstract sentences and paragraphs when presenting findings. It seems easier to tell Granny what I found than writing the findings. The enemies of clear writing include the following:

- **Long and unnecessary lead-ins.** Learn to AVOID starting sentences and paragraphs with unnecessary phrases or words, such as:
  - During the audit, it was noted. The readers must read at least six more words before getting to the real issue. By the time the readers get to "During the audit", they are certainly aware that you did an audit. When they get to "It was noted", they are overly aware that you have noted/found something. It is not easy to get this phrase out of auditors' written vocabulary. The temptation is so big, that once they have learned to avoid "It was noted", some start writing the same idea, just in a different "dialect", such as it was discovered/found/observed. The only time you should be allowed to use something like "We observed", is when you have observed the situation without having physical evidence, such as "We observed ten employees entering the premises without clocking". However, saying "We observed ten debtor reconciliations not signed" has probably been confirmed with sufficient evidence, which renders it unnecessary to say, "We observed".
  - Due to the fact that. It is likely an introduction to an abstract sentence to follow. Besides, the last four words have no meaning when on their own.
  - There, for example, "There were ten debtor reconciliations of the 20 tested that were not signed by the Financial Accountant". Rather say, "The Financial Accountant did not sign ten of the 20 debtor reconciliations tested". I usually ask the author "Where is there?", just to make the point.

    I find it is better to get rid of them immediately because trying to change the sentence with these phrases and words present will easily let us paint ourselves into a corner.
  - Providing a background to a finding is seldom necessary in my experience. One in a few hundred findings may require the reader to have the background of the finding. When required, we present the background in italics showing the background is not the finding as per the following example:

[Network capacity charge (NCC) is the R/kVA fixed network charge raised by the energy supply company for the utilized capacity requested by the client, while the notified network demand charge is the tariff raised on the actual demand (usage) for the month.]

Analysis of the NCC indicates the requested network capacity was potentially set too high for some of the premises as notified demand exceeded the NCC significantly for six of the nine premises during the ten months to October 2024 ....

Ponder this.

Do I use any unnecessary lead-ins?

Be specific as appropriate. Use specific terms such as desk, instead of furniture, the financial manager instead of management, and purchase order instead of supporting document. Paint the picture as clearly as possible depending on the purpose of your writing as in the following example:

Statement 1. Two vehicles collided in the town center this morning.

Comment: This is a vague statement possibly providing too little information, unless the readers only need to know that two vehicles crashed in the town center this morning.

Statement 2: A blue Volvo sedan crashed into the passenger door of a grey light delivery vehicle when running a red traffic light on the corner of 1st and 2nd streets this morning at around half past seven. This resulted in the delivery vehicle passenger sustaining moderate head injuries.

Comment: The clarity and detail allow the reader to visualize the observation. Unnecessary detail, if any, can be omitted depending on the purpose of your writing and the audience.

"It was noted" has been banned from being used in our reports.

Avoid up-in-the-air statements, such as "This was due to a lack of effective management controls and supervision". Or "The necessary controls need to be put in place to reduce the risk of ....". This is too vague to qualify for a proper finding and/or recommendation.

Avoid word salads. Entangling words salads is easier said than done for many people.

- Ask a colleague to read the finding(s). If the colleague does not understand it the first time, it is probably a word salad and should be revised or rewritten. When handing my first audit report to my boss in 1989, I eagerly awaited his "Good and faithful servant". Instead, he said "Barrie, this is a fruit salad. Try again", which made me realize the importance of writing clearly for readers to understand it right away. **This brings us to the importance of being teachable.** Although said without tact, I wasn't offended. Instead, this incident spurred me to always write so that the readers would immediately understand the writing.

I've observed over the years that those taking offense in such situations usually don't get it right.
- We use the *Jigsaw Puzzle Technique* to assist in entangling word salads; usually if a finding consists of multiple aspects, mostly findings where a risk has materialized. This technique helps when you feel you go around in circles, and/or if the writer has great difficulty explaining the finding.

THE JIGSAW PUZZLE TECHNIQUE – *Writing a finding by analyzing the aspects of the observation*

The purpose of this document is to identify the aspects per element of a finding if the auditor struggles to present a finding logically. By the time you realize you're getting stuck, you've usually recorded all or most of the key words, i.e., the puzzle pieces.

Step 1: Record the key aspects per finding element starting with the Criteria, Cause, and Effect. The reason for starting with these three elements is because auditors classify these easier. Determining the condition is often their dilemma.

Step 2: Record the remaining key aspects for "Condition".

Step 3: Write the rough finding using the *Condition* key aspects.

Step 4: Transfer to the report and refine.

Project: *ABC Contractor* Drop Raising Investigation
Nature of finding: Drop raise activities were incorrectly invoiced. [This is a real-life example]

Element	*Key aspects (Sort the puzzle pieces)*	*Comments/ rough finding (reorganize the puzzle pieces)*
Criteria	Contract, invoicing, actual work, operating standards.	Invoicing should be done to the required operating standards and in accordance with the contract and actual work done.

Cause(s)	Misinterpretation, ambiguities (activity descriptions & daily report sheets),
	Lack of knowledge – Contract & technical understanding,
	Ineffective review process.
		• Ambiguity of activity descriptions & daily report sheets resulted in misinterpretation.
		• The contractor admin staff lacked:
		  • Knowledge of the contract.
		  • Understanding of technical aspects of the work done
		• Ineffective review processes.
		  • Contractor
		  • Client/ company

Effect	Potential overpayments – still busy investigating	Include the summary of anomalies & detail schedules [provide preliminary results]

Condition	Incorrect invoicing:
	• Duplications
	  • Activities part of all-inclusive rate charged separately.
	  • Same work invoiced more than once.
	• Activity descriptions: site moves, site preps, set-ups
	• Drop raises
	• Quantities incorrectly transposed from sheet to invoice
	• Substitution of rates
	• Invoiced sub standard work – reinvoicing
	• Days
		ABC Contracting invoiced drop raise activities incorrectly per the observations below.
		• Duplications as follows:
		  • Invoicing separately for activities forming part of an all-inclusive rate, i.e., charged site move & site prep separately although they form part of the machine set-up rate.
		  • Invoicing twice for the same work.
		  • Re-invoicing for rectifying substandard work.
		• Off-setting (i.e. substituting) of unspecified work against items included in the schedule of rates.
		• Quantities were incorrectly transposed from the daily report sheets to the invoices.
		[Transfer to the report and refine the finding to complete the puzzle]

Avoid duplications. Common forms of duplications include:

- The period January to August. This is a period, isn't it?
- You can visibly see.
- It already exists.
- Join the two together.

"I repeat again; there should be no repetitions"

Avoid pointless words and phrases, like, undoubtedly, in fact, equally important, and obviously. They add nothing to the message and often can be removed without changing the meaning of your writing.

Use short versions of phrases. Be alert to the tendency to use phrases when one word suffices. By now many have learned some of the shorter versions through Microsoft Editor, such as "to", instead of "in order to". Other examples where people's default is to use the longer version of a word or phrase, include:

Instead of saying:	*rather say:*
Make use of	Use
Amounting to	Totaling
Take into consideration	Consider
Make available	Provide/avail
Provide an explanation	Explain
Make a decision	Decide
As a consequence of	Because

See how your sentences survive and flourish after deleting unnecessary words.

When seeing "make" or "take" in a sentence I usually look for an alternative way to structure the sentence.

Use "ing" wisely. When you are urged to use words ending with "ing", consider an alternative to enhance readability where relevant, e.g., "are not sending" can be replaced by "do not send". It is not wrong to "ing" because "inging" often improves sentences, for example, "After writing the first draft" sounds better than "After the first draft is written".

> **Tip:** Don't worry too much about getting it right while writing, as you will have the chance to perform multiple edits. It is more important to capture your thoughts as they arise rather than striving for perfection.

Use terms understood by all. Avoid technical jargon. If, for example, a document reviewed as part of the project has a description that will not be understood by all, rename the document by using a better descriptive title. Standard 11.2 [Effective Communication] urges internal auditors to avoid unnecessary technical language and define important terms that are uncommon or used in a way that is specific or unique to the communication or presentation.

Writing a technical-related finding for the non-technical readers to understand. Approximately 50% of the findings in our audit reports are technical in nature while many recipients of these reports are non-technical. Some guidelines to assist the author follow.

- Applying the clear writing principles discussed above should bring you about 80% of the way.
- Put yourselves in their shoes. Assume they have a low level of perception or insight into the technical area.
- Do not use technical jargon or explain it as is practical.

- Rather use terms that they will understand, or use both, with one of the terms in brackets.
- Use referencing footnotes to explain a term or phrase.

Use **active voice.** See the difference in the following examples.

Passive voice	*Active voice*
The reconciliation was performed by the Accountant.	The Accountant performed the reconciliation.
The meeting must be attended by at least one senior manager as required by the policy.	The policy states at least one senior manager must attend the meeting.
Discussions with the engineer indicated...	The engineer informed us ...

Use AI wisely. Using AI writing tools like grammar checking and paraphrasers can help identify oversights – from which we can learn. However, first, give it your best try by applying good writing principles to develop your writing skills before "feeding" it into AI because the garbage-in-garbage-out principle applies. Besides, AI, particularly paraphrasing tools, cannot interpret your thoughts accurately – for now at least.

AI writing tools can help teach the teachable.

Use the appropriate tone. Be mindful of the client's feelings. You may believe you merely present the facts, but a harsh tone can make enemies, while a carefully considered tone may earn respect and cooperation. Always use the softest tone as appropriate for the report. Evaluate the appropriateness of the tone by wearing the readers' hat during the review/editing of the report. Don't succumb to undue pressure from others, including:

- Someone who prompts you to use strong words to convey the alleged seriousness of the finding. I have received such requests from managers who want to use the report as ammunition, for example, to discipline an employee. Always remember it is your report.
- The auditee argues against the conclusion and/or finding(s), wanting the auditor to unduly water them down.
  - **Avoid negative language.** Negative words tend to antagonize and may dissuade rather than convince audit clients. For example, instead of saying: "the accountant refused to provide us with the information despite numerous requests made by us" – rather say: "...the information was not provided to us at request". Do not start the sentence with "no", e.g. "No evidence was provided" sounds harsher than "evidence was not provided". Other harsh phrases to avoid are "failure to" and "the lack of".

- **Do not use strong adjectives.** Avoid words like very, enormous, absolutely, intensely, utterly, and tremendously as they add to a harsh tone. It reduces the credibility of the report as it may appear the writer exaggerates. This advice extends to verbal communication as well. I tend to distrust people who often make exaggerated statements, especially if they're politicians.
- **The glass is half full.** People can easily focus on the negative and downplay the positive when preparing the audit report. Train your brain to first think half full before thinking half empty. When your tendency is to first think to conclude negatively such as controls are not adequate and effective, it may typify you as a "half empty thinker" who tends to use a harsher tone in their writing.

Focus on the findings, not the auditor. Avoid describing findings with phrases such as, "When we did this test, we found that". Instead, just tell the readers what the problem/condition is. Eliminate reference to "myself" as far as possible.

Avoid "sentimental" writing. Forcing sentimental content into the text can interrupt the flow of our writing and add unnecessary words. The core message is more important than our ego. If it doesn't belong or confuses the narrative, it must go… just like a musician scrapping a song that doesn't suit the album. I discarded many words, phrases, and sentences that I initially included in this book. It's normal to write too much with the first attempt. Some of these sentimental portions were quite difficult to let go because "I want the readers to know and appreciate them", although very few would probably even realize the "value" thereof. It helps to remind yourself that "I may be the only person whom this information will impress".

Discard everything that does not serve the primary purpose of your writing.

Editing and review

After writing the first draft, review your report with the intent of simplifying sentences and deleting unnecessary words, sentences *and* even paragraphs, e.g., "The responsibility for the submission of the VAT returns…" (nine words) can be changed to "The responsibility to submit VAT returns…" (six words).

> **Tip:** Consider performing multiple edit passes, for example, editing for active voice and sentence simplification. This may allow you to identify and revise, for example, "Discussions with the engineer indicated…", to "The engineer informed us …".

When reviewing a draft audit report, I prefer to start at the macro level, i.e., layout, logic, completeness, and general content before editing the grammar.

Starting with the grammar can be like trying to catch crabs in murky water. Rather start at the elevated level and gradually move to the details of the observations. The main purpose of the report review is not to check the spelling and grammar.

Starting with a solid finding should enhance the readers' confidence in the report. If the first finding is swept off the table, you may be outmaneuvered, particularly if the auditee takes issue with you. It may be difficult to recover from the backfoot position during the closeout meeting.

Think creatively

Ask yourself: "How can the report be made more interesting?" We use standard formats in Pro Optima but are not bound to these formats. Staff are encouraged to propose changes to the existing formats if the changes will improve the report.

The conclusion and summary of the findings should be a synopsis of the project outcome and presented in a condensed manner. To merely copy and paste findings from the detailed findings section when preparing the executive summary is, in my mind, boring. Rather use this opportunity to practice the art of plain language by capturing the essence of the finding. You may even realize how the detailed finding can be shortened. Be creative when writing the overall conclusion. Try to do better than merely concluding "controls are partially adequate and effective...", despite only having a handful of lower risk findings, which, if you are fair, may be close to a perfect score. This is playing it way too safe. Some examples of our audit conclusions follow:

It is our opinion that adequate controls are in place to effectively manage utility usage and related costs and to ensure compliance with regulatory safety standards. Opportunities were nonetheless identified that can further strengthen controls related to third-party users of electricity and water.

It is our opinion that internal controls are largely inadequate to support effective and efficient infrastructure and equipment maintenance, mainly due to the DwAP system lacking functionality and not being used effectively. However, management anticipates that internal controls will improve once the new PMSS is fully operational which is scheduled for 30 September 2024.

It is our opinion that internal controls over off-site repairs are not entirely adequate and effective, mainly due to insufficient coordination between the different departments involved in the off-site repair process and substandard discipline.

The audit close-out meeting developed into a constructive solution-driven workshop with the attendees from all the involved disciplines, i.e., asset protection, engineering, stores, finance, procurement, and safety providing practical solutions and committing to addressing the audit findings collaboratively.

It is our opinion that internal controls are inadequate to effectively address the financial control risks of the business unit under review. The findings reported herein are symptomatic of an unhealthy control environment within *XYZ* as a corporate entity, which requires a systematic approach to develop and implement more stringent controls to reduce the probability of major fraud and error occurring as well as the risk of them going undetected.

In my opinion, an audit report that contains loose findings without context to the bigger picture can easily create the impression that the team audited for findings, which alludes to an ineffective audit methodology. For example, concluding internal controls are partially adequate and effective, which is a neither-here-nor-there conclusion, and then attempting to motivate this conclusion with some generic findings, such as two of 50 documents were not signed, the review of a policy is past due, and a contract amendment was filed in the wrong folder, is unconvincing. This is playing it too safe and is often used to conceal poor auditing practices. The saying "You can fool some people sometimes, but you can't fool all people all the time" is true here. I have heard from several people who do not respect but merely tolerate their internal auditors because the audits make the auditee look good as the real weaknesses or wrongdoings aren't exposed.

Continuously refer to the project objective(s) throughout the assignment and develop a strategic action plan to achieve them. The audit program helps to identify the key controls during the first phase of the project, but in my experience, is not the complete picture. If you use the program only, you may not stumble across the hidden gems that the strategic thinker would see. View the project in the wider scheme of things as opposed to merely focusing on the risk or control at hand, for example, when performing a production bonus audit, do not only test compliance to the bonus scheme but consider the relevance and effectiveness of the bonus parameters as well as how it may affect the client's overall performance.

The main purpose of the audit is <u>not</u> to find findings.

SUMMARY OF PART 2

Developing staff to become original thinkers is a way of life for Pro Optima, which is the reason why many of our projects show tangible benefits for the clients. Initiative and creativity are important for the internal audit profession to render a good service and it involves doing more than the minimum requirements. It is of little value that we maintain independence and objectivity, do well in a quality assurance review, and issue audit reports within three weeks from the start of the project but show no or even a negative impact on the bottom line of the client's business. The person who uses initiative can deliver a good result, but the original thinker can create a masterpiece with each project that will add definite value to the internal audit function and its clients. If your internal audit function seldom or never shows quantifiable value added it is time to rethink the reason for your function's existence. Maybe the time has come to either change or terminate.

To thrive and survive in a world where stakeholders have heightened expectations of internal auditing, it is crucial that internal auditors strive for excellence. To foster a culture of excellence, internal audit leaders must be intentional about it. This mental attitude can inspire the team to deliver an excellent product with each project.

Internal auditors are often criticized for including details in reports that are of little importance to busy readers. It is senseless to try and impress the readers with an over-detailed report. It takes constant practice and awareness to develop the skill to build reports that are clear, concise, and easy to read. It is not easy to convince internal auditors to try a different approach, but the idea of Building the Report may well be worth exploring.

What happened to the 15 musicians discussed early in this chapter?

I can't say with certainty but am confident that those who didn't pursue creativity and quality were not very successful – they may not even have made it through the music industry.

TAKEAWAYS

For the internal audit function's leadership

Develop and continuously enhance your own and your staff's original thinking capabilities and strive toward excellence if you want to provide an effective internal audit service because it's unlikely that you will achieve this without these two prerequisites.

For the internal audit staff and professionals in general

There is more to internal auditing than merely auditing. You can develop and enhance your original thinking capabilities and level of excellence.

For senior and executive management, and the board

Your internal audit function should demonstrate its true value to the stakeholders. Does it make business sense to have the internal audit function or do you merely tolerate them because it is mandatory?

NOTES

1 Pav Gill provided a guest lecture at the Johannes Gutenberg University in Mainz on, 3 May 2024, https://drrainerlenz.wordpress.com/2024/05/03/thank-you-dear-pav-gill/
2 The IIA's Three Lines Model, accessed online 06 June 2024, https://www.theiia.org/globalassets/documents/resources/the-iias-three-lines-model-an-update-of-the-three-lines-of-defense-july-2020/three-lines-model-updated-english.pdf
3 GIAS://www.theiia.org/globalassets/site/standards/editable-versions/globalinternalauditstandards_2024january9_editable.pdf; accessed online 06 June 2024.
4 Accessed online on 29 May 2024, https://www.theiia.org/en/content/position-papers/2020/the-iias-three-lines-model-an-update-of-the-three-lines-of-defense/
5 I co-authored a book about Combined Assurance over ten years ago: Sarens et al. (2012).
6 Homepage: https://www.eiacg.com/
7 My blog about the event from 21 June 2024: https://drrainerlenz.wordpress.com/2024/06/21/european-academic-conference-on-internal-audit-and-corporate-governance/

REFERENCES

Drašč#ek, M. (2024), The Theory of Internal Audit – The Purpose Driven Internal Audit, EDPACS. EDPACS, 1–10. Published online: 06 February. https://doi.org/10.1080/07366981.2024.2314798

Gladwell, M. (2000), The Tipping Point, How Little Things Can Make a Big Difference, Abacus, London.

Lenz, R. (2013), Insights into the effectiveness of internal audit: a multi-method and multi-perspective study, Université catholique de Louvain – Louvain School of Management Research Institute, Doctoral Thesis 01|2013 https://drrainerlenz.wordpress.com/wp-content/uploads/2013/03/lenz-r.-2013-diss..pdf

Lenz, R., & Jeppesen K.K. (2022), The Future of Internal Auditing: Gardener of Governance, EDPACS, 66:5, 1–21. https://www.tandfonline.com/doi/full/10.1080/07366981.2022.2036314

Lenz, R., & O'Regan, D. J. (2024), The Global Internal Audit Standards – Old Wine in New Bottles? EDPACS, 69:3, 1–28. https://doi.org/10.1080/07366981.2024.2322835

Sarens, G., Decaux, L., & Lenz, R. (2012), Combined assurance: Case studies on a holistic approach to organizational governance, IIA Research Foundation, Altamonte Springs, FL.

The Institute of Internal Auditors (The IIA, 2024), Global Internal Audit Standards, Lake Mary, US, January.

The Internal Audit Foundation (2024), Internal Audit: Vision 2035, US, Lake Mary, July.

Attachment 3

EXAMPLES OF VALUE-ADDING SUCCESSES OF STAFF

Name (years employed)	Last 12 months				Total employment period			
	Source	Project	Nature of finding	Effect	Source	Project	Nature of finding	Effect
Jaques W (2 weeks)	Management request [Second Line service]	Cost savings drive	Contractor charged the incorrect unit of measure for mining activities, i.e., tons instead of m^3	ZAR 3.5m annual saving				
Martin (2.5 months)	Invoice verification [second line service]	Mining contractor management project	Contractor overstated the number of support sets installed underground	ZAR165k recoupment (not yet finalized) ZAR2.0m annual saving				
Shaun (10 months)	Invoice verification [Second Line service]	Mining contractor management project	Duplicate charges for drop raising, including transport, rigging, set-up, and drilling. (Investigation in progress – potential of further overcharges totaling ZAR6.9)	ZAR2.4m recoupment in process per settlement agreement	Invoice verification [second Line Service]	Mining contractor management project	Long hole drill & blast meters were incorrectly calculated	ZAR1.9m recouped
Ryno (12 months)	Management request [Second Line service]	Cost savings drive	Underground rail maintenance contractor performed work that was not required, and at excessive prices	ZAR7.0m annual saving	Management request [Second Line service]	Conveyor belt review	Over 3 years' value of material and equipment usage were on hand, of which 2 years' value has been issued and costed to the business units	ZAR15m cost saving
Michael (15 months)	Invoice verification [Second Line service]	Mining contractor management project	Contractor charged excessive rates for specialized crews to perform general mining activities	ZAR9.9m annual saving	Invoice verification [internal audit function)	Mining contractor management project	Incorrect rates charged for underground rock support installation	ZAR1.2m recouped, ZAR1.2m annual cost saving
Andreas (2 years)	Invoice verification [Second Line service]	Mining contractor management project	Charged incorrect quantities for casting concrete underground	ZAR222k recovery and ZAR2.7m annual saving	Invoice verification [Second Line service]	Mining contractor management project	Overstating linear meters & charging incorrect rate for equipping traveling ways underground	ZAR88k recovery and ZAR1.1m annual saving
Dudu (5 years)	ESG audits [Second Line service]	Little opportunity for savings			Management request [Second Line service) 2023	Overtime audits	Abuse of fatigue and standby overtime shifts	ZAR10.4m annual cost saving

Name (years employed)	Last 12 months				Total employment period			
	Source	Project	Nature of finding	Effect	Source	Project	Nature of finding	Effect
Katlego (6 years)	Management request [Second Line service]	Fuel audit	Diesel theft identified and stopped.	ZAR2.5m annual saving	Management request [Second Line service] (2020)	Review controls over Personal Protective Equipment (PPE).	Uncontrolled PPE issues.	ZAR2.5m annual cost saving
Johan (9 years)	Invoice verification [Second Line service]	Mining contractor management project	Charged underground rail upgrade rate for unrelated work	ZAR856k recouped & ZAR1.7m annual saving.	Management request [Second Line service] (2020)	Initial contractor management audit at new client	Charged for mine (stope) panel establishment not being done/completed, including double billing	ZAR1.8m recouped & annual saving of ZAR3.0m
Hans (8 years)	Management request [Second Line service]	Cost savings drive	Excessive prices charged for underground steel pipe replacements	ZAR13.5 annual saving	Invoice verification [Internal audit function] (2016)	Contractor cost monitoring	Wasteful spending on underground tunnel rehabilitation work	ZAR4.0m recouped & ZAR11.4m annual cost saving
Ralph (9 years)	Management request [Second Line service]	Investigate escalating costs of underground fire monitoring systems	The distributor charged the mine 197%of the contract prices due to the circumvention of the supply-under-contract procedures.	ZAR 8.6m annual saving. Recoupment negotiations in progress – amount not yet available	Own initiative: [Internal audit (2016) & Second Line service (2020)]	Fraud & error detection tests	Ralph, being a qualified rock engineer, queried the apparent over-supporting of underground tunnels at two clients following which the work was stopped	ZAR1.1m once-off saving & ZAR26m per annum saving
Nico (9 years)	Management request [Second Line service]	Cost savings drive	Rental of underground vacuum units reduced from four to one, including a reduction in the associated labor	ZAR3.0m annual saving	Fraud & error detection test [internal audit function) 2017	Investigate the outsourcing of air & water supply power packs maintenance	The maintenance was brought inhouse due to the excessive charges by the outsourced service provider	ZAR4.1m annual cost saving
Annelise (9 years)	Scheduled internal audit	Social and Labour Plan	Client not collecting outstanding home loan repayments from dismissed employees	ZAR20k per annum cost saving	Scheduled In & Out audit [internal audit function) 2023	Skills development audit	Qualifying training scheme rebates were excluded from annual income tax calculations and subsequently corrected before the tax filing	Tax assessment lower by ZAR7.3m
Cilliers (11 years)	Scheduled internal audit	Review controls over contractors	Two vendors charging for the same service	ZAR36k recouped	Own initiative [Second Line service] 2018	Mining contractor audit	Overcharging based on forged supporting documents	ZAR 912k overpaid – recouped ZAR230k from invoices pending payment.
Brandan (12 years)	Business process analysis [Second Line service]	Bus fleet optimization. (Transporting employees between residences and workplaces)	Restructuring the bus fleet configuration and bus routes thereby reducing the fleet size and eliminating additional mileage claims	ZAR2.6m annual saving	Business process analysis [Second Line service] 2023	Review of the employee/contractor onboarding processes & assisted with implementation	The onboarding process reduced from ±60 days to an average of 11 days	ZAR210m annual cost saving
Brenda (13 years)	Scheduled internal audit	Utilities audit	Electricity and water charges not recouped from third party user	ZAR13.4m recovered	Fraud & error detection test	Investigate potential incorrect occupational	Incorrect determination and declaration of dusty shifts	ZAR8.2m annual saving &

2

Name (years employed)	Last 12 months				Total employment period			
	Source	Project	Nature of finding	Effect	Source	Project	Nature of finding	Effect
					[Second Line service] 2016	health (dusty shifts) premiums	resulting in the overpayment of occupational health premiums	ZAR300k recouped
Neil (15 years)	Management request [Second Line service]	Verification of a vendor's claim of ZAR 6.9m for outstanding payments regarding surface sewerage services	The vendor's claim was invalid largely due to duplicate charges, while further duplications were discovered in the invoices previously paid	ZAR6.9m claim refuted, and an additional ZAR122k overpayment identified and recovered	Management request [Second Line service] 2014	Gas cylinders census and reconciliation	A significant liability for ±6,800 unaccounted gas cylinders was averted after identifying a system error in the supplier's stock management processes	ZAR23.8m once-off saving & ZAR2.7m annual saving
Elvis (13 years)	ESG audits [Second Line service]	Little opportunity for savings			Scheduled internal audit 2016	Vehicle workshop audit	Truck modification engineering firm charged the client for parts, which the client had provided to them at no charge	ZAR140k recouped
Garth (19 years)	Invoice verification [second Line service]	Contractor management services	Contractor charged the (higher) extend mono winch rate instead of repair and replacing of mono winch ropes underground	Potential ZAR2,7m recoupment (ZAR1,4m already agreed for repayment)	Invoice verification Second Line service] 2022	Mining contractor management project	Overstated underground mining production results	ZAR13.7m annual saving
Jacques C (20 years)	Management request (Second Line service]	Hydraulic oil audit	Hydraulic oil costs have reduced significantly after the audit exposed the poor controls had resulted in oil purchased being unaccounted for	ZAR9m annual cost reduction	Fraud & error detection test [internal audit services] 2010	Investigate potential irregularities regarding a tender for stripping of a railway line.	Distance stripped was 7.6km vs. the tender distance of 11km.	ZAR636K recouped
Donovan (22 years)	Scheduled audit [Second Line service)	Overtime audit	Unworked shifts paid	ZAR5.3m recoupment (ZAR 2.0m already recouped)	Management request [Internal audit services] 2015	Review information & communication technology (ICT) products and services	Overcharging of infrastructure loans as well as system reporting services not provided	ZAR9.5m recouped
Oosie (23 year)	Invoice verification [second Line service]	Contractor management services	Contract performing underground maintenance work invoiced the incorrect rates and quantities.	ZAR105k recouped	Follow-up audit [internal audit] 2001	Investigate potential overcharging by mining contractor (follow up)	Contractual penalties not applied, payment for work not done, duplicate charges & excessive rates charged – renegotiated following audit	ZAR414k recouped & ZAR515k annual saving

3

Chapter 3

The 3rd P is about Performance … because no business, no internal auditing

GARDENER OF GOVERNANCE ARTICLE SYNOPSIS

Internal auditing must find ways to contribute to the overall value proposition of its clients. Internal audit and good controls are not ends themselves but the means to an end, i.e., to improve an organization's governance. Auditing what truly matters in the private sector, governance, strategy, operations, and the business model are vital. There are many ways to demonstrate value in the governance arena. Internal audit professionals are typically well educated, (should) know the organization they serve well, and can emerge as true helpers in times of distress. Some internal auditing functions justify their legitimacy with contributions to the bottom line, such as hard savings, or help securing liquidity.

COMPLIANT, YET POTENTIALLY INEFFECTIVE

The Quality Assurance Review (QAR)[1] process measured conformance with the IIA Standards but did not evaluate the effectiveness of the internal audit function. It is possible that a malfunctioning internal audit department can pass a QAR. Not only is it possible; it did happen as is evident from the following case. The executive management of a listed company requested an internal audit consultant to evaluate the performance of their internal audit department, which they believed was underperforming. The department was assessed as generally conforming to the IIA Standards during a QAR some 18 months earlier. In a diplomatically worded evaluation report, the consultant concluded that ample opportunity existed for the internal audit function to increase its effectiveness. The detailed observations, however, painted a picture of an ineffective internal audit function. The client engaged the consultant to develop and upgrade the department's skills to enhance its effectiveness, which, unfortunately, the CAE and audit managers strongly resisted. They largely continued in their old ways, which culminated in the department being disbanded and the

DOI: 10.1201/9781003539001-3

function being outsourced after the inefficacy of the entity's internal control systems was subsequently exposed. This resulted in the entity realizing it could no longer express a positive opinion of the adequacy and effectiveness of its internal controls. For the ensuing four years, the entity expressed mainly negative opinions regarding the efficacy of its internal control environment. Kudos to the entity for taking the road of transparency. We are concerned many large corporations may not be as honest and transparent; mostly because, they may rely on false assurances provided by their internal audit functions … we hope we're wrong.

Conformance with internal audit standards and the effectiveness of internal auditing are equally important.

LEARNING OBJECTIVES OF THIS CHAPTER

- Providing value-adding services should be a continuous endeavor.
- Internal auditing should break the mental block caused by procedural thinking.
- Internal auditors should maintain a robust auditing mindset.
- Let's reconsider the term assurance in internal auditing.

Ponder this.

Mention at least two instances of significant value-added contributions made by your internal audit function during the past 12 months?

Part One (Rainer)

MY HOUSE OF GOVERNANCE

Mario Andretti, the Italian-born American car-racer used to say: *"If everything seems under control, you're not going fast enough"*. We need to think of performance, risks and controls as intertwined (Lenz & Chesshire 2023). Risks and controls should be embedded in the pursuit of performance.

Lenz and Chesshire (2023) picture the House of Governance with Performance Management on the top floor. Risk Management is on the middle floor, vitally, as does a hinge between door and frame, it is the only floor that directly touches and is touched by the other two. On this floor, most importantly are the "rooms" for strategic and operational risks as well as, among others, Compliance, Environment, Social, Legal, Tax and IT, for example. The ABC of organizational change is on the ground floor, the foundation on which the other two levels rely for support. It's our view that internal auditors are enablers of learning and change and are effectively builders. Internal auditing can be instrumental in enhancing the ABC, Attitude – Behavior – Culture of organizational change. Without solid foundations, the House of Governance would simply be built on sand.

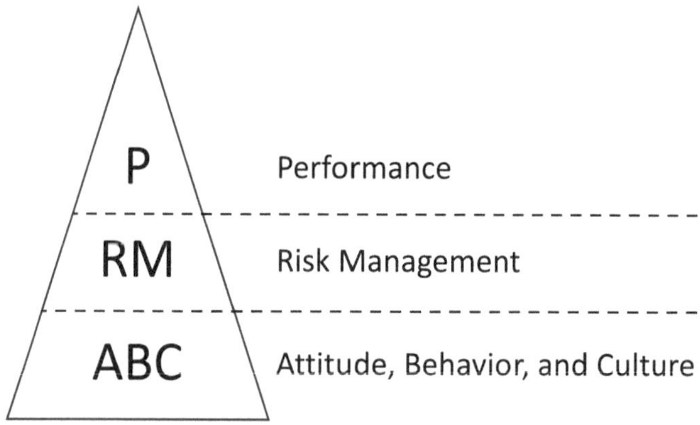

Figure 3.1 House of Governance.

WHAT A DIFFERENCE A YEAR MAKES!

We can do more. We can do better. When talking about the performance of IA, Lenz et al. (2024) demonstrate in an anecdotal fashion what a difference a year makes. To date, I have been chief internal auditor in three different multinational organizations. As Chief Audit Executive, I have always headed relatively small internal audit functions of less than five staff. In 2014, I assumed my second assignment as chief internal auditor. I joined Villeroy & Boch, a Frankfurt (Germany) listed company with about 8,000 employees generating more than EUR 800 million revenue. Family-owned since 1748, Villeroy & Boch is a global leader in ceramic production, an international lifestyle brand offering a range of tableware, home décor and bath & wellness products. Upon arrival, the internal audit department was dysfunctional and ineffective, largely disregarded by management and peers. Most internal audit observations/findings had been overdue already for a long time.

One year later, things had changed for the better. Internal audit observations were closed by management in a timely manner. The delivery time of internal audit reports was shortened from 8 weeks to less than 10 days. The productivity per full-time employee went up from six reports per annum to eight. Most importantly, the improved acceptance and effectiveness of the internal audit function was grounded in an overhaul of the overall positioning of the function. What a difference a year can make! After one year in the role and applying a different mindset, we had open access to senior management. Information flowed freely in both directions; peers and clients perceived the function as

"Guides", "Protectors" and "Change Agents", rather than the "Watchdog" and "Police" as it had been hitherto. As we can learn from the Vision 2035 survey (The Internal Audit Foundation, 2024) today many (48% of) internal auditors are still perceived as the organization's "police" force. To heighten relevance, impact and effectiveness, the positioning of the internal audit function and the profession must change (Sarens et al. 2016).

Change for the better requires, among other factors, a clear focus on our prime customers, challenging legacy wisdom and avoiding ceremonial work. Much of that is in the more immediate control of the Chief Internal Auditor and the team.

LET'S CHALLENGE OURSELVES AND AVOID ALL THE RED TAPE

Internal auditors review others' work constantly. That is part of the role. We should be more critical of ourselves, about the work and value add we render. We suggest measuring our own performance and contribution more, have our own auditing work and contribution regularly reviewed, inviting professional peers to critique what we have done. Let's challenge ourselves and avoid all the red tape, all the ceremonial components of our work and become truly outcome focused. In doing so, we must clarify who our prime customer is and what does truly matter.

You must be clear for whom you render your work, who is your prime customer and identify what truly matters to them. Ask the questions senior management and the board would ask. That clarity helps, too, in shortening your report to what MUST be said only. There are initial ideas of one-page-reports which I support. The shorter the better.

CHALLENGE LEGACY TERMINOLOGY

Building on O'Regan, I challenge "assurance", one of the pillars of the present paradigm of internal auditing, alongside consulting (advisory) services. The term assurance appears 141 times in the new Global Internal Audit Standards (GIAS). According to O'Regan (2024, 22), assurance "is **one of the most slippery of terms in the auditing lexicon**. The term is sometimes used to express a quality control review of an audit, intended to provide an opinion on the audit's accuracy; used in this sense, assurance follows an audit. Others refer to assurance as the verification of the accuracy of an accounting record, with an audit providing a higher-level evaluation of the overall accounting entries underpinning financial statements; this understanding considers assurance as preliminary to an audit" (citation with own emphasis).

We encourage further research about the core terminology and core values of the Internal Audit Profession. Twenty years after Bailey et al. (2003) and ten years after the highly influential Lenz and Hahn (2015) research agenda now enjoying over 400 citations, the profession would greatly benefit from a fresh set of research questions to help unlock the full potential of Internal Auditing.

We also challenge "objectivity" as a core component of the internal audit value proposition. Only in simple and complicated contexts, the managing zone is there such a thing as "objective truth", one right answer or a best practice. In such cases, there is nothing (or little) to decide. In complex and chaotic contexts, however, in the more relevant cases of pioneering, there is always some degree of uncertainty, here true decisions must be taken. Objectivity does not exist there. Hence, we would recommend the standard setter removing the claim of objectivity. De-emphasizing would be an alternative approach to get started.

THE VISION 2035 DEMANDS MORE VERSATILE AND AGILE INTERNAL AUDITING

Notably, the new Global Internal Audit Standards (The Institute of Internal Auditors (The IIA) (2024), effective since January 2025, do not mention "versatile" or "agile" at all. The Vision 2035 survey (The Internal Audit Foundation, 2024) published six months later, in July, acknowledges that internal auditors will increasingly be expected to render advisory services over the forthcoming decade. Stakeholders will expect more from an effective internal audit function, including being versatile and agile. The anecdotal case of Villeroy & Boch shows that much is possible in a short period of time. More internal auditors becoming change agents is a promising perspective.

In Part Two, Barrie will shed more light on what that requires in practice.

Part Two (Barrie)

CONSISTENTLY DEMONSTRATING REAL(IZED) VALUE

Providing assurance and contributing to internal control improvement, and the deterrent effect of internal auditing, are not sufficient to show real value as these are minimum basics. The internal audit profession must find ways to contribute to the overall value proposition of its clients. One way of justifying internal auditing's legitimacy is to demonstrate its contributions to the bottom line, including quantifiable savings, increased revenue, and improved efficiencies. In our experience, savings, recoveries, and efficiency improvement are mere outflows from effective auditing. High-level strategy is important, but of little value if it does not filter through to the end-product. An internal audit function that seldom or never shows tangible value-added results should reconsider its audit methodologies. If management is reluctant to request assistance from their internal audit function it may signal that they hold negative perceptions, which may include one or more of the following:

- Not adding real value.
- Lacking business insight.
- Sub-par logical thinking ability.
- Reporting mostly generic findings due to limited or superficial testing.

- Not being pragmatic.
- Rigid and slow to react to management requests.
- Lack of presence, i.e., "We seldom see our internal auditors".
- Experiencing a backlash if the internal audit function reports adverse findings higher up on management-requested projects. This dilemma requires a careful approach which we discuss in the section dealing with management requests below.

The control improvement and deterrent benefit of internal audit's work is almost a given for most businesses having an established internal audit function. The full benefit of our work is largely unquantifiable, because how do you determine the full effect of improved controls? Many large corporations, especially listed companies, have achieved a measure of internal control maturity which may create the notion with management that the internal audit function has a diminishing benefit for the business, which unfortunately, may be partially true. Perceptions are usually the Truth in people's minds, which may bring the internal auditor closer to an endangered species status when stakeholders' perceptions shift toward internal auditing as a liability. Providing value-adding services should be a continuous endeavor. We cannot keep riding the same wave, thinking we have arrived once we've identified one or two value-added opportunities.

We must question the effectiveness and efficiency of our IA function if it does not continuously, or at least regularly add quantifiable value to the business.

Create the desired perceptions.

People must associate internal auditors as:	*... instead of:*
Bringing improvement	Catching people out
Capable	Showing strength only in certain (limited) areas
Providing workable solutions	Providing reactive recommendations
Available to assist when required	Will assist when we have the time

Ponder this

Is the general perception of your internal audit function one of adding value?

How can we better support the business?

The purpose for many, maybe most people attending internal audit conferences is to learn new and better ways to enhance their work quality and the impact they have on the business. Being pragmatic, I mainly attend conferences to learn how to (practically) apply shared information in my everyday work. Unfortunately, the conferences I have attended focus mainly on **What to** do, with a scarcity of **How to** do things better. We suggest considering the following in your quest for greater value-adding internal audit services, which are discussed in more detail throughout this book.

Aspect	*Instead of:*	*... consider*
Audit universe	Limited scope.	The audit universe comprising the entire business, including all financial and operational aspects forming part of the value chain.
Audit program development	"As is" approach.	"Should be" approach.
Audit location & modus operandi	Remote, office-bound, sitting, communicating with clients primarily by e-mail.	On-site, interacting, move around, handling, observing, experiencing, hands-on, visible, eye-contact, business insight.
Walkthrough process	Sit-through.	Hawk-through.
Condition (as an element of a finding)	Predominantly identifying control weaknesses by following the audit program.	Frequently identifying that risks have materialized, including fraud and errors, which sometimes fall outside the scope of the audit program.
Effect (as an element of a finding)	Reporting that a risk may materialize.	• Identifying errors and fraud having financial and other adverse impacts. • Quantifiable value-adding, e.g., recoverable amounts, reduced cost, increased revenue, improved efficiencies, fraud detection.
Internal audit report	Compiling/writing the report.	Building the report.
Audit testing	• Tick box approach. • Standard audit programs.	• Applying your mind. • Creative audit testing. • Thorough testing, including testing to the originating records, and even the point of occurrence.
Technology	Using technology for convenience.	Using technology to optimize.
Value proposition	Cost center.	Profit center.
KPAs	Number of findings	Return on investment and realized revenue and/or savings.
Staffing	Accounting/ finance backgrounds only	Financial as well as operational and technical backgrounds.

PROCEDURAL THINKING CAN CAUSE A MENTAL BLOCK.

Individuals and groups who embrace the saying "If you can read you can do anything" will be able to achieve more in their everyday lives, including in their work. Let's add the thinking part to it; "If you can read *and think*, you can do anything." Whereas learning and understanding the theory of internal auditing is important, they are the basics only. We must develop further – just as children need to develop their fine and gross motor skills. If, after three or ten years, you're still caught up in procedural thinking, you're probably not developing satisfactorily. The internal audit leadership should lead the way in ensuring the team members develop beyond procedural thinking.

Developing our skills is a continuous process;
we should never think we've "arrived".

Ponder this

Have you developed beyond procedural thinking?

The importance of healthy thought processes

Auditors must learn to think outside the box. Otherwise, they will find it difficult to be a value-adding team member. As discussed in Chapter 2, you can develop your original thinking ability. Knowledge, combined with talent, original thinking, excellence, and people skills are prerequisites for developing into a good and effective internal auditor. Most internal auditors should be able to develop and enhance these elements in their careers if they work diligently at their craft.

Develop an operational audit mindset

In my experience, operationally minded auditors produce better audit results. They approach the project holistically and keep scanning the landscape while busy with the audit, allowing them to more often identify value-adding opportunities. They are generally more solution-oriented and know how to make practical and outside-the-box recommendations. Developing your original thinking abilities should enhance your operational mindedness, but you must be intentional about it. Operationally mindedness should be considered as an important trait when recruiting internal audit staff.

Auditing against best practice

Individuals, and entities, or sections thereof, operate at different levels of standards. It is usually easy to convince those operating at a higher level to implement a seemingly basic internal control. However, convincing someone operating at a mediocre or low standard can be challenging. Have you ever experienced an auditee looking at you funny or even ridiculing you when raising a relatively basic finding and recommending a logical solution because it seems like overkill to them? Some may use this as a tactic to water down the findings, but others may be oblivious to the obvious – they don't see the findings and recommendations for what they are. Look at the following actual finding.

"Payment vouchers do not reflect the payment make-up to enable effective review by authorizing officials and auditors, including the following information:

i. Listing the invoices and credit notes in the batch.
ii. Deductions, such as withholding taxes and pre-payments made.
iii. Treatment of VAT.
iv. Indicating whether:
    - A prepayment is made.
    - Invoices comply with VAT Act requirements.
v. Any other notes".

We recommended: "The payment voucher template should be redesigned to facilitate a proper audit trail".

The Financial Manager insisted they knew how the payments were made up, which he argued, rendered the finding invalid and the recommendation impractical.

This is in stark contrast to the following audit elsewhere where we concluded that: "*Benchmarked against security functions being audited by Pro Optima at various clients in the past,* ABC*'s Security Department is well managed. However, measured against* ABC*'s own standard, which we regard as being set at a high level, some opportunities exist to further strengthen internal controls*". Despite offering to remove from the report some of the seven low-risk findings that were quick and easy to address, the Security Manager insisted all the findings should stay in the report because "it is important that we address them". He wasn't concerned about his image but rather he strived towards internal control maturity.

Robust auditing

Maintaining a robust and resilient auditing mindset largely counteracts the risk of succumbing to intimidation, pushback, and mediocrity – both on the side of the auditor and the auditee. The standard at which the audit area/auditee operates can prejudicially affect the standard against which we audit. A low standard tends to reduce the auditor's tolerance level which can cause the auditor to overlook real control weaknesses or to water down observations. Conversely, a high standard can bring about a measure of unfair judgment, particularly if the number of findings is the key driver for formulating the audit conclusion, and/or if it is a performance indicator. In my mind, having the number of findings as a performance indicator proves little. This has never been a performance measurement for us, yet having ten or more significant findings in an audit is not uncommon.

Finding findings for the sake of finding findings undermines the objectivity principle.

The originating record of a transaction

Internal auditors often accept one of the last records in the audit trail, instead of tracing the transaction from end-to-end. We prefer going beyond the originating record of the transaction through to the point of occurrence where possible and practical. The following is an example of audit outcomes where two separate audits of the same area were performed by different audit teams around the same time.

Topic: Review controls over on-site contractors.

	Did the auditor follow the transaction back to the point of occurrence?	
	No	*Yes*
Audit test objective: Confirming the accuracy of the quantities that the contractor charged.	Vouching the invoiced quantities to the quantities reflected on the quality control report attached to the contractor's invoice.	Vouching the quantities reflected on the invoice and quality control report to (1) the survey measuring result report, (2) survey plans, (3) underground measuring record (first record), and (4) IA remeasuring the work performed (point of occurrence).
Finding	Positive finding because the supporting documents stating the quality of work and quantities invoiced were available and corresponded with the invoices.	The quality control reports attached to invoices reflected the incorrect quantities and did not correspond with the preceding records of the transactions, i.e., (1) to (3) above or the actual work performed (4).
Effect	No effect – positive finding	Overpayments to a contractor totaling ±ZAR5 million/annum (USD280,000)
Cause	Not applicable – positive finding	The invoice amounts were manipulated to agree with the monthly budget without any correlation to the work performed and measured.
Quantified value-added	Nil	Cost recovery of ±ZAR490,000, and annual cost reduction ±ZAR5 million.

THE ENEMIES OF EFFECTIVE INTERNAL AUDITING

All the "enemies" mentioned below constitute nonconformance with the GIAS, which I suspect do not always reflect as such in QAR/QAIP results.

Playing it too safe

- **Generic conclusions** such as "Controls are partially adequate and effective to ensure..." do not instill much confidence in the quality of an audit, in my opinion. This is playing it too safe. The conclusion should "talk to" the audit objective, i.e., it should tell the reader whether the audit tests prove or disprove the audit objectives. By the time the readers have reached the conclusion section they have typically already read the objective and now want to know whether it was met. Without more context, the statement "Controls are partially adequate and effective" is rather ambiguous and inconclusive. GIAS Standard 14.5 [Engagement Conclusions] requires internal auditors to "develop an engagement conclusion that summarizes the engagement results relative to the engagement objectives and management's objectives. The engagement conclusion must summarize the internal auditor's professional judgment about the significance of the aggregated engagement findings".
- **Presenting loose findings** that don't expressly support the overall objective and/or the audit conclusion is an easy way out and could be viewed as an attempt to cover up imprudent auditing. Just as the conclusion should "talk to" the audit, so must the findings relate to the conclusion. Using the "Controls are partially adequate and effective" conclusion and backing it up with a few generic findings, like documents not signed, and reconciliations not promptly done, is nonconformance to Standard 14.5.
- **Vague and flimsy findings** may be a means of escape and can affect the relatability thereof to the conclusion, whether it is intentional or not. Presenting a fair and balanced audit outcome requires auditors to explain why they reached the conclusion, and generally requires that both adverse and positive outcomes be explained, provided they are presented accurately, fairly, and in context. To list a few vague positive observations, like policies and procedures are in place, for the sake of showing we're not only trying to identify anomalies, is equally unconvincing.

Shoddy auditing

Shoddy auditing has no place in our profession. Mediocrity and imprudence like the following are harmful to the profession.

- Auditing with the purpose of finding findings. Unfortunately, too many auditors, even entire internal audit functions run after findings thinking one or more findings would cause others to think they have done their job.

- Accepting the bone fides of presented "evidence" without prudent interrogation, including blindly believing what is said and basing a finding on hearsay. This goes against the GIAS' Professional Skepticism principle requiring the auditor to question and critically assess the reliability of information. Richard Chambers (2020), the former President and CEO of the Institute of Internal Auditors, however, advises that "*internal auditors must maintain a balance between too much skepticism and too little because all audits have deadlines. Audits must be efficient as well as effective, so we can't continue to ask questions and evaluate evidence ad infinitum*".
- The tendency to AssUMe, as this can make an Ass of U and Me.
- Providing reactive response recommendations instead of (innovative) practical solutions. You can recognize reactive response recommendations when they contain predominantly the same words as the condition or the cause, for example, responding to "The accounts supervisor should approve all payment batches".
- Failing to identify the root cause of a finding. Standard 14.3 [Evaluation of Findings] states that "internal auditors must collaborate with management to identify the root causes when possible".
- Using "canned fruit" audit programs which have been passed on from generation to generation.
- Ambiguous reporting, i.e., giving up on clear reporting because it is too big of an effort.

Ponder this.

Do you have comfort about your internal audit function's overall assessment of the entity's internal control environment?

DEALING WITH MANAGEMENT REQUESTS

Internal audit and management are interdependent, and the two should view each other as part of the bigger corporate team. They should be able to rely on one another and management should trust internal audit enough to request help when necessary. However, the way we report the results of projects performed at management's request should be approached wisely.

Once bitten, twice shy

We generally have one chance to get it right the first time and show management they can rely on us. If we mess up, they might become reluctant to rely on our work or to request further assistance from the internal auditors. Consider the following risks:

- **Backlash,** for example, if the internal audit function violates management's perceived protocols, like reporting adverse findings further up the hierarchy without first seeking their consent. The general rule should be to establish and agree on the reporting protocols before starting the project, in wisdom obviously, because internal auditors must remain prudent, including in their reporting protocols in conformance with Principle 11 of the GIAS [Communicate Effectively].
- **Over promising.** Ensure you have the resources and capabilities to successfully deliver on commitments. Budgeting time for potential management requests when preparing the annual audit plan may aid in mitigating this risk.
- **Independence and objectivity.** Depending on the auditor's mindset, this can be a risk either way. Over-emphasizing independence and objectivity can result in missed value-adding opportunities, while carelessness may compromise these principles. You heard us challenging both concepts before.
- **Ulterior motives.** Be mindful of management requests that potentially originate from the wrong motives such as attention diversion, (ab)using internal audit to do management's work and wanting internal audit to prove a point on their behalf.

Ponder this

Does management in your organization have the liberty and trust in the internal audit function to request their assistance?

CAN INTERNAL AUDIT REALLY PROVIDE ASSURANCE?

Is assurance the appropriate term to use?

The GIAS defines internal auditing as *"an independent, objective* assurance *and advisory service designed to add value and improve an organization's operations. It helps an organization accomplish its objectives by bringing a systematic, disciplined approach to evaluate and improve the effectiveness of governance, risk management, and control processes".*

It surprised me that the definition of internal auditing remained largely the same as the abstract one used in the outgoing International Professional Practices Framework (IPPF). I had hoped it would have been simplified. Imagine reciting this 42-word definition (if you can remember it) to someone asking you what internal auditing is. This may explain why few of the many websites defining internal auditing use the IIA definition, and when they do use it, they usually refer to it as the "IIA's definition". When searching for other professions' definitions, all had concise and clear definitions.

The IIA webpage[2] further explains what internal auditing is, stating: *"Performed by professionals with an in-depth understanding of the business culture, systems, and processes, the internal audit activity provides* **assurance** *that internal controls in place are adequate to mitigate the risks, governance processes are effective and efficient, and organizational goals and objectives are met".*

The question is: Can internal audit **provide assurance** that internal controls in place **are** adequate to mitigate the risks, that governance processes **are** effective and efficient, and that organizational goals and objectives **are** met? This is a strong statement!

The use of assurance by the internal and external audit professions

Reasonable assurance seems fitting for use in the **external audit** context due to their focus, scope, and testing coverage, which enable them to be reasonably sure of the fairness of the financial results, provided they perform the audit well. However, the aspects of **internal auditing** as discussed below adversely affect our ability to provide assurance in the true sense of the word, as assurance is a strong expression, which may imply or be interpreted as providing full assurance. Internal audit may not even be able to provide reasonable assurance that internal controls in place **are** adequate to mitigate the risks, governance processes **are** effective and efficient, and organizational goals and objectives **are** met, as stated on the IIA's webpage.

The CPA firm, Linford & Co explains "Reasonable assurance is a high level of assurance, similar to absolute assurance but with reasonable assurance, there is still a remote likelihood that material misstatements exist. Whereas with absolute assurance, there is no likelihood of material misstatement".

Internal auditing's coverage is generally limited, which is unlikely to enable them to express a reliable opinion that there is only a remote likelihood that fraud, error, losses, and control weaknesses were not identified within the audit areas covered during the financial year, let alone the areas that were not audited. Limited coverage is typically due to the nature of our work, including the following:

- Infrequency of covering each audit area/topic.
- Incompleteness of the audit universe, which seems true for some internal audit functions.
- Limited samples and/or incomplete testing due to practical reasons, such as time constraints.

Can the internal audit function get it so wrong that they provide false assurance?

My response to this question is "YES". I have been struggling with the term assurance for many years, even with a measure of resistance when hearing internal audit's role is to provide assurance. Maybe it is because I have seen how easy (and maybe common) it is to provide false assurance. The story about the QAR at the start of this chapter provides a prime example. If internal auditors use unsuitable and ineffective audit methodologies and lack business insight, they may not be able to provide any level of assurance. The misconception of the term assurance by some has developed into the habit of performing high-level (superficial) audit testing only. The audit manager at an internal audit function who outsourced some of their scheduled audits to Pro Optima would direct us not to perform further testing when we identified suspected fraud and errors, because "internal audit's purpose is only to provide assurance". When discussing this response with him some ten years later he explained that there wasn't enough time to perform in-depth testing because they had to cover the vast audit universe in the combined assurance context and alluded to unduly sacrificing depth in favor of a wide coverage. One of the internal audit function's challenges is getting the right balance between width and depth when planning overall audit coverage, and individual assignments. In my opinion, it's better to dig too deep than too shallow. A superficial understanding and testing of the audit area is of little value.

Practice Advisory 2120–2022 – Managing the Risk of the Internal Audit Activity states that *"Risks to internal audit activities fall into three broad categories: audit failure,* ***false assurance****, and reputation risks", and "An internal audit activity may unknowingly provide some level of false assurance. 'False assurance' is a level of confidence or assurance based on perceptions or assumptions rather than fact. In many cases, the mere fact that the internal audit activity is involved in a matter may create some level of false assurance"*.

Definition of assurance in the GIAS

The GIAS define **assurance** as a "Statement intended to increase the level of stakeholders' confidence about an organization's governance, risk management, and control processes over an issue, condition, subject matter, or activity under review when compared to established criteria".

Ponder this

Without rereading the above definition, what is your definition of *assurance* in internal auditing?

Meaning of assurance in dictionaries

Considering the general meaning of assurance, the following dictionaries define assurance in (clear) strong terms, which do not support the meaning as it is used in internal auditing, or the (abstract) definition of *assurance* in the GIAS.

- Merriam-Webster

Meaning	A state of mind in which one is free from doubt, e.g., I can state with complete *assurance* that no harm will ever come to you.
Synonyms	**Strong terms/ definite** Confidence, conviction, doubtlessness, sureness, surety, certainty, assuredness, certitude, cocksureness. **Milder terms/some leeway** Positiveness, satisfaction.
Antonyms	Doubt, incertitude, nonconfidence, uncertainty.

- Collins Dictionary
  - Assurance in British English

Meaning/definition	*(Noun)* in the sense of **promise** A statement or assertion intended to inspire confidence, e.g., an assurance that other forces will not move into the territory.
Synonyms	Strong terms/ definite Promise, guarantee, pledge, commitment, vow, declaration, oath, word of honor, statement. Milder terms/some leeway Profession, assertion, affirmation, protestation (formal).
Antonyms	Lie, falsehood

  - Assurance in American English

Meaning/definition	*(Noun)* in the sense of **assertion**.
Synonyms	Assertion, declaration, guarantee, oath, pledge, promise, statement, vow, word **(all strong terms).**
Antonyms	Lie, falsehood

Is there a better term to use?

Arguing assurance must be interpreted in the context of internal audit's role in the combined/integrated assurance framework is like try fitting a square peg in a round hole – in my opinion. The definition of internal auditing in the 1980s and 1990s used the words appraisal, examining, and evaluation, i.e., "Internal auditing is an independent **appraisal** activity established within an organization as a service to the organization. It is a control which functions by examining and evaluating the adequacy and effectiveness of other controls".

What if *appraisal* replaces assurance in the current definition of internal auditing?

The GIAS definition of internal auditing would then change to "*Internal auditing is an independent, objective **appraisal** and advisory service designed to add value and improve an organization's operations [which is closer to reality in my opinion]. It helps an organization accomplish its objectives by bringing a systematic, disciplined approach to evaluate and improve the effectiveness of governance, risk management, and control processes*".

Assurance, in my view, has created unrealistic expectations and unhealthy perceptions and the belief that the internal audit activity provides assurance that internal controls in place are adequate to mitigate the risks, governance processes are effective and efficient, and organizational goals and objectives are met. This IPPF statement may not be true, fitting, or fair. It may even create the notion that internal auditors must provide assurance, irrespective of how good or bad the internal controls are.

The GIAS describe the purpose of internal auditing and uses *assurance* when describing its purpose, i.e., "Internal auditing strengthens the organization's ability to create, protect, and sustain value by providing the board and management with independent, risk-based, and objective ***assurance***, advice, insight, and foresight ...".

When replacing *assurance* with its definition, the purpose would be: "Internal auditing strengthens the organization's ability to create, protect, and sustain value by providing the board and management with an independent, risk-based, and objective *statement intended to increase the level of confidence ... when compared to established criteria*, advice, insight, and foresight ...".

- Sorry, but I don't get it. It feels like painting ourselves into a corner.

The GIAS definition of assurance being *"a statement intended to increase the level of confidence ... when compared to established criteria"*, is too abstract and confusing for my practical brain, and, in my opinion, may add to the misinterpretation by many that the purpose of internal auditing is to provide "a statement intended to increase the level of stakeholder's confidence" about an organization's governance, risk management, and control processes over an issue, subject matter, or activity under review when compared to established criteria, which I don't think is our purpose.

Ponder this.

Do you feel comfortable with the use of *assurance* in internal auditing?

Can you cite the purpose of internal auditing as defined in the GIAS (28 words)?

Shouldn't we simplify the definition of internal auditing?

We should not criticize if we don't provide an alternative, which prompted me to define internal auditing in simple terms to enable answering an uninformed person asking what internal audit is. Try fitting all the main elements describing our profession is not practical. Some elements should rather be explained separately, such as in the nature, purpose and scope statements. Herewith my attempt to explain what internal auditing is:

- *Performing audits to assist companies in mitigating the risks of errors, irregularities, and inefficiencies and to help them achieve their objectives.*

or

- *Performing audits that evaluate a company's internal controls to assist in mitigating the risks of errors, irregularities, inefficiencies and non-compliance and to help them achieve their objectives.*

SELF-EVALUATION AND PERCEPTIONS

We invite internal audit practitioners, line and executive managers, and board members to perform a self-evaluation or provide your perceptions of the internal audit function using the following matrix table.

Our internal audit function (IAF):	*True*	*Leaning to true*	*Leaning to false*	*False*	*Unsure*	*Comments/ action plan*
1. Provides an effective and efficient service.						
2. Contributes to the bottom line through quantifiable savings, increased revenue, improved efficiencies, etc.						
3. Is pragmatic in their approach.						
4. Has good logical thinking abilities.						
5. Has a fair to excellent understanding of the business.						
6. Provides practical solutions to adverse observations.						
7. Performs prudent audit testing.						
8. Reports audit outcomes clearly, accurately, and fairly.						
9. Is sufficiently flexible and promptly responds to management requests.						

NOTES

1 The Quality Assurance Review, renamed as the Quality Assurance and Improvement Program (QAIR) has been expanded in the new GIAS covering not only conformance to the standards but also assessing the effectiveness and efficiency of the internal audit function.
2 https://www.theiia.org/en/about-us/about-internal-audit/ (Sep-22).

REFERENCES

Bailey, D., Gramling, A. A. and Ramamoorti, S. (2003), Research Opportunities in Internal Auditing, The Institute of Internal Auditors Research Foundation, Altamonte Springs, FL.

Chambers, R. (2020), Internal Auditors be Trusting but Skeptical, Blog https://www.richardchambers.com/internal-auditors-be-trusting-but-skeptical/, September

Kovash, M. (2020), Reasonable Assurance: What Is it & How Does it Affect SOC Report Opinions?

Lenz, R., & Chesshire, J. (2023), Rethinking Internal Audit: Governance Needs Gardening, EDPACS, 68:3, 7–15 https://doi.org/10.1080/07366981.2023.2255432

Lenz, R. and Hahn, U. (2015), A Synthesis of Empirical Internal Audit Effectiveness Literature Pointing to New Research Opportunities, Managerial Auditing Journal, 30:1, 5–33.

Lenz, R., Karmann, O., & Druckenmueller, J. (2024), Internal Auditors as change agents: What a difference a year makes! EDPACS, 69:5, 26–38 https://doi.org/10.1080/07366981.2024.2348283

Lenz, R., & O'Regan, D. J. (2024), The Global Internal Audit Standards – Old Wine in New Bottles? EDPACS, 69:3, 1–28 https://doi.org/10.1080/07366981.2024.2322835

O'Regan, D. J. (2024). The auditor's companion: Concepts and terms from A to Z. Georgetown University Press.

Sarens, G., Lenz, R., & Decaux, L. (2016), Insights Into Self-Images of Internal Auditors, EDPACS, 54:4, 1–18 https://lnkd.in/dDJUhNr

The Institute of Internal Auditors (2024), Global Internal Audit Standards, Lake Mary, Florida, US, January

The Internal Audit Foundation (2024), Internal Audit: Vision 2035, US, Lake Mary, July

Chapter 4

The 4th P is our Purpose … because no unique selling proposition, no internal auditing

GARDENER OF GOVERNANCE ARTICLE SYNOPSIS

The profession lacks its commonly shared core and is therefore constantly at risk of overpromising and underdelivering, risking being viewed as "jack of all trades" and "master of none". If internal auditing seeks professional recognition, it will need a knowledge base that can link the profession to the work it does. The profession should not compete with external auditing and must differentiate its knowledge base from financial auditing. Internal auditing must focus on what differentiates it from external audits, such as engaging with an organization's governance processes, which external audits for independence reasons cannot do.

PUTTING PRACTICE INTO THEORY

Barrie has followed some of the approaches and applied the techniques covered in this chapter from early in his internal audit career without first recognizing it was different from the norm. The peculiarity became apparent over time while working on projects with other internal auditor functions. Some disagreed or made it clear from their responses that they did not agree with some of the main tenets of Pro Optima's audit methodologies, which was why he did some introspection in mid-2019. Barrie explains: "I couldn't help but wonder whether it was presumptuous to believe these approaches were amazing, especially when only a handful of other internal auditors seemed to agree. But then, considering the project outcomes, I regained confidence". The confusion about the apparent paradox prompted him to approach seven officials at their clients, i.e., one line manager, five senior managers, and one executive officer to rate Pro Optima's services compared to other internal audit functions. Whereas the sample was far from representative, and the face-to-face survey probably created a measure of bias, the outcome was encouraging, i.e., 84% vs. 57%, which further boosted confidence. The participants' perceptions favored Pro Optima vastly over others in the following five of the 11 performance measurement areas: trusted partner, tangible value adding, logical thinking, report quality, and operating in excellence.

DOI: 10.1201/9781003539001-4

The quest for answers led Barrie to attend the annual conference of the European Confederation of Institutes of Internal Auditors (ECIIA) held in Luxembourg in September 2019 in search of like-minded internal auditors to connect with where he met Rainer. The duo met at the welcoming supper where Barrie told Rainer why he decided to attend the conference, which was "to see whether there were other crazy internal auditors out there". Rainer invited Barrie to attend the session the next day where he presented his paper on "WRAPS – How to make better decisions". Within the first few minutes of the presentation, Barrie realized that there was indeed at least one other "crazy" auditor on planet Earth. MISSION ACCOMPLISHED.

This book covers some of the contents of the Pro Optima DNA Manual titled Beyond the Obvious compiled in 2018 to put *practice into theory* by documenting and naming their approaches and techniques. It is possible that other internal audit activities use similar approaches to increase their value proposition, and we would certainly want to hear from them.

LEARNING OBJECTIVES OF THIS CHAPTER

- Internal auditing can and should break out of monotonous procedural ways of performing audits.
- There are proven, practical methods to perform impactful assignments.

Part One (Rainer)

UNCHECKED POWER AND INADEQUATE ACCOUNTABILITY CAUSE GOVERNANCE FAILURES

Jim Collins' (2009) bestseller "How the mighty fall" is about governance failure. He argues, "Decline can be avoided. Decline can be detected. Decline can be reversed." What can internal auditors do? What is their position? We suggest viewing the effective internal auditor as THE GARDENER OF GOVERNANCE. This positioning beautifully complements Professor Mervyn King's concept of directors and senior executives as GUARDIANS OF GOVERNANCE, "*the heart, mind, soul and conscience*" of an organization with the overriding priority "to ensure the long-term health of the company" (Williams 2024). While internal auditing cannot be the panacea, the cure-all to prevent governance failure, internal auditing could become a stronger force in the governance mosaic, especially when the guardians and the gardener of governance work well together to enhance ethical and effective governance. Let's better define the position of internal auditors. Then, play your position well, dear internal auditors.

> When governance breaks down it is because of too much power concentration or not enough accountability or both.
>
> *Korine (2020)*

Korine (2020) defines 10 Archetypes of Corporate Governance Failure.

Five are attributable to **Unchecked power – "Who is running the firm?"**:

1. One-Person Rule – The Hero Problem (unfettered power, no balance of power),
2. Single Shareholder Dominance – The Too Much or Too Little Problem (firm dependent on maintaining the good will of that shareholder),
3. Interest Group Hegemony – The Ganging Up Problem (focus may be on short-term share price improvement and adoption of high-risk strategies),
4. Absolute Obedience – The Shut Up, Do as I Say Problem (a culture built upon threats and fear) and
5. Board of Director Weakness – The Lack of Backbone Problem (in-effective or paper boards).

   The other five are caused by **Inadequate Accountability – "How is accountability ensured?"**:

6. Opaque Business Models – The Blurry Windshield Problem (limited understanding of how the firm makes money),
7. Unsustainable Performance Targets – The Big Hairy Audacious Goal Problem (overpromising and underdelivering),
8. Counterproductive Incentives – The Doing the Wrong Thing Right Problem (single focus, for example, sales over everything, can lead to disastrous outcomes),
9. Concentrated Risks – The All Your Eggs in One Basket Problem (an age-old problem in corporate governance) and
10. Obsolete Control Systems – The No Way to Know Problem (poor managing and control).

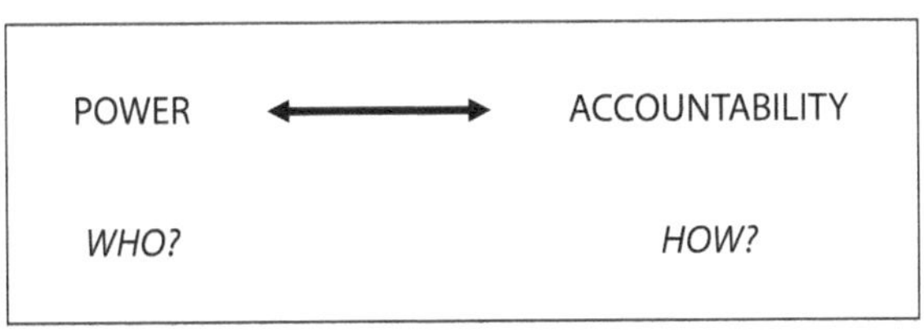

Figure 4.1 What is Corporate Governance? (Korine 2020, 16).

Avoiding unfettered power and clarifying RACI, the system to define responsibility, accountability, control and information requirements are at the heart of what internal auditing is doing. The key question here is what internal audit can do about the above mentioned Archetypes of Corporate Governance Failure. That is where I see the future direction of the internal auditing profession.

Korine (2020) references the following definitions of corporate governance: (a) "the system by which companies are directed and controlled" (Cadbury Committee 1992)[1] and (b) "Corporate governance is seen as the interactions between various internal and external actors and the board members in directing a firm for value creation" (Huse 2007).

INTERNAL AUDITING IS A COMPLEX COORDINATION CHALLENGE

I suggest moving away from portraying internal auditing as the third line as elaborated in Chapter 2 (Public). I picture the internal auditing process as a complex coordination challenge (Figure 4.2).

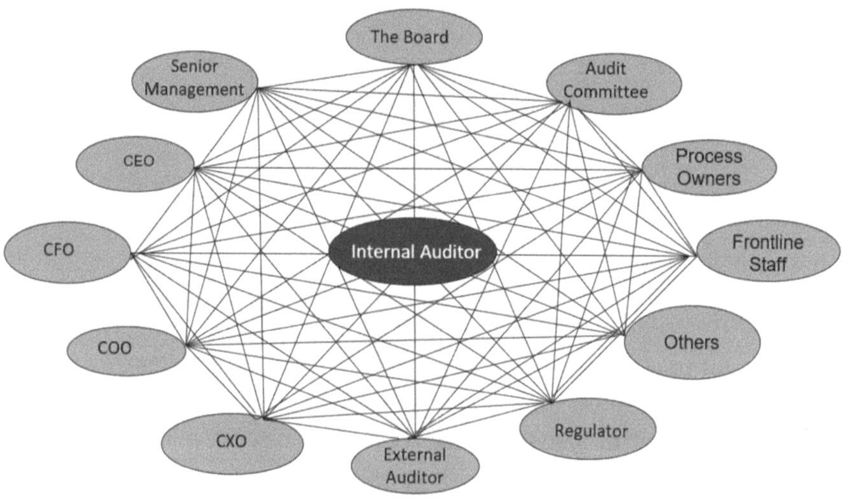

Figure 4.2 IA as coordinator in the corporate governance ecosystem (Lenz & O'Regan 2024).

In that context, I view Jody Hoffer Gittell's (2006) Relational Coordination Theory (RCT) as particularly relevant and helpful when aspiring to nurture and strengthen the corporate governance ecosystem. I regard shared goals, shared knowledge, mutual respect and effective communication (frequent, timely, accurate and problem solving minded) as key ingredients of a successful value-adding internal audit function. These are the elements of Jody Hoffer Gittell's Relational Coordination Theory (also referenced and applied to the context of IA by Lenz 2013).

In 2024, over ten years on, the time is ripe for further research exploring the power of that theory in the corporate governance ecosystem. With our book, we encourage further (qualitative) research about the role of internal auditing in the corporate governance ecosystem, contributing to or possibly chairing GRC meetings (Governance, Risk, Compliance) and/or driving the Aligned (Combined or Integrated) Assurance Agenda in organizations (Sarens et al. 2012).

PREVENTING GOVERNANCE FAILURE IS THE MISSION OF INTERNAL AUDITING

Lenz and Hoos (2023) speak about "swimming in the organization" and "surfing in the wild ocean" when contributing to the multifaceted challenges in the pioneering zone, dealing with complex and chaotic contexts, our reality in the 21st century. Lenz and Hoos (2023) suggest widening the repertoire of internal auditing, adding "Build" to the traditional pillars of the work and value rendered, that is, "Assure" and "Consult", hence, speaking about the "ABC model". We internal auditors need to be good at addressing "WHAT IS?" (Assure), "SO WHAT?" (Consult) and "WHAT IF?" (Build) type of questions. Such "WHAT IF?" type of questions become particularly important in the pioneering zone; there is no objective truth, so it is about dealing with trade-offs, alternative approaches, options, weighing up the pros and cons of the different solutions under consideration. And, this is a manager's reality when launching new products to existing or new markets, when buying and integrating new companies, when launching an Enterprise Resource Planning (ERP) software like S/4 HANA as that is presently under way – just to name a few examples.

In simple and complicated contexts, the managing zone, in cases where "objective truth" may exist, there is often one right answer or a best practice, and therefore is nothing (or little) to decide. Going forward, the machine (the robot, AI, Artificial Intelligence) will be well-equipped to fill that space. No uncertainty, no decision required, an algorithm is all you need.

In complex and chaotic contexts, however, in the more relevant cases of pioneering, there is always some degree of uncertainty, here true decisions must be taken. Only here. Most business decisions that truly matter are decisions in the context of uncertainty as defined above. Here, we are positive, internal auditors can do more, can do better. A step-up is required and expected in order to become a more respected actor in the organization. Such upskilling and upscaling would enhance the chances of heightened peer and public recognition.

Summing up, building and creating is much harder than judging. Internal auditors can render more valuable services and support, assuring, building and consulting (advising) in times of need, in cases of uncertainty. Becoming more center stage, daring more, aiming higher, entering the pioneering zone and dealing more with complex and chaotic contexts is the underlying plea.

Hence, as a promising path, Lenz and O'Regan (2024) picture Internal Auditors as coordinators in the corporate governance ecosystem. Internal Auditors may, for example, champion the Governance-Risk-Compliance (GRC) agenda in an organization. Moreover, one notch up, Internal Auditors may play an instrumental role in building and strengthening an organization's journey toward Combined Assurance (Sarens et al. 2012). I personally favor the term Aligned Assurance as applied, for example, at Adidas.[2]

As leading question,[3] we ask ourselves *"What is the greatest fear as a CEO?"* We like to believe that *"Your greatest fear as CEO is that people aren't telling the truth"*. We like to believe that governance stakeholders want to know what is going on, want the organization they manage, control and nurture to flourish and want to prevent governance failure. Internal auditors could be instrumental in becoming important contributors to asking the right questions and getting to the bottom of things when and where it matters most. We see help preventing governance failure as the main mission of internal auditors. In that regard, we advocate the suggested metaphor for the effective internal auditor (Lenz & O'Regan 2024): "The Gardener of Governance: Our Nature is Nurture".

A STICKY IDEA: THE GARDENER OF GOVERNANCE

The 28 words long purpose statement in domain I (The Internal Audit Foundation 2024, 15) reads as follows:

> Internal auditing strengthens the organization's ability to create, protect, and sustain value by providing the board and management with independent, risk-based, and objective assurance, advice, insight, and foresight.

While I particularly value the quality of strengthening, the inclusion of creation and focusing on the board as the prime customer, I am positive the internal audit profession would benefit from an overarching metaphor framing the good intentions and words chosen when crafting the purpose statement.

Heath and Heath (2008) study in their bestseller, why some ideas survive and others die. When applying their SUCCESs-model to the world of audit, it is worthwhile searching for sticky ideas that are <u>S</u>imple, <u>U</u>nexpected, <u>C</u>oncrete, <u>C</u>redible, <u>E</u>motional and/or tell <u>S</u>tories. One such trait may already be sufficient to make an idea stick.

To help becoming a more respected contributor in the corporate governance mosaic, we recommend building on the power of a sticky idea, a brand. We suggest as sticky idea: **"The Gardener of Governance: Our Nature is Nurture"**. Eight words only. A metaphor. A sticky idea, SUCCESs: <u>S</u>imple. <u>U</u>nexpected. <u>C</u>oncrete. <u>C</u>redible. <u>E</u>motional. <u>S</u>torytelling and adding a small "s", inviting internal auditors to become "**<u>surfers</u>** in the organization".

The Gardener metaphor originates from my professional journey:

In the first half of my professional career, I was in CFO type roles. In my role as Vice President of Finance, CFO Europe & Asia at Actavis, a 10,000 people and EUR 2 billion global pharmaceutical company, as leader of 20-person direct reporting team responsible for over 250 cross-functional staff I provided financial leadership, control and commercial support to all functional areas of non-US business units worth approximately EUR 1 billion in annual revenue. We conducted due diligence of over 30 mergers and acquisitions, as well as integration of 7 companies in 6 European and Asian countries, with an average purchase price of €50 million. Hence, I label that period until 2007 as my HUNTING period.

In 2007, when all the money was spent, I was invited to become the Global Head of Internal Audit, a role I happily accepted. My assignment was about leveraging the assets in hand, unearthing problems, improving processes and controls, helping to prepare for the sale of the company for the major owner at the time, was Deutsche Bank was no longer able to syndicate their investment of about EUR 4 billion due to capital market dynamics. Hence, I label that period since 2007 my GARDENING period.

We suggest "The Gardener of Governance: Our Nature is Nurture" as mantra for effective internal auditing. We suggest Preventing Governance Failure as the purpose of internal auditing. Internal auditing has unexploited potential to prevent governance failure for such failures "develop over time, often over a number of years" (Korine 2020). Internal auditing can literally watch the grass and the weed growing, to put it bluntly.

Effective internal auditing can help prevent governance failure.

I eagerly await what vision and what purpose will become reality in say, 10 years from now, in 2035.

We need to change course. There has been governance failure, again and again. The list is long, too long to reference here. Just as an example, one frightening case is Boeing[4]: "Boeing's chief executive Dave Calhoun faced a grilling from US senators about the company's culture as he apologized to family members of plane crash victims, who shouted at him throughout the hearing".

We can no longer wait, we must strengthen Corporate Governance. In that context, there are many issues and questions to address beyond internal audit, including:

Who gets on boards? Who becomes CEO? Who becomes C-Suite executives? How do we control power? How do we avoid unfettered power? How do we fight toxic leadership, toxic organizational culture? How do we nurture & secure psychological safety? What does sound accountability look like?

There are so many actors in the corporate governance mosaic. We wonder, how can all this fail, ultimately? We argue that board composition and dynamics are crucial. Top Management's character, leadership, experience, qualification and compensation matter, of course. We suspect the Peter-Principle[5] is a much bigger issue than we like to believe: *"In a hierarchy every employee tends to rise to his level of incompetence"*.

We MUST get better at controlling power and managing accountability to more successfully prevent governance failure. Boards play a crucial role here, including the Non-Executive Directors.

We suggest further research about the positioning of internal auditing in the corporate governance mosaic, our suggested GARDENER metaphor, dealing with the weeds, preventing risks and deficiencies and flourishing (nurturing) our suggested focus, PREVENTING GOVERNANCE FAILURE and about the interaction and team play with other stakeholders in the governance mosaic. The concept of directors and senior executives as GUARDIANS of governance combined with the effective internal auditor as THE GARDENER OF GOVERNANCE offers a robust and comprehensive approach to corporate governance. Now is the right time for a new research agenda. Ten years after the very popular Lenz-Hahn (2015) research agenda, the profession would benefit from a new set of research questions that may help to bring the best out of Internal Auditing.

In Part Two, Barrie will focus on the purpose of internal auditing in practice.

Part Two (Barrie)

> **Ponder this.**
>
> Off the top of your head, how would you rate the effectiveness of your internal audit function? __/**10**
>
> Mention one distinctive innovative technique that your internal audit function applies that you are aware of.

INNOVATIVE AND IMPACTFUL INTERNAL AUDIT PROJECTS

If the internal audit function is merely tolerated because of mandatory requirements, it should review the way it is doing things. My online searches for information on how to conduct impactful audit projects did not yield meaningful results, except for a few tips. Numerous articles offer valuable advice on establishing and maintaining effective internal audit functions focusing on WHAT to do, but there was limited guidance on performing innovative and impactful audit assignments, specifically on HOW to, apart from using technology, for which ample information is available.

Pro Optima has developed several methods over the years with significant value-adding effects. These methods are listed below and elaborated on further. Around 40% of our assignments have shown proven tangible value-adding results, primarily in cost savings and improved efficiencies. Since Pro Optima's inception, the direct impact of our assignments has exceeded R2.5 billion South African rand (US$170 million[6]). To put this in perspective; most of our projects are performed as a 2nd line service – with reference to the IIA's three-lines model, i.e., Pro Optima does not fulfill the internal audit function at these clients.

Most of our staff have mining technical backgrounds, such as mining engineers, surveyors, and rock engineers.

Our methodologies

- Start with Intuition Method (SWIM)
- In-and-Out Audits
- Implement Controls Before Audit Method (ICBAM)
- Fraud and error detection tests
- Risk Materialization Testing (RMT)
- Live consultative auditing

I will share a few of the thousands of examples of value-adding results throughout this chapter starting with the following:

Project	*Explosives control audits at a large gold mining company*
Value-added	• ZAR 7.8 million per annum reduction in explosives costs (conservative estimate). • Improved production efficiencies, including better advances and fragmentation.[7]
Request/ source	The Senior Manager of Metallurgy requested Pro Optima to determine the reasons for the poor fragmentation of broken rock delivered to the gold plants.
Objective	To determine whether explosives are safely and effectively used and to ascertain the impact on mining quality, with emphasis on fragmentation size.
Sub objectives	To ensure: • The mining sections receive explosives and blasting accessories as needed. • Explosives and blasting accessories are safely handled and efficiently used. • Blasting processes, i.e., rock face marking, drilling, charging up, and blasting are performed to the applicable safety and mining standards. • Appropriate decision-making regarding explosives is facilitated through relevant, accurate, and timely information.
Scope	• **Documents reviewed:** weekly and monthly explosives usage reports, explosive ordering forms, delivery summaries, explosives car control sheets, survey measuring results, mining supervisor's logbooks, planned task observation reports, safety appointment letters, and the relevant mining standards. • **In-situ inspections** were conducted at over 50 mining panels to evaluate compliance with the applicable mine standards and the Mine Health & Safety Act. • **Interviewing** representative of the explosives suppliers, explosives magazine masters, production managers, mine overseers, mining supervisors, and mining crew members.
Summarized main findings and related recommendations	Poor fragmentation occurred in most mining panels visited, which was mainly due to the deviation from the mining standards and the overcharging of drilled holes. We recommended the following: • Better oversight and the retraining of miners. [Pro Optima subsequently provided on-the-job retraining to several of the miners at management's request.] • A change in the drill pattern. • Reducing the number of explosive cartridges per drill hole.

Internal auditing is more about applying your mind than following audit procedures.

START WITH INTUITION METHOD (SWIM)

SWIM is also referred to as the *Should Be* approach vs. the commonly applied *As Is* approach. This method, along with our other methods, plays a crucial role in the Pro Optima success story as evidenced by the significant value we add to clients through our services. We have been applying the SWIM principles for as long as the company has existed. Some may, however, struggle to embrace SWIM due to conflicting professional beliefs rooted in legacy thinking. Its primary goal is to perform audits and related assignments creatively, leveraging our intuitive auditing talent to deliver valuable project outcomes. SWIM is not a one-fits-all solution though as it is not suitable for all assignments and requires a sufficient measure of skill and maturity. The more experienced the auditor or team is, the better they can draw from their intuitive auditing skills. First following the audit program when starting the fieldwork, may hamper creative thinking and cloud the broader perspective necessary to approach the project holistically. The auditor has a better thinking ability when looking from the outside before getting involved in the details. Our staff is trained to start testing whatever they feel they need to do before consulting the audit program. Interestingly enough, a large portion of the tests have usually been completed by then. Thus, the audit program is not the recipe but helps to ensure the completeness of audit testing. It can counteract shoddy auditing and prevent the audit from becoming a mere paper trail exercise. In our experience, there is often an abundance of opportunity to add value, with this approach assisting greatly in finding the hidden gems.

Benefits of SWIM

In our experience, audit outcomes are generally more successful when applying the SWIM principles compared to conventional methods in the following respects:

- Completeness of the audit testing as SWIM generally prompts more thorough and effective audit testing in areas where it matters.
- SWIM counteracts superficial auditing, such as auditing for findings, loose findings without context, accepting information at face value, and getting away with the bare minimum, i.e., SWIM enhances conformance with the new GIAS.
- Team members often stumble over value-added findings they were <u>not</u> looking for, including fraud.
- A higher likelihood of identifying value-adding opportunities with some of them falling outside the immediate scope of the audit.
- Developing staff's business insight and original thinking abilities.
- Identifying gaps in the relevant company procedures.
- Staff experience higher levels of work satisfaction due to the excellent results.

The SWIM process

Applying your mind and operating within the frame of your expertise when performing assignments are important and value-adding ingredients. This process is not set in stone and should not be followed rigidly, but rather to the extent that the auditor/team feels comfortable with. The following is a process chart and narrative explaining SWIM.

1. **The audit process starts with a scoping meeting** involving senior management to discuss and agree on the risks, objective(s), and scope of the audit and any other areas that management wants the team to address.
2. The general rule is: **do not determine how the systems in the audit area operate at the beginning of the audit** but rather gather the information while performing audit testing. Some key information should still be obtained during the kick-off meeting, preliminary survey, and project planning as appropriate.

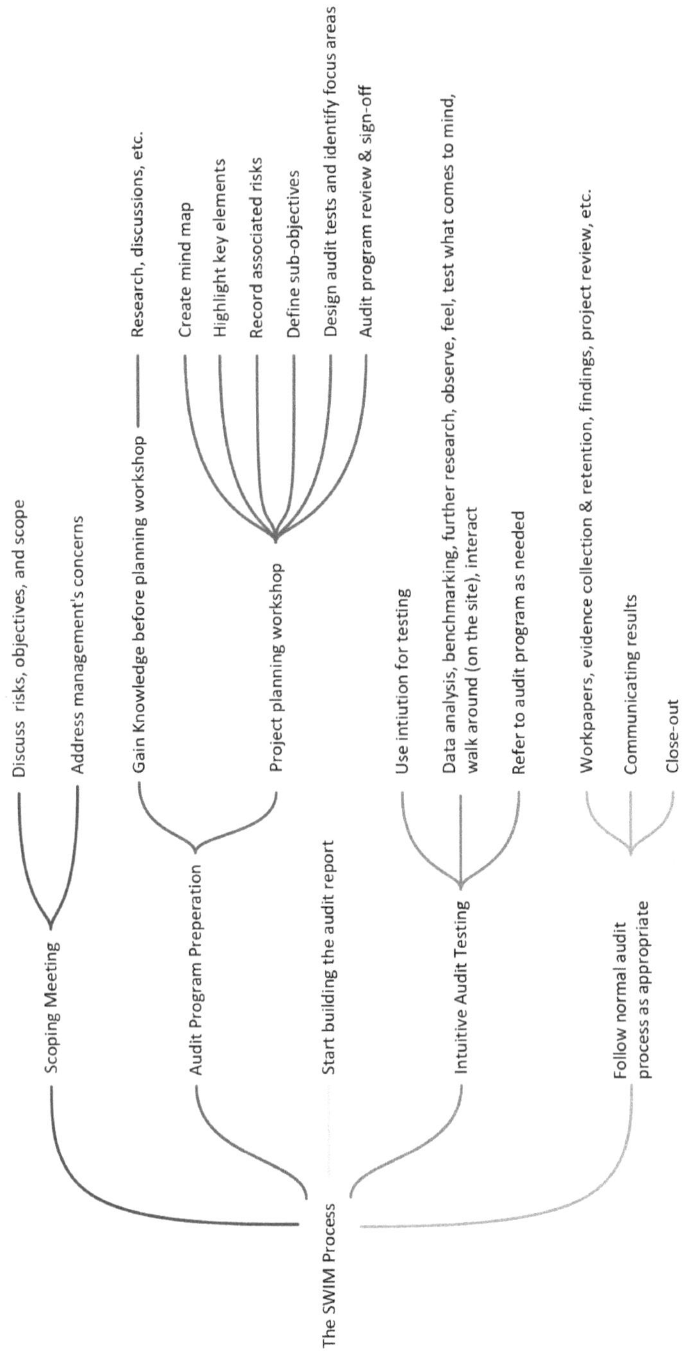

Figure 4.3 The SWIM process

3. **The team prepares the audit program** as follows:

The process is explained below using the example of a property administration audit.

3.1. **Before the project planning workshop.**
All team members should gain additional knowledge on the topic before the workshop starts, including through research, walkabouts, and discussions with people with knowledge of the topic. The rule of thumb is approximately 30 to 60 minutes per team member.
Let's get started.

Assume the following: A team member, say **an audit clerk**, noted the following when doing the research:

- How do you ensure you know which are the company's properties? – completeness.
- Getting behind on rates and taxes bigger problem than many property owners realize.
- Risk: Rent not collected – tenant screening, overdue accounts follow-ups, recons, separation of duties.
- Risk: Properties illegally transferred [discuss the Latam Gilmore Properties example].

*Note: Team members at different levels and skills will contribute, with results ranging from basic to advanced aspects of the topic. The **audit clerk's** creativity is already being pricked at an early stage, as opposed to receiving instructions only per a standard audit program.*

What you learn now, you'll know in the future.

3.2. **During the project planning workshop**, a member of the team facilitates the process and records the following on a whiteboard (or other suitable aid):

a. The mind map: Each team member mentions whatever comes to mind related to the audit topic, including the research results, which the facilitator records. Each person's contribution is accepted irrespective of whether any team member regards it as relevant.
b. Highlight/mark the key elements recorded in the mind map that the team regards as relevant for formulating/defining the overall objective.
c. Record the risks associated with the overall objective. Only the relevant and valid risks that the team agreed to are recorded.
d. Define the sub-objectives supporting the overall objective.
e. Agree on at least one creative audit test to be performed.
f. Agree on at least one value-adding focus area.

A team member is assigned the duty to prepare the detailed audit program using a template as follows:

- Record the overall objective, risks, and sub-objectives determined during the workshop.
- Determine the required controls to mitigate the risks on a macro level.
- Transfer each control to reflect under the suitable sub-objective.

3.3. **Fieldwork and reporting**

- **Perform audit testing intuitively,** yet disciplined to eliminate bias, while only later in the project consult the audit program depending on the team/auditor's maturity level in terms of skills and experience, and knowledge of the audit area. "Play" with data and information, do more research, test what comes to mind, walk around (on the site), observe, feel, and talk to people until you realize it is time to consult the audit program for completeness of the audit testing. The audit program can be consulted at any time during the fieldwork provided the SWIM principles are applied. Prepare and file/store working papers promptly and per the applicable IIA and own departmental standards.
- **Build the audit report** from the start of the project because the report will aid the team in covering the sub-objectives thoroughly. The report-building approach prompts diligent and complete audit testing by constantly asking: "How will I know"? This principle is discussed later in this chapter

Conform with all the fieldwork disciplines throughout the process.

Let's perform a hypothetical audit together...

Audit topic:	Property Administration.
Source:	Annual internal audit plan.

Figure 4.4 The team planning the audit.

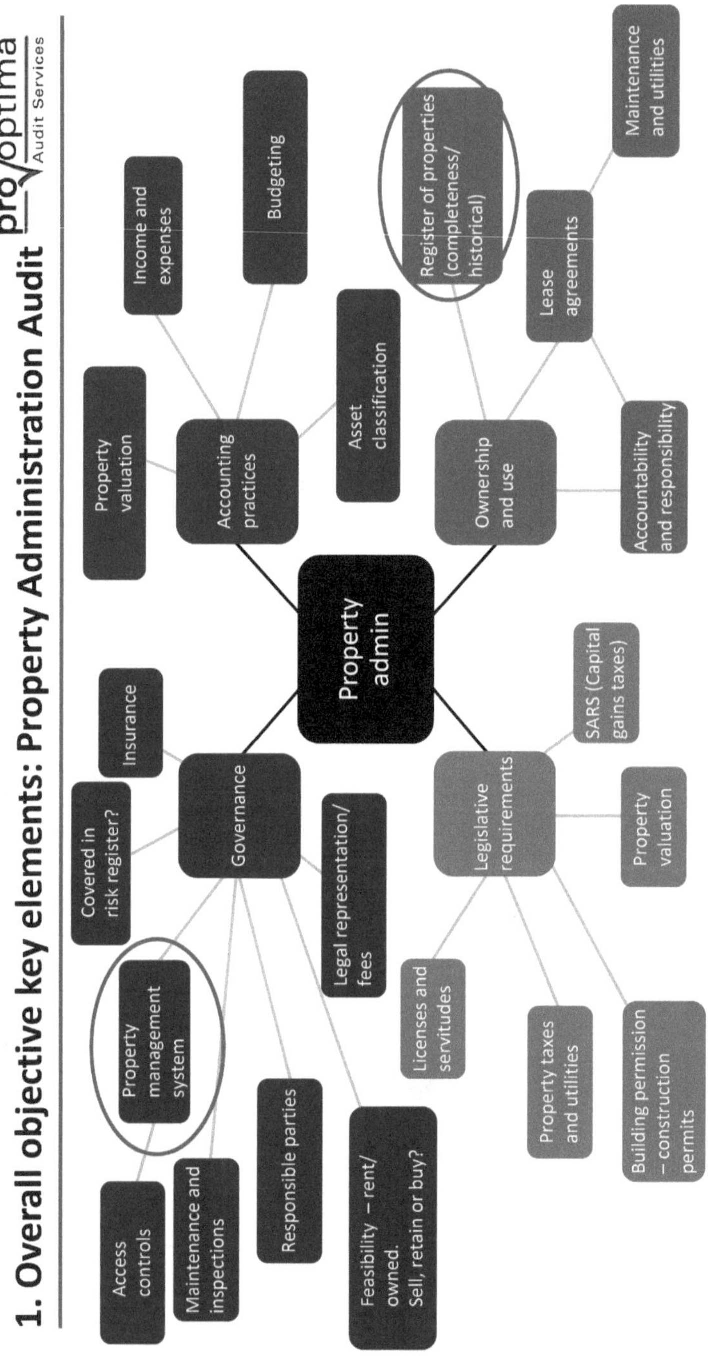

Figure 4.5 Mind mapping to determine the key elements for the overall objective.

2. Overall objective: Property Administration Audit

pro optima Audit Services

Key elements

- **Property management system**
- **Register of properties (completeness/ historical)**

Overall objective

To determine whether internal controls are adequate and effective to ensure the company's properties are optimally managed and appropriately accounted for (completeness and financial reporting).

Scope exclusions

Production sites, including factories, reduction plant, and warehouses.

Figure 4.6 The overall audit objective deduced from the mind map.

3. Risks: Property Administration Audit

pro optima Audit Services

1. Properties not properly accounted for (existence, completeness, and valuation).
2. Legal conflict risk.
3. Financial leakage/losses – excessive maintenance costs, major damage and destruction, paying levies and taxes for properties not owned, [unpaid municipal accounts – specific management request]
4. Unaccounted revenue.
5. Tenant risk – nonpayment, low occupancy, property neglect.
6. Administration risk – inadequate/inaccurate information.
7. Market risk – rental prices, inflation, interest rates, property values
8. Underutilised properties.

Associated ERM risks

1. Flooding risk at Delposoul Village.
2. Security risk at remote areas.

Figure 4.7 Determining the risks.

4. Sub objectives: Property Administration Audit

pro optima Audit Services

1. All company-owned properties are known and accounted for.
2. Rental income is optimised, and expenditure effectively controlled.
3. Properties are effectively maintained.
4. Properties are adequately secured and sufficiently insured.
5. Appropriate buy/sell/rent decisions are made. [SCOPED OUT]

Figure 4.8 Determining the sub objectives.

5. Mitigating controls: Property Administration Audit

Risks	Mitigating controls
1. Properties not properly accounted for (existence, completeness, and valuation).	1. A complete and accurate asset/ property register is in place and effectively maintained. 2. Periodically reconcile asset register with property registration authorities (Deeds office), municipality and rental records. 3. ...
2. Legal conflict risk	1. Appropriate lease agreements in place including legal conflict clauses. 2. Legal representation available. 3. ...
3. Financial leakage/losses – excessive maintenance costs, incorrect valuation, major damage and destruction, paying levies and taxes for properties not owned.	1. Property management system is in place for monitoring: - Maintenance requirements and history - Damages - Levies and taxes - Expenditure - Property valuation - Ownership...

Figure 4.9 Determining the mitigating controls for each risk.

How does SWIM differ from most conventional audit approaches?

Activity/phase	*Conventional approach*	*SWIM*
Preliminary survey.	• Perform a walkthrough/ sit-through. • Request and understand the process narratives and transaction flows. • Research if necessary.	• Perform a hawk-through. • Research the subject, e.g., Google, discuss, read, "phone a friend". [a] • Gather relevant information during the hawk-through and during the fieldwork.
Prepare the audit/work program.	Based on the processes in place (*As is*).	"Design" the internal control system that will: • mitigate the risks identified; and • ensure project objectives (and sub-objectives) are achieved (*Should be*).
Fieldwork	Follow the audit program to determine whether the systems are working as intended and identify any control gaps.	• Use the audit program to ensure completeness of testing – not as a structured program to be religiously followed. • Perform audit testing intuitively yet disciplined to enhance completeness and eliminate bias. • Generally, test what comes to mind first, including "playing" with data/ information, and perform trend analysis. • Identify focus areas and potential for value-adding. • Apply your mind and think outside the box. • Visit the site, look, feel, pick up, discuss, ask questions, and show interest.

Communicating results	Write the report after the fieldwork.	• Build the report throughout the assignment. • Use the report to enhance the quality of the assignment. • Frequently refer to the overall objective and sub-objectives while applying the "how-will-I-know" principle.

Note [a]: Standard 13.4 [Evaluation Criteria] advises internal auditors should research recommended practices and compare management's criteria to those used by other organizations.

The "How-will-I-know" principle

We apply this principle to enhance completeness and thoroughness of audit testing and the audit report. Many, maybe most, internal auditors apply this principle to some extent although not necessarily cognitively or as a technique. Whether you test the mitigating controls or the achievement of an objective, one should always ask "How will I know the risk is effectively mitigated. How will I know the overall and/or sub-objectives are achieved"? Let's apply this principle to an overtime audit:

For the achievement of the audit objective:

Objective:	*Overtime is correctly paid for actual required overtime worked.*
How will I know if this objective is achieved?	• Only bona-fide overtime hours were worked. • Only overtime hours worked were paid. • The correct overtime rates were applied. • Etc.

Continuously ask, for example, "How will I know overtime is correctly paid for actual required overtime worked"? Ask the question until you've exhausted the potential answers.

For risk mitigation:

Risk identified:	*Unnecessary overtime worked.*
How will I know if this risk is effectively mitigated, i.e., what controls should be in place?	• Formal pre-approval is required before overtime may be worked. • The TimeAxs system is set to deny a person access to the workplace after hours unless the required approval was granted. • TimeAxs is set to flag a person staying on for longer than two hours after the end of shift unless the required pre-approval was granted. • Payroll validates overtime hours booked to the TimeAxs overtime pre-approval listing before uploading the overtime hours worked listing. • Etc.

Continuously ask, for example, "How will I know people cannot work unapproved overtime" until you've exhausted the potential answers.

Success story

Financial internal controls audit – two audits performed of the same business unit two years apart.

Audit performed by:	*Conclusion*	*No. of findings per risk category*		
		Mod.	*High*	*Critical*
In-house IAF	No conclusion as the CAE did not believe in providing an overall conclusion.	2		
Pro Optima; IA co-sourcing	Internal controls were inadequate and ineffective, with board intervention advised. Refer to the sanitized report – attachment 4.	5	15	7

> **Ponder this**
>
> Can SWIM, in full or in part, assist your internal audit function to improve its effectiveness?

IN-AND-OUT AUDITS

Several audit areas forming part of the audit universe are seldom selected for inclusion in the annual internal audit plan because they reflect as relatively low risk on the risk assessment matrix. They are nonetheless important to be properly governed and should therefore be subjected to periodic auditing. Pro Optima decided to cover some of these lower-risk audit areas under the In-&-Out audits. Typical audit areas that may fall into the lower-risk category for most of Pro Optima's clients include petty cash/debit cards, travel expenses, indirect taxes and levies, leave and absenteeism, disciplinary procedures, and training administration. The objective of this approach is to facilitate a more complete audit coverage by scheduling audit areas that are continuously overlooked despite the ideal audit frequency decision matrix flagging the audit area as (over)due for audit. This is achieved by including some of these audit areas, around ten per annum, in the audit plan.

Benefits of the in-and-out audit method

- Potential full spectrum coverage over, say, five-year cycles per the ideal audit coverage matrix.
- Creating opportunities to:
  - Improve efficiency in the business.
  - Identify and address potential risks and control weaknesses in these areas.
  - Identify potential fraud and error.
- Better use of resources.

Method/process

Allocate project hours and set target dates, which are usually aligned with the annual audit planning schedule and are generally no more than 30 hours per project. The auditor's mindset should shift from performing detailed coverage of the audit area to performing a mini audit per the guidance below.

1. Set and communicate the time budget and schedule.
2. Discuss with and obtain expectations from the client.
3. Perform the "hawk-through", including site visits, where appropriate while applying the see-feel-smell-hear-taste principle.
4. Identify the key risks for the audit area – generally no more than four main risks.
5. Identify key controls required to mitigate the risks identified.
6. Determine and perform the required tests within the allocated time. Additional time may be required as circumstances dictate.
7. Follow the normal audit processes from here on.

Success story

The following is one of many successes, which would probably have gone undetected if it wasn't for this method.

Project:	*Skills development audit.*
Audit objective:	To establish whether the client optimizes on the skills development incentive grants and tax rebates offered by the government.
Value-added outcome:	• The audit identified that the company tax calculation workbook had omitted the qualifying training scheme rebates, following which management updated the information before filing the annual tax submission. As a result, the tax assessment was ±ZAR 7.3 million lower. • Mandatory grants of ±ZAR 1.6 million accumulating over three years were recouped from the government's skills development agency.

Ponder this

Would you encourage the internal audit function to consider the In-and-Out Audit method?

IMPLEMENT CONTROLS BEFORE AUDIT METHOD (ICBAM)

This method was developed in April 2020 during the COVID-19 national lockdown in South Africa to address the envisaged needs of our clients after the lockdown. We anticipated that clients may look to internal audit for help in enhancing efficiencies, including cost cutting. The overall objective of this approach is to enable the client to implement controls to address potential control weaknesses even before the start of the audit testing phase, which should accelerate the implementation of controls. It involves presenting and discussing with management a list of generic findings in the selected audit area based on the related audit reports issued to our various clients in the past. A Lessons Learned Workpaper (LLW) is used for this purpose. It is crucial to maintain confidentiality. Therefore, the clients where the adverse findings occurred, may not be divulged in the LLW or through any other means.

Application

This method is well-suited for projects where the surprise element of the audit is less important. Examples of audit areas in the mining industry where this method can be successfully applied include:

- Production-related areas, such as tunnel development and mining, underground transport, and explosives
- Ore and metallurgical accounting
- Employee transport
- Overtime
- Contract management
- Off-site repairs

Benefits of ICBAM

- A higher prospect of management buy-in, which can enhance relationships if internal audit is perceived as a supportive function rather than an enforcement mechanism.
- Accelerated implementation of controls leading to potential cost savings and recoveries, and improved efficiencies at an earlier stage.
- The client may identify control weaknesses, fraud, and/or errors while performing its own testing.
- Better use of internal audit resources.

Method/process

1. Create an LLW using the guidelines outlined below. The template in Attachment 5 and the process diagram below will aid the reader in understanding if read in conjunction with this narrative.
2. Gather all previous audit reports issued covering the audit topic and transfer the adverse findings from the reports to the LLW.
3. Arrange the findings logically by grouping related findings in one horizontal section under the Finding/Condition column.

4. Record the cause(s) for each of the adverse findings under the Cause Column.
5. Record the mitigating controls under the Recommended Control(s) column.
6. Convene a meeting with all relevant individuals of the audit area and further complete the LLW as follows:
    6.1 Explain ICBAM and present the LLW which has now been completed up to the Recommended Control(s) column.
    6.2 Discuss each finding, with its cause(s) and recommended control(s).
    6.3 Amend the contents of the recommended control during the meeting as needed.
    6.4 Complete the last four columns during the discussion with the client team.
    6.5 The client team should assign the individual(s) who will perform the testing and/or implementation for each risk/potential control weakness identified/discussed during the meeting.
    6.6 Agree on the dates when the internal audit will start, generally within two to three months.
7. Follow the normal audit processes from this point on while cognitively considering value-adding, which may require some of the lower risk controls to be excluded from audit testing to optimize the value of the audit.

FRAUD AND ERROR DETECTION TESTS

Pro Optima frequently identifies significant fraud and errors through this strategy. Each team member is required to perform at least two fraud and error detection tests per annum and issue a report for the record for each. They are free to choose a topic/area. The test results are recorded and retained, irrespective of whether any anomalies or risks were identified. The appropriate auditing and reporting protocols will be followed in case of adverse observations. For some of our clients, this activity forms part of the annual internal audit plan with around eight hours allocated per auditor for this purpose, although the auditor can request additional hours when needed, for example, to further investigate potential anomalies. We keep a SOX Parking Register to record indirect/secondary SOX observations for follow-up by the operational internal audit section. Because our employees are trained to be operationally minded, including the SOX team, they have the urge to dig deeper but also know they must strictly stay within the SOX mandate. Such observations are usually probed as part of the fraud and error detection testing strategy. Fraud and error detection tests can also be a stopgap.

Consider fraud and error detection tests as part of your fraud prevention strategy.

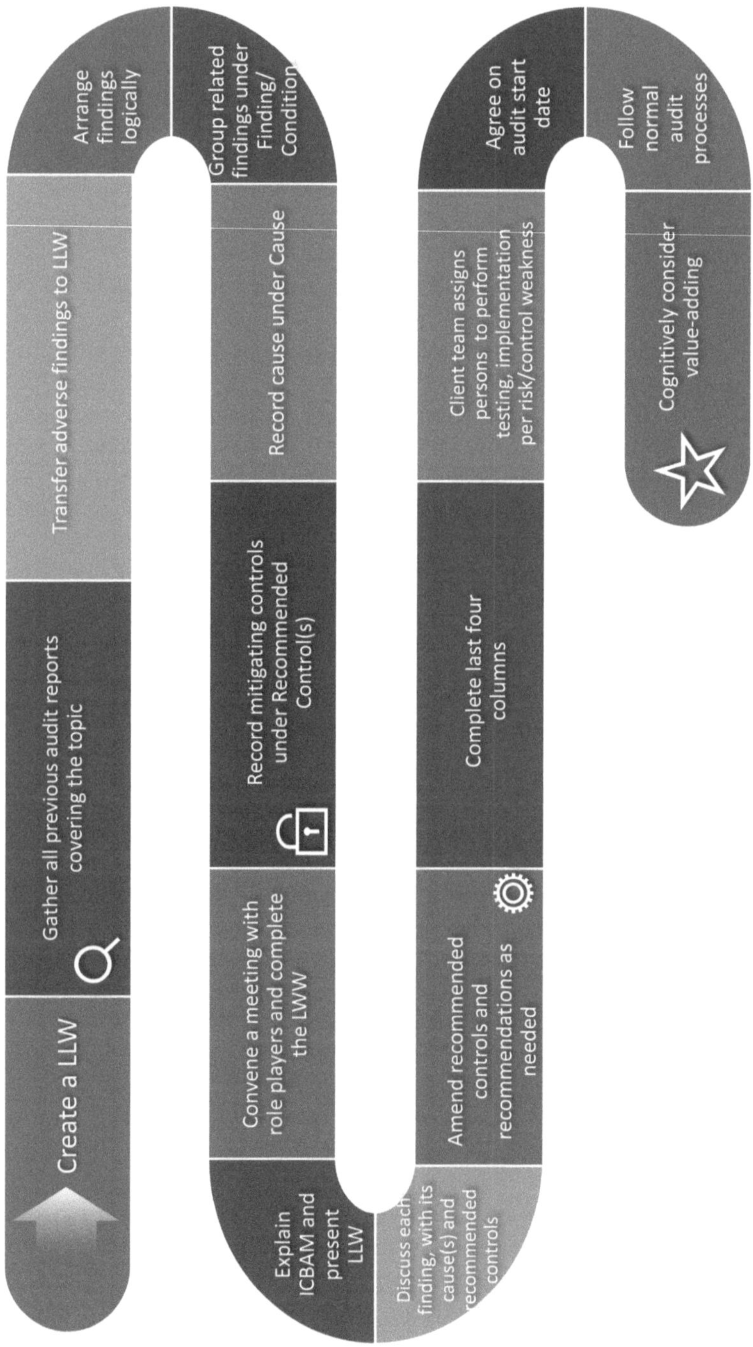

Figure 4.10 The IGBAM process flow.

Success story

Whereas we have hundreds of success stories, the following spring to mind while writing this book:

While driving past the weighbridge at a gold mine in 1999, I thought "What could go wrong at a weighbridge?". Because I have learned through experience not to ignore such a nudging, I went to the weighbridge station and asked the operator to explain their methods. They have captured the hauling truck's tare weights on the system to determine the load weight without requiring the emptied truck to proceed over the weighbridge. The risk was immediately clear – what if the fixed tare weights were wrong? This proved to be the case when directing some of the emptied trucks over the weighbridge. The investigation concluded:

- The standard/captured tare weights were understated mainly due to the accumulation of gold-bearing ore on the trucks which resulted in the double accounting of up to 1.5 tons per trip causing overpayments to the hauling contractor of around ZAR 110,000 per month, which, if converted using time value of money in 2024 totaled ±ZAR 400,000.
- The same vehicle ID was captured for both the 5t and 10t trucks of a mining contractor who delivered gold-bearing ore to the mine on a toll treatment arrangement. This resulted in the overallocation of gold revenue totaling ±ZAR 900,000 to the contractor because the smaller truck's tare weight was applied for both trucks when the weighbridge system calculated the load weights. If converted to the current time value of money, the overpayment totaled ±ZAR 3million.

RISK MATERIALIZATION TESTING (RMT)

RMT is a cognitive approach to test whether the risks associated with a control weakness identified during the audit have materialized. It is a second-nature audit procedure for our team with proven success. An internal audit function having generic control weaknesses as the predominant type of finding should rethink whether its audit testing is sufficient to provide a fair and trusted audit conclusion. Examples of generic findings include documents not signed, transactions lacking supporting documents, reconciliations not performed, and duties not segregated. The auditor who shows that the associated risk has materialized generally adds more value than the one who mainly reports that the risk may materialize. Management will be more inclined to realize the importance of addressing the control weakness if shown something has gone wrong, as opposed to something could go wrong. Each type of general control weakness has one or more associated risks, for example:

- Making irregular payments is a common result of supervisory staff not reviewing and signing relevant documents.
- Paying incorrect quantities and rates may result from vendor invoices lacking supporting documents.
- Failure to perform debtor reconciliations may result in a loss of revenue.
- Fraud risk is associated with inadequate segregation of duties.

RMT may require the team to go beyond the immediate scope of the audit to find "if and what went wrong". The following factors may adversely affect the internal audit function's ability to apply RMT as part of its audit approach:

- The lack of (suitable) resources.
- Strict time limitations placed on projects.
- Identifying the real issues in an audit area may require effort and skill.
- The internal audit function may not have the appetite to go beyond the generic finding.
- Auditing for findings, i.e., doing just enough to create the impression the team did their job.
- Insufficient insight into the audit area.

It is sensible to test beyond the control weakness *because:*

- It greatly enhances the opportunity to uncover fraud, errors, and inefficiencies.
- Offenders would rather take a slap on the wrist for deviating from the required internal controls than have their misconduct exposed. For this reason, internal audit should approach such apparent negligence strategically by performing validation checks to determine whether the associated risks have materialized.

The GIAS support RMT

Standard 14.2 of the GIAS [Analysis and Potential Engagement Findings] supports RMT as it requires internal auditors to analyze relevant, reliable and sufficient information to develop potential engagement findings. The standard requires:

- Further evaluation if there is a difference between the criteria and condition, and
- Due professional care to be exercised to determine whether additional analyses are required, in which case the work program must be adjusted accordingly.

As referenced in Chapter 3, Richard Chambers (2020), advises that "all audits have deadlines, so we must maintain a balance between too much skepticism and too little. Audits must be efficient as well as effective, so we can't continue to ask questions and evaluate evidence ad infinitum".

Make RMT part of the audit approach.

The first question should be whether there isn't a deeper problem when a generic control is not in place or not enforced. If such testing falls outside the planned scope, RMT may require additional time and resources. Consider scheduling time into the annual audit plan – as a separate line item from which you can "draw" as circumstances dictate. The likelihood of achieving a good return on investment is high in our experience. The right mindset is important here. RMT is about prudence and is not a fault-finding mission.

Unpacking the finding when the risk has materialized

The five elements of a finding are key terms that internal auditors learn early in their studies and in practice, yet academic material differs on the definitions of each element. When, for example, searching for the definition of the **condition** element of a finding, the results were surprisingly different, with the first five websites encountered offering the following explanations of what **condition** means:

1. What was discovered to determine there was a finding?
2. What is the problem/issue? What is happening?
3. The situation that exists. Or, what happened?
4. It is the statement that describes the results of the audit, i.e., the problem and how things have happened.
5. The situation found, i.e., the most relevant occurrences identified in the fieldwork.

Identifying the condition, cause, and effect becomes tricky when the risk has materialized as explained in the following hypothetical scenario:

The audit identified the risk of paying the incorrect rates because some of the paid vendor invoices tested did not show evidence of verification, like tick marks by the creditor clerk as per the Creditors Payment Procedure. The subsequent risk materialization testing revealed the risk has materialized as Vendor XYZ invoiced the incorrect rate for XXL overalls resulting in overpayments of $1,000.

When applying the websites' explanations above, you may derive different outcomes. Let's test it.

1. **Which one of the following would be the condition?**
   a. Vendor XYZ invoiced the incorrect rate for XXL overalls; **or**
   b. The overpayment occurred/went undetected; **or**
   c. The creditor clerk did not perform diligent verification checks.

2. **Which one is the effect, if any?**
    a. Vendor XYZ invoiced the incorrect rate for XXL overalls; **or**
    b. The $1,000 overpayment; **or**
    c. The error went through the system undetected.
3. **What is the cause[8]?**
    a. The creditor clerk did not perform diligent verification checks; **and/or**
    b. Non-compliance with the Creditors Payment Procedure?

My choices are: 1a, 2b, and 3a&b, although it doesn't really matter which is which as long as the finding contains all the elements.

Let's take another example, approaching it from a different angle

The security officer stole the 500g slipper[9] valued at $30,000 from the gold smelthouse vault. He gained access using a key ... because the vault door could be locked and unlocked as the combination lock has been defective for the past two months.

See how generic control weaknesses tend to become the cause, instead of the condition when performing RMT.

	Condition	*Cause*	*Effect*
Definition 1.	**What was discovered to determine there was a finding.**	**The reason for the issue or simply stated the cause for the finding.**	**The potential risk if not corrected.**
Before RMT	The vault door can be locked and unlocked independently.	The vault door combination lock has been defective for two months.	High probability of gold theft.
After RMT	Security officer stole a 500g slipper worth $30,000.	The vault door could be locked and unlocked independently.	More gold theft in the future.
Definition 2.	**What is the problem/issue? What is happening?**	**How or why did the condition happen?**	**So what? Why should the reader care about this condition? What is the impact?**
Before RMT	The vault door can be locked and unlocked independently.	The vault door lock has been defective for two months.	High probability of gold theft.
After RMT	Gold theft.	The security officer gained access because he could lock and unlock the vault independently.	$30,000 loss and risk of more losses.
Definition 3.	**The situation that exists. Or, what happened?**	**The reason or explanation provided by the local auditee that the condition exists. Or, why does the condition exist?**	**The impact of the condition. Or, what has happened, or what could happen, because the condition exists?**

Before RMT	The vault door can be locked and unlocked independently.	The vault door has been defective for two months.	Gold theft can occur.
After RMT	The security officer unlocked the door with his key and stole a 500g slipper.	The vault door combination lock has been defective for two months resulting in the vault door being locked and unlocked independently.	$30,000 loss 500g slipper was stolen, and more theft can occur.
Wiki	**What is the particular problem identified?**	**Why did the problem occur?**	**What is the risk/negative outcome (or opportunity foregone) because of the finding?**
Before RMT	The vault door can be locked and unlocked independently.	The vault door has been defective for two months.	Gold theft can occur.
After RMT	The security officer stole a 500g slipper.	The security officer had easy access because he could lock and unlock the vault door independently.	$30,000 loss 500g slipper was stolen, and more theft can occur.

Success stories

Two examples of positive results produced through RMT.

A. **Identifying overcharges caused by overstated quantities when we had a pipeline installation surveyed for which supporting documents were unavailable.**

Generic observation:	The relevant supporting documents were not provided to substantiate payments.
Risk:	Incorrect payments if the incorrect quantities reflected on the invoices.
RMT performed:	Select a measurable activity from the list of invoices related to the capital project, which, in this case were two pipelines invoiced at 6,5 km (4.04 miles) each. 1. Use Google Maps to estimate the pipeline lengths as a reasonability test. 2. Obtain the services of a land surveyor to determine the actual lengths once the reasonability test indicated the probability of the incorrect invoicing. 3. The survey confirmed the pipelines were 717m and 799m over-invoiced respectively.
RMT observation:	Overstated distances resulting in overpayments totaling ±ZAR 1.1 million.
RMT value-added:	The overpayment of ±ZAR 1.1 million was recovered. Management is better convinced there was a real risk.

B. Identifying substandard rock drill machine maintenance and repairs by the service provider due to the lack of a quality control procedure.

Generic observation:	A quality control procedure for rock drill maintenance and repairs was not in place.
Risk:	Substandard repairs resulting in additional repair costs and production disruptions.
RMT performed:	Select a sample of rock drills recently repaired to determine whether the repairs were done to the required standards by performing the following audit tests: 1. Track repair turnaround times through the review of the repair date stamps per job card. 2. Reconcile parts replaced against rock drill specifications and repair standards. 3. Perform onsite inspection of test bench processes to determine whether the rock drills were fully functional before being returned to operation.
RMT observation:	Substandard repairs were performed on 25% of the rock drills tested.
RMT value-added:	Reduced rock drill maintenance and repair costs of ZAR 29.5 million per annum. Fewer production losses previously caused by rock drill breakdowns. The need for an effective quality control procedure is proven.

Ponder this

Does your internal audit function perform sufficient testing to determine whether an identified risk has materialized?

LIVE CONSULTATIVE AUDITS

We became aware of a large capital expenditure (Capex) project, obtained the approved application for expenditure, and realized that some key internal controls were lacking. Although a Capex audit was scheduled for ten months later, we decided to perform a live consultative audit rather than waiting for the project to potentially go pear-shaped and then "criticize" when the audit was done at the scheduled time. We designed a live audit risk and control matrix to record the risks as well as the potential (and identified) control weaknesses, with recommendations for them to be implemented as the Capex project progressed. This proved to be strategically the right decision because the control weaknesses and the associated risks and errors identified during the live audit were immediately reported to the project team and line management, and promptly resolved. Otherwise, these would probably have been identified only several months later with little prospect of successfully addressing the errors and control weaknesses retrospectively.

ON-SITE CONTRACTOR INVOICE VERIFICATION

This brings us to the independence and objectivity debate. On-site services contractors' invoices are routed through our offices situated at several of our clients' premises to identify and investigate obvious anomalies, mostly underground mining contractors' invoices. We currently provide this service to four large mining companies. For the mining companies where Pro Optima does not fulfill the internal audit function, the service is rendered as a second line function. Where Pro Optima provides the outsourced internal audit services the invoice verification activity is performed with the board's approval. Since the commencement of this service in 2010 no month has passed without Pro Optima having identified significant tangible recoveries and savings through this service.

TAKEAWAYS

For the internal audit function's leadership

Evaluate the impactfulness of your internal audit function and reconsider your audit approach and techniques for efficacy if necessary.

For the internal audit staff and professionals in general

Test one or more of the methods discussed in this chapter to see how it can assist you.

For senior management and the board

We advise that you evaluate the impactfulness of your internal audit function.

NOTES

1 Cadbury Report on Wikipedia, accessed online on 09 July 2024, https://en.wikipedia.org/wiki/Cadbury_Report
2 Aligned Assurance Day at adidas on 05 June 2024, my brief blog about the event, contributing as guest speaker https://drrainerlenz.wordpress.com/2024/06/06/aligned-assurance-day-adidas-june-2024/
3 Edmondson, Amy C., 2019. The fearless organization, p.25.
4 Accessed online 23 June 2024, https://www.bbc.com/news/articles/ce7712x-l2r5o: "Boeing crash victims' families shout at CEO as he apologizes in hearing".
5 Accessed online 23 June 2024, https://professionalleadershipinstitute.com/resources/what-is-the-peter-principle-theory-and-examples/
6 Converted using the approximate time value of money.
7 Broken ore fragmentation refers to the rock size distribution (fineness thresholds) after blasting and transporting to the metallurgical plant. A constant stream of well fragmented rock reduces the risk of mud rushes and enhances plant throughput and precious metal recovery. Achieving and maintaining the optimal fragmentation size requires strict blasting-related discipline.

8 This example is for illustration purposes. The root cause may be deeper when applying the why, why, why principle.
9 A slipper is a small gold bar that is below the determined weight for dispatch to the gold refinery. The slipper should be reintroduced in the next gold smelt.

REFERENCES

Collins, J. (2009), How the Mighty Fall, HarperCollins Publishers, New York.
Gittell, J.H. (2006), in: Kyriakidou, Olivia and Özbilgin, Mustafa F. (2006), Relational perspectives in organizational studies, Edward Elgar Publishing Limited, pp. 74–94.
Heath, C. and Heath, D. (2008), Made to stick: Why some ideas survive and others die, New York, NY: Random House.
Huse, M. (2007), Boards, governance and value creation, the human side of corporate governance, Cambridge University Press, Cambridge.
Korine, H. (2020), Preventing corporate governance failure, HAUPT VERLAG, ISBN 978-3-258-08150-2.
Lenz, R. (2013), Insights into the effectiveness of internal audit: A multi-method and multi-perspective study, Université catholique de Louvain – Louvain School of Management Research Institute, Doctoral Thesis 01|2013. https://lnkd.in/dZwnhbrK
Lenz, R., & Hoos, F. (2023), The Future Role of the Internal Audit Function: Assure. Build. Consult. EDPACS, 67:3, 39–52. https://doi.org/10.1080/07366981.2023.2165361
Lenz, R., & O'Regan, D. J. (2024), The Global Internal Audit Standards – Old Wine in New Bottles? EDPACS, 69:3, 1–28. https://doi.org/10.1080/07366981.2024.2322835
Richard Chambers (2020), Internal Auditors be Trusting but Skeptical. https://www.richardchambers.com/internal-auditors-be-trusting-but-skeptical/
Sarens, G., Decaux, L., & Lenz, R. (2012), Combined assurance: Case studies on a holistic approach to organizational governance, IIA Research Foundation, Altamonte Springs, FL.
Sarens, G., Lenz, R., & Decaux, L. (2016), Insights into Self-Images of Internal Auditors, EDPACS, 54:4, 1–18. https://lnkd.in/dDJUhNr
The Internal Audit Foundation (2024), Internal Audit: Vision 2035, US, Lake Mary, July.
Williams, D. (2024), The Corporate Revolutionary: Mervyn King's Life in Law, Business and Governance, Tafelberg; 1. Edition (5. Juli 2024)

Attachment 4

Confidential

pro optima Audit Services

INTERNAL AUDIT REPORT

To: **Mr. Don Walace**
Area Production Manager
EBBE Paints

Cc: **Corporate**
Chief Executive Officer: SPL Grandica
Chief Financial Officer: SPL Grandica
Managing Director: EBBE Paints
Financial Director: EBBE Paints
Corporate Financial Manager: EBBE Paints
Human Capital Manager: EBBE Paints

Business Unit
Production Manager: EBBE no. 1 Plant
Financial Manager: EBBE no. 1 Plant

LOCATION/ AREA	**EBBE No. 1 Plant**
PROJECT TYPE	FULL SCOPE AUDIT
ISSUE DATE	15 MAY 2024

	Risk exposure (residual)	Control adequacy	Control effectiveness
Audit conclusion			

	Residual risk	Control adequacy/ effectiveness	
Audit conclusion legend	Low	Adequate/ Effective	
	Moderate	Partially adequate/ effective	+
	High		-
	Critical	Inadequate/ ineffective	

1. **INTRODUCTION**

We have conducted an audit of EBBE No. 1 Plant, a business unit of EBBE Paints (Pty) Ltd, a division of SPL Grandica Ltd, in accordance with the approved SPL Grandica Internal Audit plan for FY2024.

The business unit manufactures an extensive range of industrial primers and topcoats. The plant, which was established in 2005 is staffed with 35 permanent employees. Revenue and net profit before tax totalled ZAR481.2 million and ZAR21.1 million for FY2024 respectively. EBBE Paints use the standard costing method to determine the cost of sales. The manufacturing process is subjected to rigorous quality monitoring and testing in its laboratory.

EXECUTIVE SUMMARY

2. OBJECTIVE

The overall objective of the audit is to determine whether the internal controls are adequate and effective to provide assurance to management and the board that risks are satisfactorily mitigated.

3. APPROACH AND SCOPE

The audit approach involved the identification of the risks and associated mitigating controls. The effectiveness of the design and operation of these controls were evaluated through discussions with relevant staff, review of management information and testing of relevant transactions on a sample basis.

The audit was performed during April 2024 and the scope covered key business processes and activities during FY2024, i.e., 1 April 2023 to 31 March 2024.

The specific areas audited include the following:

- Property, plant, and equipment
- Procure-to-invoice, including contract management
- Budgeting and expenditure control
- HR and payroll
- Inventory management
- Production process

Discussions were held with the responsible management and personnel, including the Stock Administrator, SHEQ Coordinator, Production Manager, EBBE Paints Financial Director, Financial Manager, and the Divisional Procurement Manager.

Audit tests were performed on a sample of transactions, which were judgmentally selected.

The sales order-to-receipt cycle was not covered as part of this audit.

4. CONCLUSION

It is our opinion that internal controls are inadequate to effectively mitigate the risks identified at the start of the audit. It is further our opinion that the extent of the findings reported herein is symptomatic of an unhealthy control environment within EBBE Paints as a corporate entity, which requires a systematic approach to develop and implement more stringent controls to reduce the probability of major fraud and errors occurring as well as the risk of these going undetected.

PAGE 2

EXECUTIVE SUMMARY

The status of specific control objectives tested during the audit is indicated in the table below.

Audited activity	Specific control objective	Achieved ? (Y/N)	
Property, plant, and equipment	Additions and disposals are subjected to proper evaluation and approval		N
	The fixed asset register is correctly updated with additions and disposals		N
	PPE is physically secured and accounted for		N
	PPE is appropriately classified in the financial records		N
	PPE is appropriately depreciated over its useful life		N
Procure-to-invoice, incl. contract management	Proper governance is in place over the procurement of goods and services		N
	Goods and services are sourced at competitive prices		N
	Invoices are approved for payment only in respect of goods and services required and delivered to the required standard and charged at the agreed prices		N
Budgeting and financial performance monitoring	Expenses are allocated to the appropriate accounts		N
	Expenses are declared in the appropriate accounting period		N
	Budgets/targets are met, and the non-achievements are effectively dealt with		N
Inventory management	Inventory is logically stored in suitable, secure facilities	Y	
	Inventory purchased is fully accounted for		N
	Inventory is accurately and appropriately disclosed in the financial statements		N
HR and payroll	The Basic Conditions of Employment Act provisions regarding overtime is enforced		N
	Employee tax is deducted from employees in terms of the Seventh Schedule to the Income Tax Act	Partially	
Production process	Production results are accurately and appropriately declared	Partially	
	Actual performance is monitored against targets while deviations are diligently investigated and motivated	Partially	
	Raw materials introduced into the production process are fully accounted for (mass balancing)	Y	

PAGE 3

EXECUTIVE SUMMARY

Audit tests performed enabled Pro Optima to evaluate residual risk as well as adequacy and effectiveness of internal controls as depicted below.

Audited activity	Previous audit (FY2022)	Current audit (FY2024)		
	Audit opinion	Risk exposure	Control adequacy	Control effectiveness
Property, plant, and equipment	Satisfactory	High	Inadequate	Ineffective
Procure-to-invoice, incl. contract management	Good	Moderate	Partially adequate	Partially effective
Budgeting and expenditure control	N/A	Critical	Inadequate	Ineffective
Inventory management	Good	High	Partially adequate	Partially effective
HR and payroll	N/A	Moderate	Partially adequate	Partially effective
Production process	Good	Moderate	Partially adequate	Partially effective
Cash and sundry income	Satisfactory	N/A	N/A	N/A

5. SUMMARY OF FINDINGS

The main audit findings identified during the audit are summarised below and presented in more detail in Annexure A.

Finding	Risk rating*		Management response
	BU	EBBE	
*Note: The risk rating indicates whether the risk is restricted to the business unit (BU) only or whether we regard the deficiency as a divisional-wide risk, i.e., EBBE Paints (Pty) Ltd			
The control environment is weak as discussed below, and in our opinion requires Exco and board intervention. Most of the shortcomings reported herein relate to EBBE Paints as a division of SPL Grandica and requires corrective action to be taken at EBBE Paints and Grandica corporate level. EBBE Paints should embark on a structured program to develop and implement an internal control framework, such as COSO2013.	CRI	CRI	Chief Financial Officer As much as this is a harsh and concerning statement the facts presented in this audit report and our brought executive management to the realization of the seriousness of the situation. It is unfortunate that the established internal audit function presented a different status of our control environment and that external party had to alert us to this.
1. Fixed assets	CRI	CRI	**Financial Director**

PAGE 4

EXECUTIVE SUMMARY

Finding	Risk rating*		Management response
	BU	EBBE	
1.1. Significant additions during prior years were not incorporated into the fixed asset register (FAR) mainly due to responsibility and accountability for maintaining the FAR not being clearly defined in a formal corporate Capex policy and procedure. Of concern is ZAR32.3 million relating to the Factory Extension project (commissioned in November 2021) not yet being recognised in the FAR at the time of the audit. - Management informed us the project costs were incorrectly posted to the Eleanor Business Unit. This has subsequently been corrected.			An Asset Manager has recently been employed with one of his duties being to review and update the EBBE Paints FAR for the entire business. He will firstly clean up the FAR in preparation for the AX go-live in November 2024, and from there manage all disposals, transfers, and removals going forward. The Asset Manager is in the process of finalising a fixed asset policy and will provide a copy for review by Pro Optima.
1.2. An asset (fabrication of condenser) has been capitalised before commissioning, i.e., the pre-payment of R203,476 was made in Jan-24 on the asset that is scheduled to be delivered only in Sep-24. Accumulated depreciation of R5,088 was recognized on this payment in FY2024.	HI		**Financial Manager** The incorrectly depreciated amount will be reversed, and the transaction will be transferred to the CIP account.
1.3. Capital project administration processes are weak based on the following observations: - A formal Capex governing document is not in place. Instead, the informal "Capex rules" was explained to us as being the administrative standard for Capex. - ZAR 560,543 relating to the laboratory building upgrade was absorbed in Opex as the project was not subjected to formal approval aligned with Grandica's Capex rules. - Cost overruns totalling ZAR126,988 (12.5%) on the Fumes Extraction System was absorbed in Opex contrary to the Capex rule requiring overruns exceeding 10% of the approved vote to be subjected to	HI		**Financial Director** A formal Capex policy will be developed and distributed throughout EBBE Paints and its various business units. We have started an investigation into the circumvention of the Capex rules.

EXECUTIVE SUMMARY

Finding	Risk rating* BU	Risk rating* EBBE	Management response
board approval.			
2. Procure-to-invoice. Responsibility and accountability regarding contract administration are not formally documented in a policy and procedure. It is our opinion that the lack thereof has resulted in the anomalies identified during the audit. 2.1. Suitable formal agreements are not in place with any of the service providers on site. 2.2. The business unit did not perform independent benchmarking and/ or price evaluations as a standard procedure to test the competitiveness of prices charged. 2.3. Controls were not adequate to ensure payments are made only in respect of services/ goods required and rendered/ delivered to the applicable safety standards and company requirements based on the following shortcomings identified: a) Adequate supporting documents did not accompany service providers' invoices to enable effective verification of payments. b) Company representatives did not sign off on service providers' invoices in most instances observed. c) Most invoices in respect of on-site services were processed based on confirmation orders. d) Signed delivery notes were not attached to all invoices in respect of goods purchased as evidence that it had been received in good order.	**HI**	**HI**	**Procurement Manager** Contracts will be put in place with the respective service providers. We will consider establishing a centralized buying function for the acquiring of goods and services that fall outside Procurement's ambit. **Production Manager** On-site work performed will be subjected to a quality assessment by a company representative before invoices are approved for payment. Invoice substantiating documents will be requested from on-site service providers for review before invoices are approved for payment. Purchase orders will be issued to the service provider before receiving the services from the service provider. **Production Manager** Suppliers will be required to issue a delivery note for all goods purchased invoices. All delivery notes will be signed and attached to the relevant invoice before payment. Purchase orders will be issued to the service provider before receiving the services from the service provider.

EXECUTIVE SUMMARY

Finding	Risk rating*		Management response
	BU	EBBE	
			Production Manager Suppliers will be required to issue a delivery note for all goods purchased invoices. All delivery notes will be signed and attached to the relevant invoice before payment.
3. Budgeting and financial performance monitoring 3.1. EBBE Paints apply the standard costing method inappropriately for its intended purposes[1], as was obvious from the significant price and quantity variances which make up the total cost of sales (COS) section of the business unit's FY2024 trial balance. The following observations support the above statement: *a)* Variances are not subjected to effective analysis and are not formally reported to senior management to enable evaluation, thereby defeating the purpose of applying the standard costing method. *b)* Standard stock prices are reviewed monthly and adjusted when the delivered price has changed during the previous month, which is a peculiar and nonsensical way to determine standard prices in a standard costing method. *c)* The business unit experimented with the formulations within the bill of material (BOM) without having the formulations adjusted accordingly in QAD during FY2024, which compounded the usage variances.	CRI	CRI	**Financial Director** We are in the process of implementing a new accounting system. The new AX system will not be using standard costing but will be using the actual cost of material applying the FIFO valuation method. The last few months have seen an introduction of new personnel within our finance structure. We believe that the restructuring of our Finance Department will bring about the necessary changes to allow us to improve our standards and controls, including those for inventory management.

[1] *Standard costing* is a *technique that uses standards for costs and revenues for control through variance analysis.*

PAGE 7

EXECUTIVE SUMMARY

Finding	Risk rating*		Management response
	BU	EBBE	
d) EBBE Paints Finance Department did not process the necessary stock quantity variance adjustment journals during Nov-23 to Feb-24, resulting in COS and inventory being incorrectly declared during said months, including at Dec-23 quarter-end. The adjustment journals were only processed at financial year-end which resulted in significant adjustments being made, i.e. ±ZAR8.5 million decrease in inventory value with COS increasing with the same amount in Mar-24.			
3.2. Controls are not adequate to ensure transactions are appropriately allocated to the relevant cost centres and expense elements due to insufficient supervision over the assigning and reviewing of cost codes and expense elements.	**HI**	**HI**	<u>**Financial Director**</u> The duties of the new Costing Department will include the reviewing of cost centres and expense elements for the entire division to enhance the accuracy of cost allocations.
3.3. The 2024 actual vs. budget analysis of expenditure reflects significant variances for most expense elements of the business unit, with a net overspent of 19%. This is an indication that the budget was either not realistically set and/ or expenditure was not effectively monitored.	**HI**	**HI**	<u>**Production Manager**</u> There are justifications for the variances however going forward we will provide more details regarding the variances.
3.4. The business unit does not accrue expenses incurred (where relevant) as a standard practice, which resulted in certain expenditure not being posted during the period when it was incurred.	**HI**	**HI**	<u>**Financial Director**</u> Part of the duties of the new Costing Department will be to review cost centres and expense elements for the entire division to monitor cut-off to ensure they have been correctly allocated.

EXECUTIVE SUMMARY

Finding	Risk rating*		Management response
	BU	EBBE	
3.5. Cost reporting formats are not adequate to facilitate effective management of actual financial performance against targets. The failure to effectively monitor and report on cost variances as discussed above limits the BU's ability to identify account misallocations, wasteful spending, and inappropriate accruing of expenses.	HI	HI	**Financial Director** We have designed a business intelligence dashboard on AX that will allow for standardised review of financial performance targets.
4. Inventory management. **4.1.** The failure to process the necessary stock quantity variance adjustment journals during Nov-23 to Feb-24 as mentioned in 3.1(d) above, resulted in inventory being incorrectly declared during said months, including at Dec-23 quarter-end.	CRI	CRI	**Financial Director** The last few months have seen an introduction of new personnel within our finance structure. We believe that the restructuring of our Finance Department will bring about the necessary changes to allow us to better accounting standards and controls, including those for inventory management.
4.2. Maintenance spares that are kept in the workshop and valued at over ZAR 1.2m, had not been brought into stock. The failure to treat maintenance spares as stock items increases the risk of theft going undetected as well as inappropriate financial reporting.	MOD		**Plant Manager** A record of maintenance spares will be properly maintained after the implementation of the AX system. The current QAD system does not cater for a module to maintain a record of spares stock per site.
5. HR and payroll 5.1. Production employees booked overtime more than what is permitted in the BCEA, which creates the risk that the Department of Labour could impose penalties on the company.	HI	HI	**Plant Manager** We consult with HR and ER to determine whether the current shift pattern is compliant with the substantive agreement between EBBE Paints and the National Bargaining Council of the Chemical Industry (NBCCI). Based on the outcome of the consultations necessary corrective action will be taken.
5.2. Overtime hours worked were incorrectly calculated resulting in underpayments to employees totalling ZAR2 301.09.	MOD	MOD	**Plant Manager** As above

EXECUTIVE SUMMARY

Finding	Risk rating* BU	EBBE	Management response
5.3. Shift workers were not taken up on the payroll at the correct shift-type codes resulting in the business unit manipulating the system by booking an additional two hours Sunday overtime in respect of normal Sunday shifts worked to ensure employees are correctly remunerated. The payable amounts were correctly determined but the overtime statistics were incorrect as a result.	**MOD**	**MOD**	**Plant Manager** We are working with HR and ER to determine whether the shift pattern is compliant with the BCEA following which Payroll will create a code specific to the shift pattern decided upon by the BU. The relevant employees' shift code will then be updated on the payroll accordingly.
5.4. The reviewed employee timesheets do not comply with acceptable documentary standards which increases the risk of irregular additions and alterations being made.	**MOD**		**Plant Manager** A new timesheet format will be implemented, and the documentary standards will be enforced.
5.5. Nimolala Consult (who performs maintenance in the plant) is not a registered business. The way the owner operates will cause the Revenue Authority to view him as an employee of EBBE Paints for personal income tax purposes. This creates the risk that the Revenue Authority may claim unpaid taxes plus penalties and interest from EBBE Paints.	**MOD**		**Area Productions Manager** Nimolala Consult will be reviewed against the Revenue Authority's requirements. This will be discussed with HR and Payroll departments and the appropriate action will be taken to ensure compliance to the tax laws.
6. Production Process Actual production performance is monitored against targets, but deviations are not sufficiently motivated, which may result in inefficiencies not being diligently investigated and addressed as well as fraud and error can go undetected more easily.	**HI**	**HI**	**Financial Director** We have designed a business intelligence dashboard on AX that will allow for standardised review financial performance targets.

Elvis Sefitlhlolo
Audit Manager

Barrie Enslin
Audit Partner

PAGE 10

ANNEXURE 1, PAGE 1

Finding	Recommendation/corrective action	Management comment	Implement date

1. Property, plant, and equipment (PPE)

Specific control objectives	Achieved?
Additions and disposals are subjected to proper evaluation and approval	N
The fixed asset register is correctly updated with additions and disposals	N
PPE is physically secured and accounted for	N
PPE is appropriately classified in the financial records	N
PPE is appropriately depreciated over its useful life	N

Audit conclusion	Risk exposure	Control adequacy	Control effectiveness
	High	Inadequate	Ineffective

Finding	Recommendation/corrective action	Management comment	Implement date
The FAR was not effectively maintained, resulting in the anomalies as mentioned below. Maintenance of the FAR is, however, a SPL Grandica-wide problem as Internal Audit has been reported on during the past three years.		Financial Director	
1.1. Significant additions and disposals during the current and prior years were not incorporated into the FAR mainly due to responsibility and accountability for maintaining the FAR not being clearly defined in a formal Capex policy and procedure. The following anomalies were identified with regards to the GL and FAR:	SPL Grandica should embark on a project to bring all FARs up to date to ensure accurate take-on in AX. A formal Capex policy and procedure should be put in place, which should cover maintenance of the FAR among others.	An Asset Manager has recently been employed with one of his duties being to review and update the EBBE Paints FAR for the entire business. He will firstly clean up the FAR in preparation for the AX go-live in November 2024, and from there manage all disposals, transfers, and removals going forward. **Responsible person: Asset Manager**	30-Sep-24
1.1.1 Additions not taken up in the GL and FAR: Project costs totalling ZAR32.3 million relating to the Factory Extension project that was commissioned in November 2021 have not yet been taken up in the business unit's GL and FAR at the time of the audit. Management have since discovered the project costs were posted to the Eleanor Business Unit.	The business unit should update the FAR as a matter of urgency.	The Asset Manager is in the process of finalising a fixed asset policy and will send Pro Optima a copy to review. The fixed asset policy will be separate from the Capex policy, which will be the Risk & Compliance Manager's responsibility. **Responsible person: Asset Manager**	30-Jun-24
1.1.2 Disposals not incorporated into the FAR: The following assets being disposed of reflected on the FAR at the time of the audit.			

Table 1: Disposed assets reflected in FAR

Acquisition date	Description	Cost	Net book value 31-Mar-24
31-Dec-13	Element tank (ZT2)	R 32,020.00	3,419.08
06-Dec-06	Honda 23 Generator	R 9,246.95	1.00
31-Aug-09	Venter Trailer MNX10	R 16,111.21	1.00

Finding	Recommendation/corrective action	Management comment	Implement date
1.2. An asset (fabrication of condenser) has been depreciated although delivery is scheduled for 30 September 2024. A deposit of R203,475.97 was paid on 16 January 2024 and asset has already accumulated depreciation of R5,087.66 on 31 March 2024. This was due to the transaction being posted directly to Capex instead of the Capital in Progress (CIP) account resulting from inadequate oversight and review controls at Corporate Finance.	The incorrectly depreciated amount should be reversed, and the full transaction amount (excluding VAT) transferred to the Capital in Progress account. The recommended Capex procedure should describe the procedures regarding expense recognition for capital projects in progress and commissioned.	Agree. The incorrectly depreciated amount will be reversed, and the transaction will be transferred to the CIP account. **Responsible person: Financial Manager** Financial Director	31-Jul-24
1.3. Capex amounting to ZAR687,531.30 was absorbed in operational expenditure, which adversely affected the FAR values as discussed in more detail in finding 3.3 related to budgeting and cost control.	The Capex procedure should clearly define responsibility and accountability relating to Capex budgeting, preparation, submission, and project approval.	Agree. A formal Capex policy will be developed and effectively distributed throughout EBBE Paints and its various business units. **Responsible person: Corp. Financial Manager**	30-Sep-24

ANNEXURE 1, PAGE 2

Finding	Recommendation/corrective action	Management comment	Implement date

2. Procure-to-invoice

Specific control objectives	Achieved?
Goods and services are sourced at competitive prices	N
Invoices are approved for payment only in respect of goods and services required	N
Invoices are approved for payment only in respect of goods and services received/ rendered to the required standards and charged at the agreed prices	N

Audit conclusion	Risk exposure	Control adequacy	Control effectiveness
	Moderate	Partially adequate	Partially effective

Finding	Recommendation/corrective action	Management comment	Implement date
Controls were not adequate or effective to facilitate the achievement of the specific control objectives mentioned above. Most of the control deficiencies are divisional and group related and should be addressed at the Group level. Findings were as follows.			
2.1 Contract administration.		**Procurement Manager**	
Responsibility and accountability regarding contract administration are not formally documented in a governance document. It is our opinion that the lack thereof has contributed the anomalies identified during the audit as detailed below.	A contractor should not be permitted to perform work without a duly signed contract (or order for lower value projects) being in place.	Agree. Contracts will be put in place with respective service providers. We will formulate and communicate the requirements and thresholds for tendering and contracts.	30-Jun-24
2.1.1 Suitable formal agreements are not in place with any of the on-site service providers. Service level agreement (SLA) of two of the service providers are on file, but none of the agreements are adequate to facilitate effective controls as discussed below. The lack of formal agreements precluded Pro Optima from effectively validating the accuracy and validity of payments to these vendors.	Contracts should be in the Grandica contract format as opposed to SLAs in the vendors' standard formats, with the Procurement Department driving this intervention ensuring all necessary contracts are in place. The Legal Department should review draft contracts per the Board Resolution and the Delegation of Power Framework. Where (due to unforeseen circumstances) the contract is not in place when the contractor is required to start work, a letter of intent should be in place setting out the scope and rates.	All contracts will be subjected to the Legal Department's review. **Responsible person: Procurement Manager**	

Table 2: Issues pertaining to vendor SLAs.

Vendor (annual value)	Service	Issue/s
Banksil Rentals (±ZAR670,000)	Rental of mobile equipment	SLA is not signed
Mantle Asset Protection (±ZAR790,000)	Security services	Does not include clear specific conditions of the agreement. A schedule of rates is not included. Signatories did not initial all pages.

Finding	Recommendation/corrective action	Management comment	Implement date
		Production Manager	
2.1.2 The business unit did not perform independent benchmarking and/or price evaluations as a standard procedure to test the competitiveness of prices charged by the on-site service providers.	Where contractors are required to perform services on-site, such services should be formally planned, typically monthly. Orders should be placed with the contractor under the formal, signed-off planning sheet.	Agree. Work instructions will be issued based on monthly planning. **Responsible person: Engineering Supervisor**	Already in place.
2.2 Invoice certification and processing.		**Area Production Manager**	
Controls were not adequate to ensure payments were correctly made for services required and rendered to the applicable safety standards and company requirements. The following shortcomings exist in the system in operation:	All on-site work should be subjected to a formal quality assurance process performed by a suitable company representative before invoices are approved for payment.	Agree, will implement as recommended. **Responsible person: Plant Manager**	30-Jun-24
2.2.1 Adequate supporting documents did not accompany service providers' invoices to enable effective verification of payments per the	The following supporting documentation should accompany on-site service providers' invoices during the	As above.	30-Jun-24

ANNEXURE 1, PAGE 3

<table>
<tr><th>Finding</th><th>Recommendation/corrective action</th><th>Management comment</th><th>Implement date</th></tr>
<tr><td>following observations:

Table 3: Inadequate vendor supporting documents.
<table>
<tr><th>Vendor</th><th>Service</th><th>Monthly ave. spend</th><th>Issue</th></tr>
<tr><td>A&L Bus Service</td><td>Employee transportation</td><td>ZAR105 914</td><td>Trip log sheets not available to verify the number of trips and distances invoiced.</td></tr>
<tr><td>ACE Trading</td><td>Mechanical repairs and maintenance</td><td>ZAR 97 981</td><td>Invoices not referenced to job cards.</td></tr>
</table>
- Formal agreements were not in place with A&L Trading and ACE Trading to enable verification of the amounts charged.</td><td>invoice certification process:
• Works order.
• Measuring/quantification results e.g. job cards, timesheets, trip log sheets, etc.
• Quality control sheet, which may form part of the measuring/quantification results if practical.</td><td></td><td></td></tr>
<tr><td>2.2.2 The responsible company representatives did not sign the service providers' invoices in most instances observed as proof that the invoices were reviewed and duly approved.</td><td>The responsible managers should sign invoices as evidence of review and approval.</td><td>As above.</td><td>Already in place.</td></tr>
<tr><td>2.2.3 Most on-site services invoices were processed based on confirmation orders, i.e. the orders were created after receiving the invoice. This increases the risk of unnecessary services being provided, and/or it may result in the creation of duplicate orders which in turn may cause duplicate payments.</td><td>Purchase orders should be issued in advance of incurring costs. Exceptions, e.g. where it is not practical to create purchase orders in advance, such as Telkom and Eskom should be determined and clearly communicated to the administrative staff.</td><td>As above.

<u>Financial Manager</u></td><td>Already in place.</td></tr>
<tr><td>- In one instance two orders were created for the same service, i.e. hiring of a mobile lifting during 24 December 2023 to 23 January 2024. Both orders were receipted in QAD during February 2024. At the time of the audit, the business unit had not identified the error, mainly due to overdue orders not being followed up as a standard procedure. The invoice was however only paid once, presumably due to the accounts payable module, which flags an invoice number that has been previously loaded for payment for the same vendor.</td><td>The duplicate order should be reversed, and costs written back.
An overdue orders report should be provided to the business units to respond to Procurement for follow up on overdue orders.
(Also refer to recommendation 3.5 relating to cost accruals)</td><td>Procurement Department will review the outstanding purchase order report monthly to ensure that all open (unpaid) purchase orders are investigated and can either be cancelled or paid.
Responsible person: Procurement Manager

<u>Production Manager</u></td><td>30-Jun-24</td></tr>
<tr><td>2.2.4 Signed delivery notes were not attached to all invoices in respect of non-stock purchases as evidence that the goods were received in good order. This was due to responsibilities regarding invoice certification not being assigned in an administrative procedure.</td><td>Signed delivery notes should support all invoices in respect of goods purchased before payment processing is performed.</td><td>Agree, will implement immediately.
Responsible person: Financial Manager</td><td>Already in place.</td></tr>
</table>

ANNEXURE 1, PAGE 4

3. Budgeting and financial performance monitoring

Specific control objectives	Achieved?
Expenses are allocated to the appropriate accounts	N
Expenses are declared in the appropriate accounting period	N
Budgets/targets are met and the non-achievements are effectively dealt with	N

Audit conclusion	Risk exposure	Control adequacy	Control effectiveness
	Critical	Inadequate	Ineffective

Finding	Recommendation/corrective action	Management comment	Implement date
Significant control weaknesses exist in the budgeting and financial performance monitoring processes as discussed below.		<u>Financial Director</u>	
3.1. EBBE Paints does not appropriately use the standard costing method of determining the cost of sales for its intended purposes[2]. This is evident from the significant variances which make up the total cost of sales section of the business unit's FY2024 trial balance which remained largely unexplained at the time of the audit. The following observations support the notion that the additional effort required to administer the standard costing process is not justified because at present it involves the preparation and processing of multiple manual journals to adjust, among others, stock levels and standard stock prices, with no apparent benefit for cost monitoring.	The costing method should be reconsidered in its entirety. Standard costing should either be discontinued, or the application should be revised to make it fit for purpose. In any event, usage and price variances should be calculated at least monthly and the results should be declared as part of KPI reporting. Significant variances should be investigated, effectively addressed, and the results declared in the KPI report.	We are busy implementing a new accounting system. The new AX system will not be using standard costing but will be using the actual cost of material using the FIFO valuation method. **Responsible person: Corporate Financial Manager** <u>Financial Director</u> The last few months have seen an introduction of new personnel within our finance structure. We believe that the restructuring of our Finance Department will bring about the necessary changes to allow us to better comply with accounting standards and controls, including those for inventory management. **Responsible person: Corporate Financial Manager**	Oct/ Nov-24 Nov/ Dec-24
3.1.1. Variances were not subjected to effective analysis and justification as well as these are not formally reported to senior management to enable evaluation of actual performance against set standards.	The plant should provide valid reasons per variance to Corporate Finance before adjusting.		
3.1.2. Standard stock prices are reviewed monthly and adjusted when the delivered price has changed during the previous month. This is a peculiar way of applying standard stock prices in a standard costing system since this method will not provide a logical efficiency measurement against a target/budget (which is the purpose of using standard costing).	The price adjustment rules should be clearly defined and communicated.	Agree. We will implement define and communicate the rules. **Responsible person: Corporate Financial Manager**	31-May-24
3.1.3. The business unit experimented with the formulations within the bill of material (BOM) without having the formulations adjusted accordingly in QAD during FY2024, which compounded the usage variances.	The BOM formulation adjustment rules should be clearly defined and communicated.	Agree. We will implement define and communicate the rules. **Responsible person: Corporate Financial Manager**	31-May-24
3.1.4. The business unit does not report the usage variances as part of its KPIs, thereby defeating the purpose of applying the standard costing method.	Usage and price variances should be calculated and explained at least monthly, and the results should be declared as part of KPI reporting.	This be included in the Rules mentioned above. **Responsible person: Corporate Financial Manager**	31-May-24
3.1.5. EBBE Paints Corporate Finance did not process the necessary stock quantity variance adjustment journals during November 2023 to February 2024, reportedly due to under-staffing during the departmental restructuring phase. This resulted in inaccurate monthly and quarterly financial reporting during the four months to February 2024, i.e. cost of sales was overstated, while raw material inventory was understated. The net stock adjustment processed for the Plant at	The Financial Director issued an instruction to staff to promptly process the quantity variance adjustments after identifying the anomalies in February 2024.		

[2] *Standard costing is a technique that uses standards for costs and revenues for the purpose of control through variance analysis.*

ANNEXURE 1, PAGE 5

Finding	Recommendation/corrective action	Management comment	Implement date
the 2024 financial year-end was ZAR8,490,912 consisting of ZAR10,828,116 write-downs and ZAR2,337,204 write-ups.		**Financial Director**	
3.2. Controls were not adequate to ensure transactions are appropriately allocated to the relevant cost centres and expense elements. There is insufficient oversight regarding the assigning of cost codes and expense elements as well as a lack of detection controls as the Stock Coordinator who prepares most of the non-stock purchase orders does not have sight of the detail expenditure report for review, i.e. to identify potential inaccurate expense allocations.	Detailed and summarised cost reports in a suitable format should be provided to budget holders and the Stock Coordinator who should review the reports for the validity of costs allocated to their budget accounts. The Financial Manager should diligently interrogate the cost reports for accuracy and validity.	The duties of the new Costing Department will be to review cost centres and expense elements for the entire division to ensure they have been correctly allocated, and to train budget holders on cost monitoring controls. **Responsible persons: Corporate Financial Manager & BU Financial Managers**	Already in place and ongoing.
3.3. Instances of expense misallocation occurred when capital expenditure (Capex) was posted to working cost as follows:	The misallocation of the capital expenditure should be transferred to the fixed assets.	As part of the duties of the new Finance Department will be to review cost centres and expense elements for the entire division to ensure they have been correctly allocated. **Responsible person: Financial Manager**	Already in place and ongoing. Nov/ Dec-24
3.3.1. Laboratory building extensions costs (ZAR560,543.21) included in the 2024 Capex budget was absorbed in operating cost under the repairs and maintenance expense code.	The circumvention of the Capex rules should be investigated.	We have already started with the investigation.	
3.3.2. The business unit circumvented the 5% overrun board approval requirement by posting the ZAR126,988.09 (11.6%) overrun on the Fumes Extraction System project to the labour hire expense code. This has resulted in incorrect financial reporting for FY2024. The failure to formally motivate budget variances contributed to the misallocation going undetected during FY2024. Capex procedures have not been formalised. Instead, the undocumented Capex rules "governs" the Capex processes. Failing to define responsibility adversely affects accountability when procedures are breached.	The Capex rules should be formalised in a Capex governance document, clearly assigning/ defining responsibilities, and accountability.	A Capex policy and procedure will be put in place. **Area Production Manager**	30-Nov-24
3.4. The FY2024 actual versus budget analysis showed significant variances for most of the expense elements of the business unit which is an indication that the budget was either not realistically set and/ or expenditure was not effectively monitored. Refer to Table 4. Explanations were not provided for the variances in the KPI report, which increases the risk that wasteful spending, as well as fraud and error will go undetected. **Table 4: Budget /actual variances re expenditure for EBBE Paints Plant 1 - FY2024 (excluding year-end adjustments).** (see table below)	The budgeting and expenditure control processes within EBBE Paints should be re-engineered, incorporating amongst other the following: • Restructuring the cost accounting function within EBBE Paints to better support the business units. This may include assigning certain of the cost accounting functions to the administrative staff at the business units as well as establishing closer liaison between the central cost accounting function and the business units. • Introducing timely, user-friendly, and transparent cost reporting, which will require designing fit-for-purpose weekly and monthly summary *and* detailed transaction reports. The costing function should provide weekly cost reports to the relevant budget holders (electronically or hard copy).	There are justifications for the variances however going forward we will provide more details regarding the variances. **Responsible person: Financial Manager** **Financial Director** See comments in 3.1 above. We have designed a business intelligence dashboard on AX that will allow for standardised review financial performance targets. **Responsible persons: Corporate Financial Manager and Business Unit Financial Managers**	31-May-24 Already in place.

Table 4: Budget /actual variances re expenditure for EBBE Paints Plant 1 - FY2024 (excluding year-end adjustments).

Expense Item	Actual (R)	Budget (R)	Variance (R)	% Variance
Cleaning	147,223	69,000	78,223	113%
Consumables	391,075	361,436	29,639	8%
Electricity & water	1750,032	2,062,300	-312,268	-15%
Insurance	140,262	333,664	-193,402	-58%
Motor & vehicle costs	65,265	58,956	6,309	11%

ANNEXURE 1, PAGE 6

Finding	Recommendation/corrective action	Management comment	Implement date

Printing	77,958	36,000	41,958	117%
Rental	612,306	484,000	128,306	27%
Repairs & maintenance	4,576,609	1,928,880	2,647,729	137%
Safety	94,264	35,520	58,744	165%
Security	962,821	900,000	62,821	7%
Staff employment	10,749,107	9,147,275	601,832	6%
Subscriptions	0	200,544	-200,544	-100%
Telephone	104,316	125,304	-20,988	-24%
Training	305,458	207,900	97,558	47%
Travel	252,707	174,048	78,659	45%
Vehicle tracking	29,509	0	29,509	Infinite
Other	383,127	115,348	67,779	58%
Total expenditure	**20,542,039**	**16,240,175**	**4,301,864**	**26%**

Cost reporting formats are not suitable to facilitate effective management of actual financial performance against targets. The failure to effectively monitor and report on cost variances limits the BU's ability to identify account misallocations, wasteful spending, and inappropriate accruing of expenses.

Recommendation/corrective action:

- Explaining significant variances between actual and budgeted performance (down to BU level and prepared by the costing function in liaison with the budget holders) should be prepared and incorporated into the monthly financial and operational business review reporting, e.g., KPI report.
- Verifying the appropriateness of expense allocations, including the correctness of expense elements, cost centres as well as correct allocation to Opex vs. Capex.
- Administrative staff at the business units should assume greater responsibility in the annual budgeting process.

Finding	Recommendation/corrective action	Management comment	Implement date
3.5. Expenditure was not always posted during the period when it was incurred. This is due to the business unit not accruing expenditure when an invoice has not yet been received by the end of the relevant reporting period, and the use of confirmation orders per finding 2.2.3. For example, Banksil Rental's standard monthly invoices of R49,944.32 for the hiring of lifting equipment during October 2023 to January 2024 were all costed in February 2024. The creation of a duplicate order as discussed in 2.2.1. (c) exacerbated the effect, meaning that R89,229.44 was expensed in February 2024, while the hiring of the forklifts did not reflect in the costs during October 2023 to January 2024.	The costing function's duties should include the appropriate accruing of expenses in the relevant accounting period.	**Financial Director** See comments in 3.3 above.	Oct/ Nov-24
3.6. Quotations are not obtained from prospective suppliers as a standard practice to enhance the opportunity of obtaining goods and services at optimal prices.	EBBE Paints should consider establishing a centralized buying function for the acquiring of goods and services that fall outside the scope of Procurement's ambit.	**Procurement Manager** Agree. We will consider establishing a centralised buying function. **Responsible person: Procurement Manager**	Nov/ Dec-24

4. Inventory management

Specific control objectives	Achieved?
Inventory is logically stored in suitable, secure facilities	Y
Inventory purchased is accounted for	N
Inventory is accurately and appropriately disclosed in the financial statements	N

Audit conclusion	Risk exposure	Control adequacy	Control effectiveness
	Moderate	Partially adequate	Partially effective

Inventory is logically stored in suitable, secured facilities, but we do not regard financial controls over inventory as entirely adequate, with a resultant likelihood of inventory and cost of sales being incorrectly declared in the financial statements as discussed below.

Finding	Recommendation/corrective action	Management comment	Implement date
4.1. As mentioned in finding 3.1.5 stock quantity variance adjustment journals	Refer finding 3.1.5.		

ANNEXURE 1, PAGE 7

Finding	Recommendation/corrective action	Management comment	Implement date
were not processed during November 2023 to February 2024 which resulted in raw material inventory being understated by ZAR8 490 912. 4.2. Maintenance spares valued at over ZAR 1 million kept in the workshop had been expensed and not brought into stock. Failure to treat maintenance spares as stock items increases the risk of theft going undetected as well as inappropriate financial reporting.	Detailed stock records should be kept for all maintenance spares on hand at the workshop.	**Production Manager** A record of maintenance spare will be properly kept after the implementation of the AX system. The current system QAD does not cater for a module to maintain a record of spares stock per site. **Responsible person: Production Manager**	Oct/ Nov-24

5. HR & Payroll

Specific control objectives	Achieved?
The Basic Conditions of Employment Act provisions regarding overtime is enforced	Y
Employee tax is deducted from employees in terms of the Seventh Schedule to the Income Tax Act*	**Partially**

*Note: the scope is limited to determining whether employees receive any fringe benefit that is not declared in accordance with the Income Tax Act

Audit conclusion	Risk exposure	Control adequacy	Control effectiveness
	Moderate	Partially adequate	Partially effective

Finding	Recommendation/corrective action	Management comment	Implement date
Compliance with the Basic Conditions of Employment Act (BCEA), Compensation for Occupational Injuries and Diseases (COID) and the Income Tax Acts has not been effectively enforced as discussed below. 5.1. **Overtime booked more than the BCEA rules.** Production employees booked overtime above what is permitted in the BCEA[3], i.e. for the sample of timesheets tested showing the following instances of excessive overtime:	Overtime should be closely monitored. Employees working more than the required limit should not be allowed to work the next working shift. The Foreman should monitor the employee overtime hours worked on a daily/weekly basis to ensure compliance with the BCEA.	**Production Manager** We consult with HR and ER to determine whether the current shift pattern is compliant with the substantive agreement between EBBE Paints and the National Bargaining Council of the Chemical Industry (NBCCI). Based on the outcome of the consultations the necessary corrective action will be taken. **Responsible person: Production Manager**	30-Jun-24

Table 5: Overtime exceeding BCEA allowable hours

Employee	Week ending	Overtime hours
AM Claasen	05-Feb-24	40
S Mandabele	19-Feb-24	32
S Snow	19-Mar-24	24
MA Shonki	08-Jan-24	20
MA Shonki	05-Mar-24	20
MA Shonki	05-Apr-24	14
TT Mthimu	16-Apr-24	16
CB Gelderblom	16-Apr-24	21
CB Gelderblom	08-Jan-24	24

[3] *In terms of the Basic Conditions of Employment Act 75 of 1997, overtime is regulated by Section 10 of the BCEA and it provides that an employer may not require or permit an employee to work:*
- *more than 10 (ten) hours per week;*
- *in terms of subsection (1) may not require nor permit an employee to work more than 12 (twelve) hours on any day.*

Finding	Recommendation/corrective action	Management comment	Implement date
5.2. **Inaccurate overtime hours worked.** Overtime hours worked were incorrectly calculated resulting in underpayments to employees. This underpayment relates to the substantive agreement in place between EBBE Paints and the National Bargaining Council of the Chemical Industry (NBCCI) which has reduced the normal working hours to 42 hours for the continuous shift workers. However, this reduction has not been applied correctly to the overtime calculation as EBBE Paints determines overtime hours worked by considering only hours above the daily normal working hours (8 hours). Of the sample tested, 106 hours had been underpaid per table 10.	The operations should familiarise themselves with the bargaining council agreement in place with the regarding the reduction of the normal working hours to 42 per week, which should be applied to overtime going forward.	Production Manager We consult with HR and ER to determine whether the current shift pattern is compliant with the substantive agreement between EBBE Paints and the National Bargaining Council of the Chemical Industry (NBCCI). Based on the outcome of the consultations the necessary corrective action will be taken. **Responsible person: Production Manager**	30-Jun-24

Table 10: Employees underpaid on overtime.

Employee name	Month	OT hrs not paid
S Mandabele	Feb-24	6
S Snow	Mar-24	6
S Snow	Apr-24	18
MA Shonki	Jan-24	20
MA Shonki	Mar-24	6
MA Shonki	Apr-24	6
TT Mthimun	Apr-24	6
PD Tshabalala	Apr-24	14
CB Gelderblom	Jan-24	18
CB Gelderblom	Apr-24	6

Finding	Recommendation/corrective action	Management comment	Implement date
5.3. Shift workers were not taken up on the payroll at the correct shift-type code resulting in the business unit having to book an additional two hours Sunday overtime for normal Sunday shifts worked to ensure compliance with the BCEA, requiring that "an employee who ordinarily works on a Sunday must be paid at 1.5 times the normal wage" (refer BCEA Section 16, paragraph 2.8.2). Business unit management stated they believed that the payroll system was unable to automatically calculate the remuneration for normal Sunday shifts correctly; hence the need to manipulate the system accordingly. Although this practice did not cause employees' remuneration to be incorrectly determined, statistical data with regards to overtime is incorrect, which affects the reliability of management information with regards to overtime.	Shift types codes for all EBBE Paints staff should be reviewed for accuracy and the payroll should be updated accordingly.	Production Manager This will be resolved as part of our consultation with HR. **Responsible person: Production Manager**	30-Jun-24
5.4. Adequate documentary standards were not enforced on timesheets, which increases the risk of irregular alterations and limits the opportunity to detect fraud and error, e.g.:	Strict documentary standards should be enforced, including: • Reflecting names and designations of originators and	Production Manager A new timesheet format will be implemented, and the documentary standards will be enforced. **Responsible person: Production Manager**	31-Aug-24

ANNEXURE 1, PAGE 9

Finding	Recommendation/corrective action	Management comment	Implement date
• Timesheets do not provide for control totals, including totals in words and figures. • Unused lines were not cancelled. • Unauthorised alterations occurred, including corrections using correcting fluid. • Reasons for overtime were not recorded on all the relevant timesheets.	approvers. • Showing evidence of review and supervisory checks. • Stating the date generated and authorized. • Unused lines cancelled. • Alterations duly authorized/ initialled and no correcting fluid used. • Providing for control totals, including totals in words and figures.	**Production Manager**	
5.5. Nimolala Consult is not a registered business and is likely to be viewed by the Revenue Authority as an employee of EBBE Paints for personal income tax purposes for the following reasons[4]: • The person is a natural person receiving remuneration and is residing in South Africa. • The person does not employ three or more unrelated employees throughout the year of assessment. • Services are rendered mainly at the client's premises and under the control of the client. This creates the risk that Revenue Authority may claim unpaid taxes plus penalties and interest from EBBE Paints.	The applicable employee status of Nimolala Consult should be reviewed considering the Revenue Authority's requirements to decide whether to take the person up in the payroll.	Agree. Nimolala Consult will be reviewed against tax requirements. This will be discussed with HR and Payroll and the appropriate action will be taken to ensure compliance with the tax laws. **Responsible person: Financial Manager**	31-Aug-24
6. Production process			

Specific control objectives	Achieved?
Production results are accurately and appropriately declared	Partially
Actual performance is monitored against targets while deviations are properly investigated and motivated	Partially
Raw materials introduced into the production proves are fully accounted for (mass balancing)	Y

Audit conclusion	Risk exposure	Control adequacy	Control effectiveness
	Medium	Partially adequate	Partially effective

Finding	Recommendation/corrective action	Management comment	Implement date
The underlying internal controls are in place to facilitate accurate and appropriate declaration and accounting of production results, with the key controls listed below being in place. However, cost variances were not effectively identified, investigated, and reported.		**Plant Manager**	
6.1. The suppliers of the bulk raw materials provide a certificate of conformance with each delivery, while the business unit also performs its own analysis to ensure the raw materials conform to the required specifications before being introduced into the production process.	Positive finding, no recommendation.	Noted.	
6.2. A mass balancing spreadsheet is maintained to reconcile raw materials usage with production output, with no significant variances between raw material usage, production output and sales being recorded for July 2023 to 31 March 2024, being the files obtained during the audit.	Positive finding, no recommendation.	Noted.	
6.3. Formally documented standard operating procedures (SOPs) for the main	Positive finding, no recommendation.	Noted.	

[4] Refer to the interpretation note: no. 17 (issue 3) relating to the Income Tax Act no. 58 of 1962, fourth schedule relating to employees' tax: independent contractors.

Finding	Recommendation/corrective action	Management comment	Implement date
plant processes are in place, with the relevant procedures being presented in a user-friendly format and posted on the noticeboards at working places. The safety officer and the operations foremen perform regular planned and unplanned task observations to test compliance with the SOPs while recording and following up on reportable deviations. Task observation reports are securely and logically retained.		<u>**Financial Director**</u>	
6.4. Actual performance is monitored against targets, but deviations are not always formally explained/motivated, which may result in inefficiencies not being diligently investigated and addressed as well as fraud and error going undetected.	The KPI report should explain the variances, including investigation results and agreed corrective as well as the status of the corrective action plans.	We have designed a business intelligence dashboard on AX that will allow for standardised review financial performance targets. **Responsible person: Production Manager and Financial Manager**	31-May-24

Attachment 5

IMPLEMENT CONTROLS BEFORE AUDIT METHODOLOGY

LESSONS LEARNT WORKPAPER (LLW)

pro optima Audit Services

Project description: **Review of the Ore Accounting Processes at XYZ Mine**
Project code: **XY2403**
Kick-off meeting: **20 September 2024 @ 13:30 (online)**
2nd meeting: **02 October 2024 @ 14:00 (online)**
Planned audit start date: **Earliest: Third week of November 2024 (dates to be finalized)**

The purpose of this document is to present generic findings which may assist clients in identifying potential similar risks and anomalies in their own organisations, and to implement controls to mitigate such risks before the audit is conducted. Following are summarised extracts from audit reports issued by Pro Optima about ore accounting at various clients.

The last four columns have been completed following the kick-off meetings held as follows:

20-Sep-24: In attendance: xx

02-Oct-24: In attendance: xx

	Finding per audit reports at various clients	Cause(s)	Recommended control	Likeli-hood H/M/L	Impact H/M/L	Control effectiveness G/M/P	Management response/ action
	Complete this portion before meeting with client			Complete this portion during meeting with client			
1	An Ore Accounting Code of Practice (COP) is not in place, which may adversely affect compliance with mine (and industry) standards, and to hold employees accountable for deviations when roles and responsibilities are not defined.	Not deemed necessary. Not a priority.	The relevant standards and procedures should be drafted, reviewed, communicated, and enforced. COPs should provide for supervisory checks and PTOs. The relevant persons should sign acknowledgement of having read the governance documents and a commitment to comply therewith.	H	H	M	GAVIN: Not yet in place. We will draft an Ore Accounting COP to be finalised before start of audit. IA will provide high level guidelines.
2	Industry standards relating certain sub-sections of the ore accounting process were deviated from on a large scale, including the sampling and measuring standards.	The survey and sampling procedures are too high-level and do not cover all the relevant aspects. Lack of diligent supervisory checks, including PTOs.	The survey and sampling procedures should be revised to ensure completeness. The need for diligent supervisory checks should be addressed during the revision.	M	M	M	GAVIN: Revised procedures for the different facets of sampling drafted, awaiting sign-off. The survey procedure will be revised to cover all relevant aspects.

	Finding per audit reports at various clients	Cause(s)	Recommended control	Likeli-hood H/M/L	Impact H/M/L	Control effectiveness G/M/P	Management response/ action
	Complete this portion before meeting with client			**Complete this portion during meeting with client**			
3	<u>**Sampling**</u> results were not reliable due to the following: a) **Insufficient sampling coverage** A large portion of panels did not have any valuation results due to poor sampling coverage, thereby compelling the Chief Sampler to use estimations. For the panels where sampling was done, only the latest sampling results were used in the panel valuation process instead of both the current and previous sampling information. b) **Deviation from sampling standards** The process followed to valuate on-reef working places is not effective to derive reliable valuation data due to the following: i) Deviations from the sampling standard were observed underground during the rock face sampling process: • The sampler deviated from the required start and intervals when marking the sampling positions, resulting in three sample sections being taken from the face instead of five as follows: - The first sampling position was located at 6m instead of at 1.5m from the edge of the panel. - The sampler omitted the last required sampling position. • The sample pan was not properly cleaned after completing each sample, increasing the risk of sample contamination. • The sampler did not record the geological features, e.g., faults and different reefs/ veins in the field book per in the Underground Sampling Standard.	The mine does not employ sampler assistants to assist with tasks such as measuring, tagging as well as carrying of sample bags and equipment. Samplers were assigned the responsibility to perform backlog sweeping and vamping measuring in addition to their sampling duty, without an increase in complement being allowed.	Additional resources should be considered, e.g., by assigning at least one sampling assistant per sampler. A list of all stope panels should be prepared, and the chief sampler should closely monitor daily sampling to improve sampling coverage. Regular PTOs to monitor and enforce compliance. Samplers should be required to sign acknowledgement annually of having read, understood, and committing to comply with the sampling standards.	L	M	G	<u>Derick:</u> PTOs are being done & will be continuously enforced. We have confidence in the quality of sampling as we have seasoned samplers. Also, samplers are rotated as a double check to identify adverse trends. Samplers will receive refresher training once the revised sampling procedure is finalized.
4	**Survey measuring not accurately performed.**	Lack of oversight, including the failure to perform PTOs resulted in the errors going undetected.	Supervisory checks should be enforced.	M	M	M	<u>Jesica:</u> We have made good progress. Controls have improved through training and supervision. Development quality has improved but we're not yet there.

pg. 2

	Finding per audit reports at various clients	Cause(s)	Recommended control	Likeli-hood H/M/L	Impact H/M/L	Control effectiveness G/M/P	Management response/ action
	Complete this portion <u>before</u> meeting with client			Complete this portion <u>during</u> meeting with client			
5	**The Mineral Resources Management (MRM) report does not provide sufficient and accurate information, such as:** a) **The MRM Report contains nonsensical information.** The gold lock-up figures reported appeared nonsensical. It is unlikely that the MRM Report, Mine reflects the Call Factor (MCF) correctly considering the reported gold lock-up as well as the lock-up that was omitted from the MRM Report. b) **Declared MCF not accurately presented.** The high occurrence of current month gold lock-up does not reflect in the MCF calculations. c) Capturing errors resulted in some sweeping distance-to-face results to reflected incorrectly in the MRM Report.	Potential manipulation of the declared lockups and other key production figures. Inadequate supervisory checks.	Diligent oversight procedures. The current Excel-based system in use should be replaced with an MRM software system.	M	M	M	<u>Jesica:</u> Reliability of info has improved through supervision and PTOs. This is an ongoing process. A review of controls will assist in reducing risk. Controls will improve once Syncromine software is implemented – expected in the next two months.
6	Sweepings and gully lock-up tons had not been captured onto the MRM Report.	Oversight	The MRM report should include all sweeping and lock-up tons.	n/a			Not a risk at XYZ Mine.
7	Excessive lock-up tons underground.	Negligence	A new drive to identify and hoist the lock-up tons is necessary.	n/a			Not a risk at XYZ Mine.
8	Waste development lock-up tons were not determined or captured onto the MRM Report, which adversely affects the reconciliation of broken vs. trammed tons.	Oversight and poor work practices.	Waste development lock-up tons should be determined and captured onto the MRM Report.	n/a			Not a risk at XYZ Mine.
9	Tons treated and hoisted reflected in the MRM Report were not effectively reconciled based on the following audit test results: a) The reef tons hoisted figure presented in the MRM Report differed from the aggregate daily tramming sheets. b) We observed dirt accumulation in the bowls of the trucks ranging from 1 to 2 tons, which equates to 3% to 6% of the loads being double accounted for.	Oversight and poor work practices.	Management should determine the reasons for the differences. Supervisory staff should provide meticulous oversight as is expected from them. If a discrepancy occurs, it should be referred to the survey manager for a decision and sign off. Management should consider applying a penalty for double accounting on the Monthly Hauling Tons Report if accumulation of dirt is observed on the haul trucks.	H	H	H	<u>GAVIN:</u> This is a problem at the mine. We are busy investigating to resolve the differences and to reduce the need for adjustments. Hauled tonnages (load weights) do not affect ore accounting though but it affects payment to the transporters.

pg. 3

	Finding per audit reports at various clients	Cause(s)	Recommended control	Likeli-hood H/M/L	Impact H/M/L	Control effectiveness G/M/P	Management response/ action
	Complete this portion before meeting with client			**Complete this portion during meeting with client**			
10	The plant applies a fixed 8% moisture factor in their declared total tons as opposed to the actual sampled moisture factor of around 6% that Survey applies. This adversely affects the reliance that can be placed on the tonnage reconciliation between survey and the plant.	Oversight and poor work practices.	The plant and sampling function should agree monthly on the appropriate moisture factor to be applied in the calculations	H	M	Poor	GAVIN: Moisture is an issue. More data collection and analysis are required. I will follow up.
11	Cross tramming resulted in gold loss and dilution.	Oversight and poor work practices.	The introduction of the material into the production stream should be properly managed to ensure optimal recovery. The mine should embark on a new drive to eliminate cross tramming and reduce dilution, including weekly audits.	H	H	Poor	GAVIN: Needs some work to determine the extent of the problem/ risk. This is Mining's responsibility. IA to discuss with Mining.
12	Excessive water resulting in gold loss; more particularly fines being washed away.	Excessive water leakage from one of the hydro power machine hoses observed during our visit indicates potential drilling equipment maintenance issues.	An analysis should be performed of the site characteristics combined with the consideration of mining methods (e.g. Flow3D) to determine the most appropriate water control method.	L	L	G	GAVIN: Not a risk at XYZ Mine. No work needed
13	Broken rock fragmentation not optimal. We observed the particle size of blasted rock to be generally less than 50mm, which increases the risk of gold loss and mud rushes considering the excessive water.	Poor drilling and blasting discipline.	There should be a renewed drive on drilling and blasting discipline to optimize fragmentation to enhance optimal gold recovery.	M	M	G	GAVIN: This is a Mining issue. IA to discuss with Mining.
14	**Drilling into the reef contact.**	Lack of discipline, poor oversight.	The miners and shift bosses should enforce the correct marking of face drilling positions.	L	L	G	GAVIN: Not a risk at XYZ Mine
15	**Recontamination of cleaned panels**	Lack of discipline, poor oversight and deviation from standards, incl. the incorrect use of blasting barricades. Inadequate/ ineffective planning.	The Mine should embark on a "Clean Mining" drive, including awareness campaigns, retraining, regular gold loss audits, formal pre-planning sessions, and effective oversight. The correct use of blasting barricades requires special focus.	n/a			GAVIN: Not a risk at XYZ Mine
16	The mine does not use the MRM software to populate and present the monthly production statistics. Instead, the various sources of information, such as sample results, survey measuring, and valuation is manually captured onto an Excel file creating the following risks:	It was decided to discard some of the software's functions due to the manual intervention needed to facilitate	Full use of the MRM software should be enforced to consolidate the complicated functions, such as resource to reserve conversion forecasts and the continuous re-	H	H	M	GAVIN: We're implementing Mineware. Geology already started with

	Finding per audit reports at various clients	Cause(s)	Recommended control	Likeli-hood H/M/L	Impact H/M/L	Control effectiveness G/M/P	Management response/ action
	Complete this portion before meeting with client			**Complete this portion during meeting with client**			
	a) Lack of a proper audit trail with regards to valuation data used for each panel. b) Data manipulation and errors going undetected due to insufficient built-in controls, e.g., cell protection, cell limits, etc. as is evident from findings mentioned earlier.	accurate processing of data due to the following: • Inconsistency with allocating workplace names. • low sampling coverage.	classifications to enable budgets, plans, actuals, sampling, drilling, inspections, and evaluation to be expressed in real time.				the process. Survey is in progress, i.e., input side done, busy with reporting. Info side expected before year-end.
17	Plant stockpiles were estimated instead of being measured, which reduces the reliance that can be placed on the lock-up/ release figures applied when determining delivered tons.	Oversight and poor work practices.	Survey should measure all the stockpiles at month-end.	L	L	G	GAVIN: Survey measures accumulations and include results in the calcs as standard practice.
18	The plant used the declared belt/ hoisted tons from the shafts to determine the total Surface Rock Dump (SRD) tons, by calculating the difference between total milled tons and plant tons. The following observations demonstrate the inappropriateness of applying this method: a) The ore accounting investigation team identified that no. 10 Shaft's tons may have been overstated by ±20% due to inaccurate weightometer readings, which implies those tons were incorrectly deducted from SRD. b) The calculated trucked tons, *based on truck tallies and load factors*, exceed tons allocated to SRD by 14%. - The transport contractors' tonnages for invoicing purposes were potentially unjustly reduced to match the tons allocated to SRD.	Deviation from the COP for Metal Accounting (which is based on the AMIRA principles) by failing to investigate biases which have been evident over at least eight months. SOPs have not been defined. Haul trucks not weighed because the weighbridge is out of their way.	The matter requires urgent executive management intervention.				GAVIN: Plant responsibility. IA to discuss with Metallurgy.
19	The declared hoisted tons exceeded the underground measuring results significantly, with supporting documents not provided at request to explain the excess tons hoisted. Conversely, the declared contained gold and grades have dropped significantly from the underground measured face to the mill, which is a peculiar inverse relationship.	As above.	As mentioned above, the matter requires urgent executive management intervention.	H	H	M	GAVIN: Tonnage discrepancies is an issue, which we're working on.

pg. 5

	Finding per audit reports at various clients	Cause(s)	Recommended control	Likeli-hood H/M/L	Impact H/M/L	Control effectiveness G/M/P	Management response/ action
	Complete this portion **before** meeting with client			Complete this portion **during** meeting with client			
20	Excessive spillage occurred along the tramming routes due to overloaded and severely worn hoppers.	Poor work practices and ineffective rolling stock maintenance.	The importance to not overfill hoppers should be reiterated. All officials, including safety officers should be instructed to report instances of over (and under-filling) of hoppers. Engineering should embarked on a rolling stock maintenance program – to be performed inhouse as far as possible.	L	L	G	GAVIN: Haulage spillage is cleaned, this is not an issue at XYZ Mine.
21	Sampling reports were not available for 10 of the 50 face samples selected for testing.	The chief sampler was unable to explain the mystery, with unconfirmed rumours that fake sampling reports were prepared but were subsequently destroyed.	The matter was still under investigation at the time of issuing the audit report.	L	L	G	GAVIN/ Derick: Sampling side is well controlled per 3 above.
22	Sampling method not consistently applied. a) For certain panels the face value was calculated using the weighted mean, while using the arithmetical mean for the rest. b) Inconsistent rounding at no. 1 Shaft, i.e., the channel width was rounded to the nearest 10 cm and gold grade to the nearest gram. Due to primary and subsequent rounding of a 5 to the next higher figure, this will have a compounding effect, which may cause some degree of over-valuation.	It was not clearly communicated to grade officers what mean should have been used in calculating the face value. Deviation from good practice, lack of standardization throughout the mine, and lack of oversight.	The importance of the relevant statistical principles should be stressed to staff through periodic training sessions.	L	L	G	Gavin: We've recently checked, we do regular checks to evaluate the appropriateness of our averaging method. Analysis will show if there is a problem, but we can check during the audit as well. Again, considered. More reliable data in the new system will assist with analysis.
23	A shale parting occurring after measuring day was not considered in the tonnage calculations resulting in trammed and hoisted tons of two mining sections being overstated, and thereby compilated the tonnage reconciliations.	The affected sections failed to alert Survey to the problem as they argued the extent of the additional tons was underestimated.	Survey should consider the shale parting tons in the monthly measuring results.	H	H	M	GAVIN: We've tried to do void scans. Quality of surveying improves continuously. GAVIN will do the long-term tonnage recon before the audit.

Additional information:

A. The above may not be complete list of controls within the audit area. Internal Audit may cover required controls during the audit testing that are not mentioned above.

pg. 6

B. Audit focus areas/ sub objectives.

To determine whether:
1. Gold mined is accurately quantified and reported.
2. Gold lock-up and gold loss are minimised.
3. All the gold mined is delivered to the plant.

C. High-level risks

1. Substandard staff performance
2. Inaccurate measuring/ tonnage determination
3. Inaccurate grade determination
4. Gold loss and theft
5. Inappropriate decision-making

D. Internal Audit is looking forward to a positive audit outcome and finding the 'house in order'.

Chapter 5

The 5th P is our Planet ... because no planet, no internal audit

GARDENER OF GOVERNANCE ARTICLE SYNOPSIS

ESG (Environment, Social, and Governance) is no longer a "nice to have", and internal auditing has a role to play. The challenge is real and will not disappear even if ignored by some. ESG becomes a question of "Do or Die" for society, companies, and internal auditing. ESG measurements have become formally embedded into decision-making by investors and by private equity firms.

E (environment) is directly related to the climate change threat. There are further environmental challenges. Internal auditing must become a more prominent and respected player providing due assurance to management on strategic and operational environmental goals.

S (social) is relevant as a company's legitimacy will depend on more than just profits. A company will need to show how it contributes with broader value to society to attract investments and talented employees. The profession needs to provide assurance that the company's objectives in this regard are met, and its external reporting is correct.

G (governance) – Internal auditing has the potential to render more added value in the arena of governance, determining how an organization is directed and controlled.

ESG has great potential for the profession to demonstrate value to business and society by providing the basis for recognition by society while simultaneously differentiating internal auditing from external auditing. We view G (Governance) as the overarching concept. We regard sound Governance as prerequisite for effectively managing the E (Environment) and the S (Social) dimensions of this acronym. Hence, we prefer spelling ESG as "esG".

DOI: 10.1201/9781003539001-5

HAS BUSINESS TURNED THE CORNER ON ESG?

The conflict between economic advancement and the exploitation of our natural resources has reached a stage where the former is no longer the sole or dominant factor. The preferences of investors have changed and are likely to change further. Investors are increasingly far more sensitive to externalities, environmental and social issues (Lenz and Chesshire 2023). Hart and Zingales (2022) offer practical solutions about how to consider environmental and social responsibilities in the equation. In their landmark article, "Shareholder Welfare Maximation (SWM)" is the suggested new paradigm of corporate governance: "The New Corporate Governance".

The accelerated emphasis on reserving natural resources has caused a major shift in businesses that can't get away with "murder" so easily as investors and consumers' appetite for responsible preservation of our planet increase.

LEARNING OBJECTIVES OF THIS CHAPTER

- Expand your repertoire to include WHAT IF questions, alongside the traditional WHAT IS and SO WHAT approaches, to enhance critical thinking and strategic foresight.
- Analyze and reflect on the implications of internal audit evolving into a primary function, exploring the potential benefits and challenges.
- The audit universe should cover every aspect of the business and not be limited to financial and administrative areas, including ESG.
- ESG offers great potential for internal auditing to provide value to business and society.

Part One (Rainer)

OUR PLANET IS AT RISK

Lenz and Jeppesen (2022) summarize that all sensible minds have realized by now that our planet is at risk. No planet, no (internal) audit. There is no plan(et) B. However, internal auditors have not yet satisfactorily staked a claim in the ESG debate. Why is that so? Lenz and Hoos (2023) hypothesize that the ESG challenge is so big and the threats for the role of the internal audit function are so real, that the profession reacts like an animal in the face of a threat: it freezes. To that date, the internal audit profession and its professionals had only slowly taken (insufficient) actions. Lenz and Chesshire (2023) "sound the alarm": "it is a fact that the world is not on track to meet the Goals by 2030. To prevent a climate catastrophe, more effective and timely climate action, focusing here on SDG 13 (Goal 13 aims to combat climate change), is required now. The time is now. There is no more time to waste. We need to change course. At pace". Lenz and Chesshire (2023) reference the scientific consensus that our planet is at risk, for example, in the Global Risks Report 2023 environmental challenges account for 6 out of the top 10 risks over a 10-year period (World Economic Forum 2023).

In my humble view, the acronym ESG is misleading. Governance (G) is more than the third letter of ESG, it is the overarching concept: *"Corporate governance is the system by which companies are directed and controlled"* (Cadbury Committee 1992).[1] "RIP ESG" is too radical, says Olga Goncharova.[2] I agree. While authoring her thesis on ESG auditing recently, she has abbreviated "ESG" as "esG". I like that. That is an elegant way of expressing that effective Governance is a prerequisite for successfully addressing the E and the S. When meeting Prof. Mervyn King SC in person while in Johannesburg in October 2024, he suggested spelling the acronym as "GES". I like that, too.

INTERNAL AUDIT'S ROLE

We must ask ourselves: "How best can internal auditing contribute and support the mitigation of these global challenges?" We can do more. We can do better. We must change. The inertia is self-inflicted in parts. In Chapter 4, (Purpose) we posit: PREVENTING GOVERNANCE FAILURE IS THE MISSION OF INTERNAL AUDITING. We argue that sound Governance is the enabler of more effectively addressing both the Social and the Environmental dimensions of ESG. Considering the vital risks associated with our stressed planet, we must ask ourselves the hard questions: what do we internal auditors de facto contribute to prevent catastrophes from happening, what else, what more we can do? Talking about Third Lines and such will not do the trick. Being a bystander, to put it harshly, no longer meets the challenges we are facing. According to the 2024 report by The Internal Audit Foundation 37% of internal auditors were categorized as "Purists" who hold traditional views of internal audit. This Vision 2035 report rightfully demands the professional community of internal auditors to change its mindset, suggesting a greater openness *"to new technology, approaches, and attitudes"*. We need *"greater adoption of a growth mindset characterized by adaptability, flexibility, confidence, and innovation"*. We agree with Anthony Pugliese, the President and CEO at The Institute of Internal Auditors Inc.: *"We must transform now or risk becoming irrelevant by 2035"* (The Internal Audit Foundation 2024, July).

We suggest that we can do more and do better. Internal auditing is a profession full of well-educated, business-minded, smart and ambitious individuals. We fundamentally challenge the present value proposition of internal auditing.

Lenz and Hoos (2023) argue that the traditional two pillars of what internal auditing is about are no longer adequate and are no longer good enough to meet the heightened challenges of the 21st century:

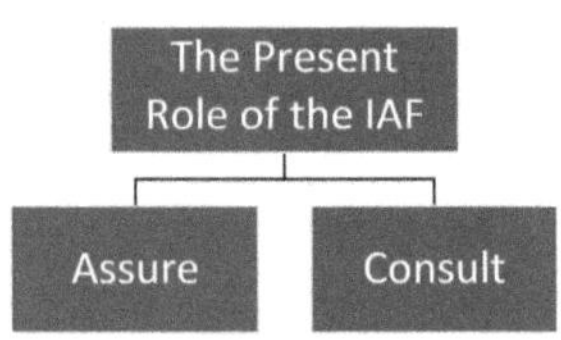

Figure 5.1 Two traditional pillars of internal auditing: Assure and Consult (Advice).

We demand that internal auditors overcome self-inflicted constraints and widen their scope. The ABC article (Lenz & Hoos 2023) advocates a pragmatic way of better serving the purpose of the organization we work for by adding "Build" to our repertoire, so "doing stuff", becoming, for example, project team members, becoming (co-) architects and where possible be truly value adding, especially when considering that the planet is at stake.

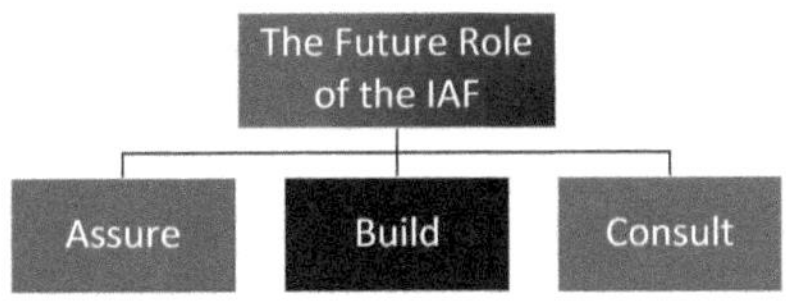

Figure 5.2 Adding "Build" to the traditional pillars of internal auditing.

That suggestion is beautifully in line with the professional plea to transform the internal auditor's mindset to become more proactive (The Internal Audit Foundation 2024). Value creation often demands more than rendering assurance or consulting (advisory) service. There is nothing good unless you do it. Rightfully, the profession of internal auditors demands the professional community to become "Proactive", embracing new ideas, new ways of working and driving change that creates value.

In the context of ESG, especially as far as the E (Environment) part is concerned, we must move from being just a bystander, however, smart the advice provided may be, to become a "doer", to co-create adequate responses to help find better, practical solutions. A little less conversation and navel-gazing about independence and objectivity, a little more action, please, in the paraphrased words of another: Lenz and Hoos (2023) argue that the pioneering zone, dealing with complex and chaotic subject matters, like environmental challenges, is the arena where we need effective and value-adding internal auditing the most. This is the future space of human beings in the internal auditing arena, supported by technology as much as possible. In the pioneering zone, there is more than one single truth. It is about "WHAT IF" type of questions, dealing with trade-offs.

If we are courageous, if we truly dare go down that path, time is right to challenge legacy thinking, including the paradigm of "objectivity". Why? Because there is no such thing as "objectivity" in the pioneering zone. We enter unchartered, unknown territory. Hence, we recommend the internal audit profession should at least de-emphasize their pursuit of "objectivity". There is only "objectivity" when dealing with mundane matters, in the managing zone, dealing with simple and complicated matters. Here, you often have best practices and the single truth, "objective" truth to say so. When presenting to diverse audiences in 2024 - ranging from hundreds of students at universities such as the University of Johannesburg and the University of Pretoria in South Africa, the University of Malaya and the Johannes Gutenberg University, to global internal audit practitioners at organizations like Adidas, Steiermärkische Sparkasse, and the WÜRTH Group - I posed a rhetorical question whether anyone in the audience had found their partner in life based on an objective scoring model? ... You know the answer: Nobody. What does that tell you?

De-emphasizing objectivity as a pillar of internal auditing might be a bridge too far for some professional peers. In our fast-paced and interconnected world, we challenge the profession to ask itself some fundamental questions, including, what are the true Unique Selling Propositions (USPs) of internal auditing, what is the legitimacy of internal auditing, why does the profession exist and who needs and demands its services in the 21st century and beyond. Mainstream thinking has brought us to the place where we are now. We need better. We need to change course. The Vision 2035 project report (The Internal Audit Foundation 2024) rightfully demands change: *"If the profession chooses not to confront its challenges and focuses exclusively on its traditional responsibilities or progresses slowly without keeping pace with a fast-changing global landscape, the internal audit profession will become irrelevant".*

We argue for Humphrey (2019), now is the right time to rethink audit. Are we asking the right questions? Are we focusing on the right thing? Humphrey (2019) suggests agonizing less about independence, reporting and evidence collection, while encouraging the profession to break free from the constraints and limitations of its conceptual past. In his view, audit can be more than just a form of assurance. He asks, *"what if we allow audit to become more of a primary function"* and challenges, *"why that something 'else' cannot count as audit"?*

We are on the same page. Re-emphasizing Lenz and Hoos (2023): We recommend CAEs to discuss with senior management and the board: *"How best can internal audit help the organization successfully manage ESG and associated risks?"* Such a discussion may reveal new opportunities for internal auditors to enhance the value of their services. ESG is a hot topic and will be for all forthcoming generations. However, so far, internal audit's contribution to it has been too little.

The new global internal audit standards (The IIA 2024) are pointing in the right direction. The purpose statement in domain I states (we emphasize create): "Internal auditing strengthens the organization's ability to create, protect, and sustain value by providing the board and management with independent, risk-based, and objective assurance, advice, insight, and foresight".

We interpret the new wording of the purpose of internal auditors as an encouragement to "do more" to become co-creators, value generators, to step out of the box, labeled "Third line" and become actors in the governance arena. Internal auditors can do more and do better. Demonstrate your full potential. There is no more time to waste. There is no planet B.

Part Two (Barrie)

A COMPLETE AUDIT UNIVERSE

The audit universe should cover every aspect of the business and not be limited to financial and administrative areas. Environmental, Social, and Governance individually, and ESG as a combined audit area should form part of the entity's audit/risk universe. Pro Optima has, since its establishment in 1997, included

E, S, & G in the audit universe of each client where we performed the internal audit function and have recently included ESG as a separate audit area. The completeness of the audit universe should not be a daunting thought, especially for the smaller internal audit function having limited resources and skills. Referring to Rainer's discussion in Chapter 2 on "Internal Auditing Can be More Than the Third Line", the internal audit function does not have to do all the ESG-related audits themselves because the services of third parties (Second Line), including in-house departments, can be used to cover some of these areas, while the internal audit function may coordinate and review such third line coverage as appropriate. Pro Optima has a dedicated ESG and compliance audit section, performing ESG and compliance audits for some of the largest mining companies in South Africa – as a Second Line service.

Environmental

Environmental-related regulations have been affecting business for many years and are doing so now more than ever. The International Organization for Standards (ISO) has developed ISO14001, which specifies the requirements for an environmental management system to assist organizations improving their environmental performance through the efficient use of resources and reduction of waste. ISO14001 requires that an organization must provide recorded evidence that its environmental management system meets specified criteria. Related audit areas in the mining industry, which we include in the audit universe are the following:

- Environmental management, including environment management plans, policies, and regulatory compliance.
- Environmental liability, incorporating annual assessments, reconciliations, and accounting.
- Financial provisioning for rehabilitation, including trust funds and guarantees.
- Environmental rehabilitation (concurrent and non-concurrent).

Performing an environmental audit remotely can be less effective than visiting the site(s) in my opinion, obviously depending on the geographic and purpose of the audit. As one would expect, most adverse findings involve noncompliance with legislation and/or company procedures, as well as company procedures not being adequately defined. Window-dressing may be easier to spot when the auditor is "on the ground".

Social

The Social aspect looks at the company's management and development of its human resources and the communities which they come from, ensuring they provide for a safe and healthy working environment, protecting employee rights and freedoms in the workplace, and enhancing the overall well-being of employees and communities. Businesses in developing countries are increasingly required to demonstrate responsibility and accountability to invest in the communities in which they operate through socio-economic development projects and activities.

The GIAS mentions ***Internal Auditing and the Public Interest*** as one of the Standards' fundamentals,[3] stating further that

> Internal auditing plays a critical role in enhancing an organization's ability to serve the public interest. While the primary function of internal auditing is to strengthen governance, risk management, and control processes, its effects extend beyond the organization. Internal auditing contributes to an organization's overall stability and sustainability by providing assurance on its operational efficiency, reliability of reporting, compliance with laws and/or regulations, safeguarding of assets, and ethical culture.

The Mineral and Petroleum Development Act requires from mining companies in South Africa to submit a Social and Labour Plan (SLP) to the Department of Mineral Resources and Energy (DMRE) as part of their applications for mining rights. The SLP contains various commitments made by the mining company to bring about socio-economic transformation, empowerment of historically disadvantaged persons and poverty eradication in the affected communities. An annual report is submitted to the DMRE detailing the extent of the mine's compliance with the SLP. The result of this review is the decision on whether to approve a new SLP developed for the next five years. The DMRE, when deciding on the review, must consider the extent to which the company has complied with the SLP, input, comments and reports from the mining right holder, mining community and interested and affected people and the changing needs of communities. Pro Optima reviews the declared progress on SLP commitments annually for one of our clients.

Audit areas covered under the Social category in South Africa include socio-economic development, incorporating social policy, grievance redressal mechanisms, fair compensation, livelihood restoration, and corporate social investment, as well as employee safety and development.

Social may be regarded as the moral high ground but is often the most misguided of the three factors encompassing ESG. My daughter Lana explains:

> My journey in humanitarian work started when holding a starving child who hadn't eaten in days. His cry was something I've never heard before; it was a hunger cry which haunts me to this day. This moment propelled me into humanitarian work. It's one thing to be aware of the existence of human suffering; it's a completely different thing to have had a visceral experience. It's different when you've seen it, it's different if you realize how misplaced funds could have made a difference here. Funds still fall through the cracks and some fail to reach the rightful beneficiaries due to lack of enlightenment on this subject. The corporate world is often out of touch with human suffering as they try to alleviate the plight of those in need from afar, while legislation in many, maybe most countries, is hopelessly inadequate to curb charity fraud and related schemes. Donors, especially business leaders, should be alerted to the prevalence of charity fraud. Legislators and internal auditors should also take action. It is difficult to believe that some so-called do-gooders have

malicious intent, yet this happens all too often. Knowing the difference between humanitarian aid and so-called foundations, charity galas, and other fundraisers is useful. Foundations are particularly vulnerable to money-laundering.

We call on the internal audit profession to help curb the onslaught of charity fraudsters, using funds that our clients allocate to supporting those who are in desperate need of humanitarian aid. Accountability can be difficult to spot if internal auditors exclude humanitarian aid from their audit universe.

Donors should be alerted to the pitfalls and dangers of charity fraud.

Warning signs

It is important to validate the beneficiaries of our clients' well-intended contributions. I suggest a vetting process that includes a requirement to route the final approved charity funding documents through the internal audit function for review; obviously considering practicality and independence. Knowledge of the following common pitfalls should assist in identifying potential irregular organizations:

1. The most basic test would be to obtain and confirm with the relevant authorities the registration number of charity/non-profit organization. However, our vetting must not stop here because it may be relatively easy for scrupulous persons to register such an organization under false pretenses.
2. An organization being defensive when asked to provide the necessary governance documents or to open their books to show specifics of how funds are accounted for, is a red flag. Some charity trustees keep the money for themselves, calling it operational costs.
3. Vague descriptions of charity work, for example, "Please donate to our organization where we help orphans in Africa" without stating which country and city, orphanage setup, ages of the children, and the specific needs apart from cash funding. Fake charities tend to exploit the voiceless, like children and animals for self-enrichment. A good internal control and audit testing would be going to "see for yourself".
4. Fundraisers showing pictures of vulnerable people to play on potential donors' emotions, such as children in tattered clothes. I think that is unethical.

What can internal auditors do?

1. Start by scheduling a humanitarian aid audit, and maybe in the next audit planning process if not yet included. I see it as a separate audit area under the Social factor of the audit universe. Below is an example of a planning in progress for a corporate social investment audit.
2. Become knowledgeable about charity fraud and related schemes.

Example of an audit planning process using SWIM (incomplete)

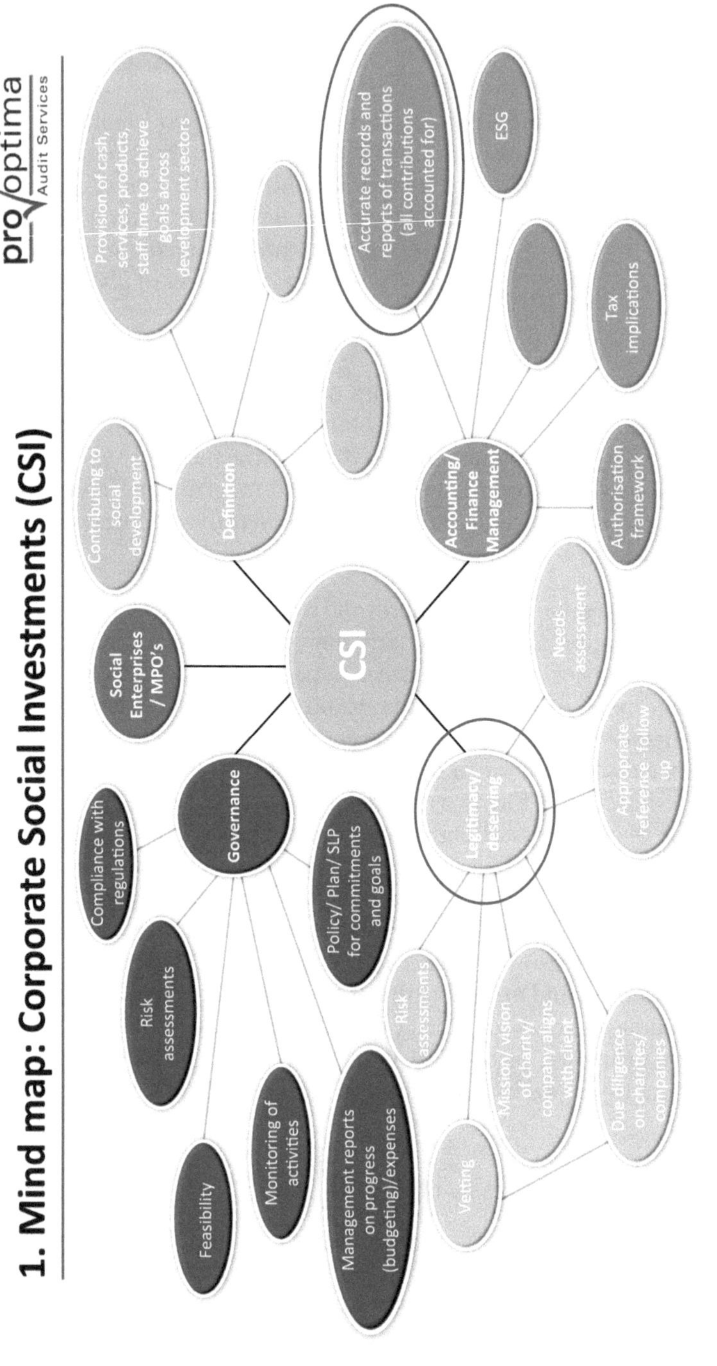

Figure 5.3 Mind mapping performed for a CSI audit.

2. Overall objective: Corporate Social Investments (CSI)

Key elements

- Legitimacy and deserving
- Accurate records or reports of transactions (all contributions accounted for)

Overall objective

To determine whether internal controls are adequate and effective to ensure that the CSI contributions are disbursed to legitimate and deserving organisations as well as being appropriately and fully accounted for.

Figure 5.4 Defining the overall audit objective deduced from the mind map.

3. Risks: Corporate Social Investments (CSI)

1. Contributions not fully accounted for (completeness).
2. Contributions not appropriately accounted for (financial reporting).
3. Contributions made to illegitimate/non-deserving/non-qualifying entities (reputational).
4. Beneficiary entities unable to account for donations disbursed.
5. Beneficiaries fail to deliver on their mandate/commitment/obligation.
7. Money-laundering (hiding origins of funds).

Associated ERM risks

1. Socio-political instability/social unrest.
2. Threat to social license to operate (stakeholder pressures and demands).

Figure 5.5 Determining the risks.

4. Sub objectives: Corporate Social Investments (CSI)

1. Company contributions are appropriately and fully accounted for.
2. Contributions are only made to bona-fide entities.
3. Beneficiaries account for donations received in accordance with their obligations.

Figure 5.6 Defining the audit sub-objectives.

5. Mitigating controls: Corporate Social Investments (CSI) pro optima Audit Services

Risks	Mitigating controls
1. Contributions are appropriately and fully accounted for.	1. Regular reconciliations of CSI accounts and related contributions. 2. Management reports on progress of contributions. 3. Appropriate approval framework.
2. Contributions are only made to bona-fide entities.	1. Vetting of entities (due diligence, reference checks, site visits) 2. Monitoring of activities 3. Legal compliance.
3. Beneficiaries account for donations received in accordance with their obligations.	1. Agreements with beneficiaries outlining specific obligations for accounting and reporting on donations received.

Figure 5.7 Determining the mitigating controls per risk identified.

Governance

The GIAS defines Governance as "*The combination of processes and structures implemented by the board to inform, direct, manage, and monitor the activities of the organization toward the achievement of its objectives*". The Standards stress the importance of the appropriate governance arrangements to enable the internal audit function to be effective, which include internal audit's own governance processes. Corporate governance involves promoting a fair and transparent way of doing business and ensuring adequate internal controls for managing risks. This may be an uncomfortable path to tread on as it affects senior executives. Governance audit areas may include the following:

- Entity level controls.
- Transparent disclosure of senior management incentive schemes, including share options, bonuses, profit share, and discretionary payments.
- Maintenance and disclosure of annual reports and financial statements.
- Business Continuity Management Planning.
- Adoption of policies such as:
  - Anti-bribery.
  - Anti-corruption and anti-money laundering.
  - Anti-Corruption, Counter-Fraud (ACCF).

We cover much of the above annually during ICOFR/SOX testing, while also attesting all the short- and long-term-incentive scheme calculations and payouts for one of our clients as part of the internal audit service and reporting the results to the remuneration committee before finalizing the calculations and disbursing the payments as a safety net.

ESG as a separate audit area

ESG criteria measures an entity's ability to conduct its business sustainably in a manner that primarily meets its needs without compromising the ability of future generations to meet their own needs. To this end, entities must be committed to the responsible stewardship of the ecological environment, ensuring compliance with safety, health, environmental, and sustainability requirements in their operations. Alignment with the United Nations Sustainable Development Goals (SDGs) and compliance with ESG-related laws, regulations, and industry-specific standards should form part of the company's audit universe. For example, compliance with the following:

- UN Principles for Responsible Investment (UNPRI).
- Responsible Gold Mining Principles (WGC RGMPs) of the World Council.
- International Council on Metals and Minerals (ICMM), which defines the ESG principles for the mining industry.

Large corporates increasingly require their vendors to become ESG-compliant; a process in which Pro Optima has become involved through our ESG and Compliance section. The first round of audits mainly serves as an opportunity to educate the vendors following which compliance testing becomes the tool to enhance their compliance levels. For one of our clients, a member of the ICMM, these audits evaluate the level of compliance with the Mining Principles and Performance Expectations of the ICMM. In determining a vendor's level of compliance to ESG and the ICMM's guiding principles, the audits assess each vendor's compliance in the following areas:

- Legislative compliance to specific statutory requirements.
- Broad-Based Black Economic Empowerment (B-BBEE) Act.
- ESG sustainability criteria.

Legislative assessment

Determining whether suppliers doing business with the mining company conduct business in accordance with 33 generally accepted (South African) legislative and good practices including the laws covering the following aspects:

- Basic conditions of employments.
- Occupational health and safety.
- Compensation for occupational injuries and diseases.
- Skills development.
- Employment equity.

B-BBEE is defined as viable economic empowerment of all black people, in particular women, workers, youth, people with disabilities, and people living in rural areas, through diverse but integrated socio-economic strategies. Some refer to it as black empowerment and intends to redress the inequalities created by Apartheid. The B-BBEE Act defines black people as Black, Colored, and Indians, being regarded as previously disadvantaged persons in South Africa. Referencing the three categories comprising black people, which may be derogative terms in some cultures or countries, are generally accepted terms in South Africa. These audits evaluate the B-BBEE structure and transactions, including confirming the validity of the entity's annual B-BBEE accreditation certificate and performing tests to determine the presence, if any, of the following fronting risks:

- Window-dressing, i.e., appointing black people based on tokenism.
- Benefit diversion, i.e., initiatives in which the economic benefits received based on its B-BBEE status do not flow to black people in the ratio as presented.
- Opportunistic intermediaries, i.e., having agreements with other enterprises purposed to leveraging the opportunistic intermediary's favorable B-BBEE status.

ESG testing covers the following aspects for each of the three ESG elements:

Element	Condition
Environment	Register of regulations
	Pollution abatement and testing
	Resource efficiency
	Greenhouse gas emissions reduction
	Environment policy and organization structure
	Environment management system
	Disclosure and reporting
	Environment management plan
Social	Social policy
	Grievance redressal mechanism
	Monitoring ESG and safety incidents
	Minimize impacts and provide fair compensation and livelihood restoration
	Emergency plans
	Health and safety policy and training
	Minimum wage, medical, and retirement benefits
	Occupational injury and disease insurance
	Skills development and employment equity
Governance	Promoting a fair and transparent way of doing business
	Ensure good governance practices at the company *
	Ensure adequate internal checks for managing risks

Levels of compliance are applied as follows against each legislative area:

Level of compliance			
N	Non-compliance		
P	Partial compliance	(+)	(–)
G	General compliance		

TAKE AWAYS

For internal audit, management, and the board

- Ensure a complete audit universe that includes Environmental, Social, and Governance, and if feasible ESG as a separate area as well.
- Help curb the onslaught of charity fraudsters through audits and awareness.

NOTES

1 Accessed on 18 October 2024, https://en.wikipedia.org/wiki/Cadbury_Report
2 Blog from 31 January 2024: "esG", https://drrainerlenz.wordpress.com/2024/01/31/esg/
3 Public interest encompasses the social and economic interests and overall well-being of a society and the organizations operating within that society (including those of employers, employees, investors, the business and financial community, clients, customers, regulators, and government).

REFERENCES

Hart, Oliver D., & Zingales, Luigi, The New Corporate Governance (April 25, 2022), University of Chicago Business Law Review, Summer 2022, Vol.1, Issue 1, University of Chicago, Becker Friedman Institute for Economics Working Paper No. 2022–55, Available at SSRN: https://ssrn.com/abstract=4094175 or http://dx.doi.org/10.2139/ssrn.4094175

Humphrey, C. (2019), Thinking differently is 'audit'. Audit Futures, ICAEW. https://auditfutures.net/blogs/thinking-differently-is-audit

Lenz, R., & Chesshire, J. (2023), Rethinking Internal Audit: Governance Needs Gardening, EDPACS, 68:3, 7–15. https://doi.org/10.1080/07366981.2023.2255432

Lenz, R., & Hoos, F. (2023), The Future Role of the Internal Audit Function: Assure. Build. Consult. EDPACS, 67:3, 39–52. https://doi.org/10.1080/07366981.2023.2165361

Lenz, R., & Jeppesen K.K. (2022), The Future of Internal Auditing: Gardener of Governance, EDPACS, 66:5, 1–21. https://www.tandfonline.com/doi/full/10.1080/07366981.2022.2036314

The Institute of Internal Auditors (The IIA) (2024), Global Internal Audit Standards, Lake Mary, Florida, US, January.

The Internal Audit Foundation (2024), Internal Audit: Vision 2035, US, Lake Mary, July.

World Economic Forum (2023, January), Global Risks Report. https://www.weforum.org/reports/global-risks-report-2023

Epilogue

We started this book by saying, this is NOT just another book about internal audit. This is OUR book about the profession and this is our only book about it. Our joint journey started over a drink at the social event in the evening just before the start of the ECIIA 2019 conference in Luxemburg.

Co-authoring this book has been a pleasure for both of us. We share the same ambition, our professional purpose (our WHY) is to make the internal audit function and the internal auditing profession more effective in practice.

In 2023, Rainer was the winner of the Bradford Cadmus Memorial Award[1] from The Institute of Internal Auditors Inc.

Picture 1 Global IIA conference 2023 in Amsterdam (July), with Anthony Pugliese (President and CEO at The Institute of Internal Auditors Inc.) and Benito Ybarra (Chair IIA Global Board 2023).

In Rainer's THANK YOU video, he says:

> We usually have about 20 seconds to say what we want to say. It is easy this time because all I want to say is THANK YOU! Thank you for the award, thank you for this recognition. I am grateful. For about 20 years I have

> been working in the internal auditing profession. My purpose has been all along the way to make internal auditing more EFFECTIVE in practice. I see value in the metaphor GARDENER OF GOVERNANCE. Let's see. The jury is out. I think, we can do more. We can do better. Bye for now.

If interested, you can view this THANK YOU message here on YouTube: https://www.youtube.com/watch?v=NDd37-rx958

Barrie and I see value in the metaphor "**The Gardener of Governance**" as purposeful for the effective internal auditor in the 21st century. Hence, we structure this book around the 5 Ps, five paths strengthening internal audit on a macro and on micro level, as suggested in Lenz and Jeppesen (2022): People, Public, Performance (Prosperity), Purpose (Profession) and Planet.

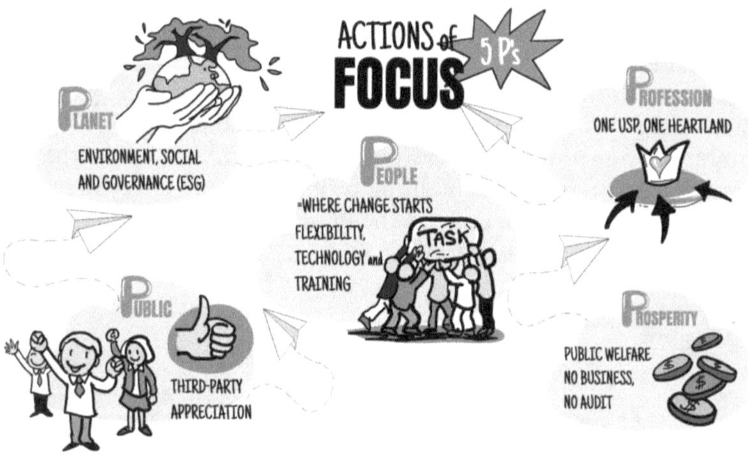

Picture 2 Five P's Lenz-Jeppesen 2022.[2]

As metaphor for the effective internal auditor we suggest:

THE GARDENER OF GOVERNANCE: OUR NATURE IS NURTURE

This idea originates from Rainer's keynote at the 70th anniversary of the IIA Nordics in October 2021.[3] The popular Lenz-Jeppesen 2022 article is known as the GARDENER article.

We have chosen to cite Prof. Dr. Florian Hoos (Professor of Sustainability and ESG Accounting at IMD Business School) as a closing comment to our book:

> This book is full of hands-on and more detailed content and guidance for internal audit practitioners. The hands-on part is missing in internal auditing that is based on internal audit principles without much guidance of how to apply them in practice. Less than the technical skill set, internal

auditors need the empathy, political compass, and communication skills to be a valuable function with an organization, and to really be a gardener of governance. The Lenz-Enslin 2025 book fills this gap. You can find real life examples, stories, and exercises for concrete behavior of internal auditors in the book. A must-read for internal audit professionals.

We are grateful to Prof Kato Plant and Prof Mervyn King SC for writing the forewords to our book. When meeting Mervyn on 08 October 2024 in Johannesburg we enjoyed an inspiring conversation and learning about his perspective on Corporate Governance and Internal Audit. Mervyn views both as intertwined. He sees a strong symbiosis of the Guardians and The Gardener of Governance, both aspiring to the long-term health of their organization, seeking to prevent governance failure. We agree. It is high time for change. We propose a path forward. We recommend that THE GUARDIANS and THE GARDENER OF GOVERNANCE join forces.

Picture 3 Dr Rainer Lenz and Barrie Enslin meeting Prof Mervyn King SC on 08 October 2024 in Johannesburg.

NOTES

1 Accessed online on 11 June 2024, https://www.theiia.org/en/about-us/initiatives-and-awards/awards-and-designations/bradford-cadmus-memorial-award/:

> The Bradford Cadmus Memorial Award, established by The Institute, is a tribute to the memory of Bradford Cadmus, author, educator, researcher, and the first managing director of The Institute. It officially recognizes individuals, whether or not they are members of The IIA, who have made outstanding contributions in research, education, publications, or other developments and activities in the field of internal auditing.
>
> Nominations for the award will be accepted from any member, group of members, or chapter of The Institute of Internal Auditors. Each nomination must be supported by a detailed explanation as to why the nominee should receive the award.

The number of awards to be made in a single year is at the discretion of the Award Committee. Current members of the Global Board and Awards Committee, and paid employees of The Institute of Internal Auditors are not eligible to receive the award.

The award consists of a suitably inscribed plaque, scroll, or other types of memento, a lifetime membership in The Institute of Internal Auditors, and complimentary registration to all IIA International Conferences attended.

Individuals or groups of individuals who have received the award in prior years shall not be eligible to receive the award in subsequent years.

2 Kudos to Axelle Vanquaillie (www.drawify.com) for the slide-deck and the drawings when presenting the Lenz-Jeppesen 2022, for example, at the ECIIA 2022 in Brussels https://drrainerlenz.wordpress.com/2022/10/07/eciia-2022-in-brussels/

3 Rainer's presentation at the 70th anniversary of the IIA Nordics on 08 October 2021: https://drrainerlenz.wordpress.com/2021/10/08/the-future-of-internal-auditing/

FSC
www.fsc.org
MIX
Papier | Fördert gute Waldnutzung
FSC® C083411

Kolibri 360 GmbH
Ferdinand-Jühlke-Straße 7
99095 Erfurt, Deutschland
produktsicherheit@kolibri360.de